Paradores
of
Spain

Entrance court of Parador Nacional Hernán Cortés, Zafra.

Paradores
of
Spain

Unique Lodgings
in State-owned Castles,
Convents, Mansions,
and Hotels

Sam & Jane
Ballard

MOORLAND PUBLISHING

The Harvard Common Press
535 Albany Street
Boston, Massachusetts 02118

Printed in the United States of America

Library of Congress Cataloging-in-Publication Data

Ballard, Sam.
  Paradores of Spain.

  Revision of 1978 ed.
  Companion vol. to: Pousadas of Portugal.
  Includes index.
  1. Hotels, taverns, etc.—Spain—Directories.
I. Ballard, Jane. II. Title.
TX910.S7B35 1986   647'.9446   86-314
ISBN 0-916782-76-X (pbk.)

Cover design by Jackie Schuman
Text design by Linda Ziedrich

10 9 8 7 6 5 4 3 2 1

Published in the United States by the Harvard Common Press.
ISBN: 0-916782-76-X.

Published in the United Kingdom by Moorland Publishing Co
Ltd, 8 Station Street, Ashbourne, Derbyshire DE6 1DZ.
ISBN: 0-86190-166-5.

Cover photo: Parador Nacional Hernán Cortés, Zafra

Grateful acknowledgments are made to Doña Elena de Ferro, Subdirectora General de Comercialización, Administración Turística Española, Madrid, and to our editor, Kenneth Hale-Wehmann.

CONTENTS

Introduction

SPAIN HAS SO MUCH TO LURE THE TRAVELER: AN infinite variety of landscapes that seem to change every 75 kilometers, vibrant cities, innumerable relics from previous civilizations, and immense collections of riches in churches and cathedrals. But perhaps most alluring to the perceptive visitor are classic scenes of life in rural hamlets unchanged for centuries.

One cannot grasp completely the quality of a different land and its people without traveling to remote areas. To see Spain only from Barcelona, Madrid, or resorts along the Mediterranean is to be cheated of the thrill of discovery. To get the taste and feel of Spain, take advantage of the network of paradores, inns owned and operated by the Spanish government, each reflecting the character of its region and each affording opportunities for exploration nearby.

How rewarding to stumble upon a village such as Besalú, with its unusual angular medieval bridge spanning the Fluvia River, or to chance upon Congosto de Ventanillo, a spectacular gorge with rocky sides reaching heights of 1000 feet. Where but in Spain could you hear a rooster crow in a twelfth-century cathedral? He and his clucking mate are ensconced in a lighted glass cage commemorating the medieval rescue of a condemned pilgrim by Saint Dominic in Santo Domingo de la Calzada.

How better to spend a Sunday than in Guadalupe, seated at an outside cafe facing the cathedral, watching the parade of village life. Blue-scarved nuns lead burros to drink from the town fountain. Smiling señoras joyfully hawk bags of nuts and dried figs. Sudden eruptions of song and dance occur when young people pause before entering the great doors of the cathedral. A harried local magistrate tries to solve the problem of where to park the elephantine tour buses.

Today the traveler to Spain is assured of fine accommodations in paradores, where prices and standards are set by the government. You may be a seasoned traveler, but unless you have experienced a parador you have missed a rare treat. The Marquis de la Vega Inclán held the post of royal commissioner for tourism in 1926 and it was under his guidance that the concept of paradores was developed. He envisioned three distinct types of paradores: those built in areas of great natural beauty; those reconstructed from ancient castles, monasteries, and mansions, thereby preserving national monuments; and those placed along the major highways of the country as restful stopovers for motorists.

Efforts were made to avoid areas in which private investors might be interested and to establish paradores in each of the fifty provinces, to promote tourism and aid local economies.

Originally, some of the government's lodgings were called *albergues*. Paradores were generally established in historic buildings and scenic areas, while *albergues* were more like motels. Over the years the differences between *albergues* and paradores have diminished and now all are called paradores.

Travelers on their first parador junket may find themselves not wanting to leave one parador, yet eagerly anticipating the next, wondering what it will be like. Although no two paradores are the same in setting, historical background, or decor, each meets high standards of cleanliness and efficiency, and is given a rating of either three or four stars by the government. Every parador has a fine restaurant.

Room rates in 1986 were as follows (current price lists are available from Spanish National Tourist Offices):

	3-star Paradores	4-star Paradores
Jan. 9–March 21	5000–7000 ptas	5000–9000 ptas
Jan. 1–8	5000–7500 ptas	5000–9000 ptas
April 1–June 30, Nov. 1–Dec. 21, and July 1–Oct. 31	5000–6500 ptas	5500–9000 ptas
Easter week and Christmas	5000–7500 ptas	6500–9000 ptas

In addition to 74 paradores within Spain, Paradores de Turismo operates two government-owned *hosterías* and two hotels. An *hostería nacional* is an outstanding restaurant set in a historic building, where exceptional food and wine are served. The two hotels are the incomparable San Marcos in León and the Reyes Católicos in Santiago de Compostela.

How to Use This Guide

The paradores, *hosterías,* and hotels are covered under their respective regions; within a region, lodgings appear alphabetically by the city or town where they are located. The regions themselves are also presented in alphabetical order.

Each write-up contains not only details about the parador, but information about what to see and do in the immediate environs, and, at the end, suggestions for day-trips to interesting places near the parador or other sights to see en route to the nearest lodgings.

Two indexes and the table of contents provide the key to finding what you're looking for. If you want to know whether a certain city has a parador, *hostería,* or government hotel, and where the establishment appears in this book, use the Index by Locale. For a run-down of the lodgings in a particular region, consult the table of contents. If the name of a parador is known, but not its location, see the Index by Establishment. The subject index will also help you find points of interest.

Numerous maps help to pinpoint paradores and plan your own routes. A map of each region, appearing at the opening of each section, shows the various types of government-run lodgings and restaurants, along with principal highways. A small map appears at the start of each write-up, pinpointing the establishment's location with respect to towns and highways. These maps are not designed to replace road maps but are schematic drawings showing recommended routes. On these maps:

   🏰 denotes a parador in a castle or monastery

   🏰 denotes a parador of modern or regional architecture

   🏰 denotes an *hostería nacional* or a government hotel

In the Recommended Itineraries section, each itinerary is accompanied by a map to show at a glance the general outline of the route.

Throughout this book, the abbreviation "km" is used for kilometers. In general, names of people, places, and geographical terms are given their Spanish spelling. A list of historical and art-historical terms travelers will encounter frequently is presented in the Glossary.

SPANISH NATIONAL TOURIST OFFICES

- 665 Fifth Avenue, New York, NY 10022   (phone 212/759-8822)
- 1 Hallidie Plaza, #801, San Francisco, CA 94102 (phone 415/346-8100)
- 60 Bloor Street West, 201 Toronto, Ont., Canada M4W 3B8 (phone 416/961-3131)
- 57 St. James Street, London SW1A 1LD (phone 499 10 95)

Reservations

Tourist season begins June 1 as thousands of Europeans arrive on the Iberian Peninsula. Their exodus starts the last of August. It is essential that those traveling during this peak period make reservations months in advance. Even during off season, it is wise to have reservations at the first few paradores to be visited. A member of the parador staff will be glad to telephone for subsequent bookings. Try to book two or three paradores ahead. Reservations may be made in the following ways:

- *Write to the parador.* Envelope should be addressed:
  Parador Nacional Costa Blanca (*name of parador*)
  Javea, Alicante (*city, province*)
  Spain
  Enclose a personal check equal to one night's lodging. If you did not receive confirmation before leaving home, telephone the parador when you arrive in Spain. It has been our experience to find our personal check awaiting us at the parador desk.
- *Marketing Ahead,* owned by Antonio Alonso, one-time director of public relations of the Spanish National Tourist Office in New York, is one of two official parador booking agencies in the United States. Confirmation is possible 24 hours after your check is received by Marketing Ahead. The room costs charged by Marketing Ahead are quoted per person and include breakfast, lunch or dinner, and Spanish taxes. Marketing Ahead, 433 Fifth Avenue, 6th Floor, New York, NY 10016 (phone 212/686-9213).
- *Marsans International,* 3325 Wilshire Boulevard, Suite 508, Los Angeles, CA 90010 (phone 213/738-8016); and 205 East 42d Street, Room 1514, New York, NY 10017. The other official U.S. booking agent.
- *Central Reservas* is in the Parador office complex in Madrid. Write: Velasquez, 18, Apartado de Correos 50043, Madrid 1, Spain (phone 435-97-00; telex 46865 RRPP).

Tour Operators

Guided tours and fly-drive do-it-yourself packages featuring paradores are offered by the following companies:

- *Encore Tours,* 1299 Kingsway, Vancouver, B.C., Canada V5V 3E2
- *Extra Value Travel,* 437 Madison Avenue, New York, NY 10022
- *Iberia Airlines Skyway to the World Tours,* 97-77 Queens Boulevard, Rego Park, NY 11374

- *Isram Tours & Travel Ltd.*, 630 Third Avenue, New York, NY 10017
- *JM Sun Spree Vacations* (general sales agent for RNVT of Portugal; works with travel agencies only), 421 Eglinton Avenue, West, Suite 3, Toronto, Ontario, Canada M5N 1A4
- *Marketing Ahead*, 433 Fifth Avenue, 6th Floor, New York, NY 10016 (phone 212/686-9213)
- *Marsans International*, 3325 Wilshire Blvd., Suite 508, Los Angeles, Calif. 90010 (phone 213/738-8016); and 205 East 42d Street, New York, NY 10017
- *Memo Tours*, 310 Madison Ave., New York, NY 10017

Border Crossings

Locations and times of opening are given in the table below.

Portuguese-Spanish Border Crossings

Portugal	Spain	April–Oct.	Nov.–March
Caminha	LaGuardia	9 A.M.–6 P.M.	9 A.M.–6 P.M.
Valença do Minho	Tuy	7 A.M.–1 A.M.	8 A.M.–midnight
São Gregório	Puentes Barijas	7 A.M.–midnight	8 A.M.–9 P.M.
Portela do Homem	Lovios	7 A.M.–9 P.M.	closed
Vila Verde da Raia	Feces de Abajo	7 A.M.–midnight	8 A.M.–9 P.M.
Quintanilha	Alcañices	7 A.M.–midnight	8 A.M.–9 P.M.
Miranda do Douro	Torre Jamones	7 A.M.–midnight*	8 A.M.–9 P.M.*
Barca d'Alva	La Fregeneda	7 A.M.–midnight	8 A.M.–9 P.M.
Vilar Formoso	Fuentes de Oñoro	7 A.M.–midnight	8 A.M.–midnight
Segura	Piedras Albas	7 A.M.–midnight	8 A.M.–9 P.M.
Marvão	Valencia de Al- cántara	7 A.M.–midnight	8 A.M.–9 P.M.
Caia	Caya	7 A.M.–midnight	8 A.M.–midnight
São Leonardo	Vila Nueva del Fresno	7 A.M.–midnight	8 A.M.–9 P.M.
Vila Verde de Ficalho	Rosal de la Fron- tera	7 A.M.–midnight	8 A.M.–9 P.M.
Vila Real de Santo António	Ayamonte	8 A.M.–midnight	8 A.M.–9 P.M.

*Closed Jan. 16–May 31.

There is a ferry from Plymouth, England, to Santander. Write Brittany Ferries, Millbay Docks, Plymouth PL1 3EF, England. Trains run daily between London (Victoria Station) and Lisboa via Paris and Hendaye (France) / Irun (Spain).

Automobiles

Although cars may be rented at major airports, it is best to make prior arrangements through your travel agent. For extended stays you may want to purchase a car to be delivered in Europe, then shipped home. (Make sure to order it to U.S. specifications.) Agencies such as Europe-by-Car can handle details for you. Consult your travel agency or Europe-by-Car, 1 Rockefeller Plaza, New York, NY 10020 (phone 800/223-1516). Another alternative is a purchase-repurchase plan, in reality a long-term lease. The advantage to this plan is that you are assured of a new car. Disadvantages are that you must arrange pick-up and drop-off points and then plan your itinerary around them. Seat and Renault continue to be popular cars in Spain, with service garages in even the most remote parts of the country.

Defensive driving is essential on the Iberian peninsula. Try to avoid driving in major cities, because traffic moves at a fast clip and if you don't know where you're going it can be a nightmare. Even in cities the size of Granada, with just over 200,000 people, driving can be harrowing. We have arrived at this solution to being lost: After making a couple of unsuccessful attempts to find a particular place, we hail a cab and ask the driver to lead us to our destination, cautioning "Despacio, por favor," slowly, please. The drivers are very obliging and helpful—once, unknowingly, we were so close to our destination that the driver refused a fee! Cab fares, incidentally, are the best bargain in Spain.

Outside cities, on the highways, trucks are the number one hazard because they are underpowered and crawl along, causing impatient drivers to take chances, passing even on curves. So try to keep well back of the car in front of you in case the one behind you, determined to overtake a truck, attempts a pass and has to duck in for safety.

Occasionally when roadwork is in progress in outlying areas and traffic is restricted to one lane, a signal man may hand you a stick if you are the last car in a line to be let through. You are to carry this stick to the end of the construction zone, where you hand it over to another signal man. This notifies him that there are no more cars coming, so cars can be let through in the other direction. A simple substitute for using walkie- talkies.

Regional maps published by Firestone are for sale in bookstores (*librerías*) and are excellent at detailing points of interest easy to miss when using a larger-scale map. If the road on a Firestone map is yellow (denoting secondary roads) and twisting, plan on it taking three times longer to reach your destination than usual. Study your route thoroughly. Know what cities lie in your path, because suddenly towns other than the one you're heading for will appear on highway signs. Don't deviate; forge ahead. Your town will appear.

Roads are good and well-maintained. The *autopista* (freeway) is much less trafficked than the federal highways (wide red on Firestone maps) because tolls are relatively high. You can make good time on the *autopistas* and avoid problems with slow trucks, but will not see intriguing sights.

Use of seatbelts is mandatory. Foreigners must have an international drivers license, available through the American Automobile Association. (Be sure to take along a passport-size picture for your license.)

Never let the gas supply get too low. In some remote areas not every town has a service station. There's no need to shop for better fuel prices, as they are the same throughout the country, regulated by the government.

Trains

Spanish trains are clean and run on time, and the fares are inexpensive. We met several people traveling through the country by train, stopping off to stay at paradores wherever possible. Their comments were so enthusiastic that we have determined to go by train on our next trip. There are no porters to help with luggage. Taxis usually stand at train stations; if there are none in sight, one can be procured for you.

Get a Thomas Cook Continental Timetable at a travel bookstore or order from Forsyth Travel Library, P.O. Box 2975, Shawnee Mission, KS 66201. You can spend hours making up your own itinerary. We suggest three itineraries using the trains in the Recommended Itineraries section of this book.

Even if you don't see Spain solely by train, do take some short trips out of Madrid—to Segovia, Avila, Toledo, or the Escorial, for instance. If you have been traveling by car, the driver will welcome a day off to relax and enjoy the scenery.

A word of caution: Try not to sit in the back coaches, because some train platforms are not as long as the train, which could mean a tremendous step down.

Airlines

Iberia is the national airline of Spain, almost wholly owned by the government. One of the largest airlines in Europe, Iberia flies to 52 countries. It is the number one carrier of passengers to Spain.

There are daily non-stop flights from New York to Madrid, three times a week from Boston, and weekly from Miami. Non-stop charter flights are scheduled from Dallas and Los Angeles to Madrid and from Chicago to Málaga. From June to September (exact dates vary year to year) Iberia flies non-stop between New York and Santiago de Compostela.

Iberia flies between major Spanish cities, while Aviaco, the national domestic airline, serves others.

Iberia has an interesting "Visit Spain" program whereby travelers can visit up to 29 cities in Spain, including the Balearic Islands, for just $199 over round trip fare. The Canary Islands can be included for just $249. Tickets must be purchased ahead of time in the U.S. and are valid for 45 days from first use. However, it would be a challenge to come up with an itinerary using this fare because you can stop in any city only once (except Madrid). In order to visit paradores on this program, car rentals would have to be arranged at the various airports.

Here is a list of Spanish cities served by either Iberia or Aviaco: Alicante, Almería, Badajoz, Barcelona, Bilbao, Córdoba, Gerona, Granada, Jerez de la Frontera, La Coruña, Madrid, Pamplona, San Sebastián, Santander, Santiago de Compostela, Sevilla, Valencia, Vigo, and Zaragoza.

Language

Very little English is spoken outside of large resort-type hotels. But don't let the fact that you are not fluent in Spanish prevent you from traveling in Spain. Brush up on a few courtesy words and phrases. Carry a Spanish-English dictionary, the more complete the better. Don't be afraid to try. Your meager attempts may elicit smiles, but they will be friendly ones.

A necessity is the word for restroom. If you need to ask where the toilet is, say "Por favor, donde está el lavabo?" Other terms used are *servicios* and *aseos*. Take heed if signs read Señores and Señoras. The *-es* ending is for men, the *-as* for women. Quite often, the doors will bear masculine and feminine silhouettes or paintings. (In Cataluña, Homes is for men, Dones for women.)

Cartas (menus) in paradores have English, French, or German translations. Take your pick. If you are purchasing an item, ask that the price be written: "Escriba, por favor."

The use of regional languages is increasing. Highway signs often appear in two languages: Spanish first then Catalán if in Cataluña, Valenciano if in or around Valencia, Euskera if in the Basque region, and Gallego in Galicia.

Business Hours and Holidays

With the exception of large department stores in major cities, restaurants, bars, and service stations, everything shuts down from about 1 to 4 P.M. six days a week. The times can vary thirty minutes either way. Also, hours may be different from town to town. If you plan on being any one place for more than a day, inquire at once about business hours. Just knowing may ease frustration. Stores reopen in the late afternoon and stay open until 8 P.M. or thereabouts.

Museums, closed on Mondays, also observe the three-hour afternoon closure. In the past, this period was a boon to travelers on the highways because truck drivers rested. No more. They may stop for thirty minutes or so, but then they're back to work.

Banks are open Monday through Friday from 9 A.M. to 2 P.M. and on Saturdays from 9 A.M. to 1 P.M.

Another thing to check out is whether a holiday will occur during your stay. It would be impossible to list all the *fiestas* and saint's days in Spain, as each town and region has its own. The following is a list of national holidays:

January 1	New Year's Day
January 6	The Epiphany
March 19	St. Joseph's
variable	Easter (including Thursday before Good Friday and Good Friday)
May 1	May Day
June 6	Corpus Christi
July 25	Feast of Santiago
August 15	Feast of the Assumption
October 12	Spain's National Day
November 1	All Saints Day
December 8	Feast of the Immaculate Conception
December 25	Christmas Day

Tipping

The Spanish almost never have their hands out, but tips are accepted and appreciated. Even though a bill (*cuenta*) states *servicio incluido,* it is customary and proper to tip 10 to 15 percent.

There are two ways of doing this at a parador: either on the spot, or in a lump sum at the desk when checking out. This is shared by all employees. We usually follow this procedure, an exception being the porter who helps with luggage.

Cab fares are so reasonable that a tip should always be given. You may want to be lavish in your gratuity to the hairdresser who has just revamped you at a fraction of the cost back home. (Without exception, they are top-notch even in tiny pueblos.) For some reason, it is customary to tip station attendants a small amount even though they never clean the windshield or check the tires. They do perform the oil routine, however, when asked.

Pharmacies

Every town, however small, has a *farmacia.* By law, there must be a 24-hour pharmacy in each area. Location of the specified store is posted on the doors or windows of every pharmacy. You may be surprised to find remedies that require a prescription in the U.S. being sold over the counter in Spain.

Pharmacists are knowledgeable about common ailments and act as medical consultants much the same as in the United States years ago. From personal experience on three occasions, we can attest to their competency.

The usual drugstore items such as shampoo, toothpaste, facial tissues, and sanitary napkins are found in pharmacies. The tissues, called *pañuelos*, come in little packages and are sturdy, rather like heavy paper napkins.

Clothing

The first and most important item on any clothes list should be shoes. It is impossible to become familiar with Spain without walking miles on cobbled streets, climbing over castle ruins, struggling to the tops of ancient citadels. Sandals won't do. Neither will shoes with too thin a sole—you will seem to be walking on marbles. Take shoes well broken in with substantial rubberized soles. (One of the wonders of the Iberian world is how *señoritas* can scurry at top speed in spike heels!)

The type of clothes to take will depend upon your season in Spain. Check the climate chart. Pantsuits for women are acceptable. In some cathedrals women may be asked to cover arms and heads, so make sure to take a lightweight jacket and scarf. Men will be glad to know that a tie at dinner is not mandatory. However, a Toledo *bolo*, a decorative clasp on leather or cord, adds a touch of class. Be sure to take a sweater or two and a weatherproof coat.

Ease of laundering is another factor in determining the type of clothing to bring. Coin laundromats have not yet appeared in Spain. But there are *lavanderías*, where you can leave your clothes to be done. If permanent press, be sure to specify "no agua caliente—agua media." Also specify *media* for the dryer (*el seco*). You can usually pick up your clothes nicely folded the same day. To have laundry done in a parador requires 48 hours, except in Segovia where they have a dryer!

Using a *lavandería* can be a hassle to go through too often. Every third day we manage to spend two nights in the same parador to allow time to catch up on the chore. Par-

Maximum and Minimum Daily Average Temperatures (Degrees Fahrenheit)

Region	Jan.	Feb.	Mar.	Apr.	May	June	July	Aug.	Sept.	Oct.	Nov.	Dec.
Costa Blanca (Alicante)	61–43	65–43	68–47	73–50	78–55	84–62	90–67	89–68	83–64	75–57	68–50	63–45
Costa Brava (Barcelona)	55–42	57–44	61–48	67–51	74–55	77–61	84–65	84–69	77–64	69–58	61–50	55–44
Granada	53–34	57–35	63–40	68–43	74–48	86–57	92–62	90–62	84–57	71–48	62–41	53–39
Costa del Sol (Málaga)	60–46	64–46	69–50	75–56	78–57	82–64	86–67	87–70	84–65	77–59	70–53	65–48
Madrid	47–34	51–35	59–41	65–45	73–50	83–57	88–64	91–62	78–57	64–49	55–41	50–35
Northern Coast	50–39	55–40	59–42	61–43	66–43	70–59	75–59	75–59	69–53	60–45	55–48	53–42
Sevilla	60–42	63–44	69–48	74–52	80–56	89–63	96–68	95–68	89–64	78–57	68–50	60–44
Costa del Azahar (Valencia)	59–42	61–43	65–46	68–49	73–55	79–62	83–67	85–69	81–64	74–56	67–49	60–45

ador bathrooms often have two sinks, one that can be used for soaking, the other for rinsing. Take along plastic fold-up hangers, blow-up hangers, extra wire hangers, and clip-on clothespins. (Hotel and parador closet hangers are no good for laundry.) Position all dripping hangers on shower head and curtain rod and let the bathmat catch the drips. Take a supply of plastic bags for soiled or not yet dry clothes. Tuck in a bar of Lava soap, a great spot remover. No need to take liquid or powdered soap as laundry soap is available everywhere. Look for the box or bottle with a picture of a baby holding a soft blanket to its cheek.

Finally, try to remember that on previous trips you have always taken too many clothes. Leave room in your bags for some of Spain's wonderful products.

Money Matters

The most common credit cards are accepted throughout Spain. If you are using credit cards, have at least two—one for paying expenses and one for obtaining cash (Visa or American Express). In this case, take a minimum of travelers checks to be used in emergencies. It is usually possible to find at least one bank in every area that will give you cash on your credit card or cash travelers checks. We found the Banks of Bilbao very accommodating. However, don't let your reserves get too low before seeking a bank.

Before leaving home, buy just enough pesetas to get you through a couple of days until you can get to a bank. The money exchange rate is much better in Spain.

Security

It is sad to have to issue warnings about an unfortunate fact of life everywhere in the world and in Spain: theft. The traveler hears all kinds of horror stories and runs the risk of becoming paranoid. So, here are a few common sense hints on how to avoid such unpleasant and costly incidents.

Women should hold on to their purses. Don't put them down for a minute anywhere. Shoulder bags are not very wise, as they can easily be whipped away. If you and a companion are walking down a street, keep your bag on the inside. Better still, carry your purse in a nondescript shopping bag.

Men shouldn't carry billfolds in hip pockets. Keep larger bills in one front pants pocket, smaller ones in the other.

Know your passport number and take along an extra picture. The photography is what holds up quick passport replacements.

Use hotel and parador safes or lock jewelry, credit cards, purse, passports, and travelers checks in your luggage and hang a No Molestar sign on the door.

If you are driving and stopped at a signal light in a larger city, make sure your doors are locked and that your purse, camera, etc., are out of sight. Keep windows up past half-way. Never leave valuables exposed in the car—cover them up with coats or a bag of dirty laundry. Try not to leave telltale tourist lures—maps, guidebooks, shopping bags, and so on—in plain sight.

Women should avoid taking expensive jewelry. A gold necklace or bracelet can be easy picking for a thief.

Tips on Photography

The Iberian peninsula offers excellent photographic opportunities for the amateur as well as professional. Brilliant sunshine enhances medieval streets and colorful fishing villages. The wealth of photo subjects is unlimited.

For some dramatic scenic shots, try shooting in early morning, late afternoon, and even at sunset. The shadows and reddish colors at these hours will add more dimension to your photos.

When going through airport security, in spite of the claim that the machines will not harm your film, we recommend that you either request hand inspection of your camera kit and film, or carry all film in lead-laminated bags available at photographic supply stores. This is a must if you are carrying some of the new high-speed films. We found it easier to carry all film in the lead bags, avoiding hassles and delay at the inspection stations.

Try to purchase enough film before leaving home, as it is still more expensive in Spain, even though film costs have come down substantially because of the dollar ratio to the peseta.

Food

It is surprising how many North Americans think Spanish food is the same as Mexican food. Wrong. For instance, a Spanish *tortilla* is an omelette. *Tortilla española* is the traditional omelette of potatoes and onions. Others may contain ham, asparagus, spinach, herbs, or mushrooms.

Every parador has a dining room that serves three meals a day. Breakfast, *desayuno,* has been expanded from the "continental" snack of yore. It is served buffet-style from 8 to 10 or 10:30. A bountiful table holds choices of cold cereals, fruit, cheese, sliced meats, breads, and even scrambled eggs. Understandably, this substantial meal is no longer included in room rates.

Lunch, *almuerzo,* is served from 1 to 3:30 or 4. The same menu appears at dinner, *cena,* served from 8:30 or 9 to 11 P.M. Guests enjoy two-course and three-course meals of regional foods, as well as traditional dishes popular all over the country. Those who don't want two heavy meals a day may order a la carte. In most of the paradores, light snacks such as bread and cheese are served in the bar, which is open for coffee, tea, wine, spirits, and ice from 11 A.M. until 11 P.M.

Many foods are cooked in or seasoned with olive oil, rarely overpowering. Salads are served with do-it-yourself cruets of oil and vinegar, though other dressings are beginning to appear in Spanish cuisine. Garlic is the predominant herb and it is used liberally.

Piquant sauces flavor many dishes. *Chilindrón* is a spicy tomato sauce in which chicken, lamb, kid, veal, and pork may be simmered. *Pil pil* and *ali oli* are Catalán concoctions heavy on garlic. *Romesco* is a fish sauce combining olive oil, pepper, crushed hazelnuts, and Priorato, a robust red wine. *All i pebre,* a very peppery sauce, is popular in Albufera and other parts of the Levant.

There are four basic native dishes and they have countless variations: *cocido, fabada, paella,* and gazpacho. *Cocidos* are meat stews using pork, veal, lamb, kid, or chicken, usually cooked and served in earthen bowls. Fish stews are called *zarzuelas,* or *suquet de peix* in Cataluña. *Fabadas* are bean dishes made primarily with dried white beans (larger than the largest North American lima beans) flavored with ham or *chorizo* sausage or both.

Paellas consist of many kinds of local fish and shellfish

served on a bed of saffron rice. Gazpacho is an uncooked tomato-base soup garnished with chopped celery, green pepper, cucumber, onion, tomatoes, and croutons.

Meat and poultry include pork, veal, lamb, kid, rabbit, chicken, wild quail, and partridge (*perdiz*). Roast meat is called *asado*. In the past, Spanish steaks were nothing to rave about. However, we found the *entrecot a la pimienta* (pepper steak) to be consistently good.

Sausages are used extensively in cooking and also served cold and sliced as hors d'oeuvres. Three of the most common are *chorizo, butifarra,* and *morcilla,* the latter a blood sausage whose name is sometimes translated as "black pudding." Morcilla looks a bit ghastly but close your eyes and try it. You will discover it to be very tasty.

An item appearing on almost all parador menus is *entremeses,* normally ordered only at lunch. The tabletop will be covered with tiny dishes, from 12 to as many as 20. The delectables range from succulent spears of white asparagus, stuffed hardboiled eggs, and potato salad, to sausages, sardines, chunks of cod, anchovies, and smoked oysters—the sky's the limit.

Travelers will likely not be able to keep track of the many varieties of fish. There are those familiar in North America, such as trout, swordfish, sole, bass, and turbot. Mussels, prawns, clams, lobster, oysters, and crayfish are also common. Three excellent whitefish to look for are *merluza, besugo,* and *lubina.* Be brave and try octopus. Squid (*calamares*) are delicious sliced in rings and deep-fried, but you may be reluctant when *calamares* are touted on menus as *en su tinta* (cooked in their own ink). And then there is *bacalao.* Dried cod, *bacalao,* is the fish that predominates in the Spanish diet as it has for centuries. Legend has it that there are as many ways to cook *bacalao* as days in the year. Every visitor to Spain should try it at least once. In some recipes it is quite bland, while in others a strong white wine accompaniment is called for.

Soup, *sopa,* is a universal first course. It comes in many guises, from consommé to hearty one-dish meals. Garlic soup (*sopa de ajo*) is very popular with the Spanish. Served in an earthen bowl, it is almost always topped with a poached egg. Sometimes a slice of bread will be afloat, but underneath is sure to be a sunny-side-up. If you do not care for the egg addition, specify "sin huevo, por favor." *Pote gallego* and *caldo verde* are flavored with ham and enhanced with chopped leaves of Galician cabbage.

Migas is another traditional Spanish dish often appearing on parador buffet breakfast tables. *Migas* are coarse bread crumbs fried with onion, garlic, and other seasonings in olive oil or bacon drippings.

Vegetables are fresh, tasty, and prepared in many ways. There are supposedly fifty ways to prepare potatoes. French fries are marvelous in Spain, always served piping hot and done to the right crispness. Green beans are much wider than those in the U.S. and may be cooked in a tomato sauce or with bits of ham. Asparagus spears are long, plump, and white. Often asparagus *con dos salsas*, with a mayonnaise and a tomato sauce, will appear as a luncheon entree. Artichokes are quite small and delicious, and appear on most menus. *Menestra de verduras* is a pleasant mixture of fresh vegetables.

Sobres, desserts, invariably include flan, a cold custard that is a reliable standby. Fruit is on every menu. Melons and dessert grapes are excellent. A *tarta* consists of two layers of cake with a custard or fruit sauce as filling. We have found that the quality and variety of desserts depend on the finesse of the chef.

It is wise to order bottled water, pure (*sin gas*) or carbonated (*con gas*). Order a large bottle at the evening meal and remember to take it to your room.

Coffee is flavorful and powerful. At breakfast, *cafe con leche*, half coffee, half hot milk, is poured in large cups. At all other times of the day, it is served in small cups. If you want a larger amount, order "cafe con leche doble." If you drink your coffee black say "cafe sin leche," "cafe negro," or "cafe solo."

Wine

Spanish table wines are rated good to excellent and in the opinion of wine experts are on a par with many French wines. Traveling the parador circuit can become an adventure in wine tasting. Paradores offer a selection of wines in addition to the *vino de casa*, or house wine, ordered by either the carafe or the bottle. Because travelers will pass through thousands of acres of vineyards and may be curious about their fruit, we give an overview of the wine industry.

Sherry is perhaps the most well-known Spanish wine. There are five types of sherry: *manzanilla*, the driest and lightest of sherries; *fino*, a little heavier and darker; *amon-tillado*, medium-dry, amber in color; *oloroso*, robust and dark gold; and cream sherry, sweet and smooth.

Eight large wine-producing sections of Spain are made up of distinct, demarcated areas called *denominaciones del origen*, shortened to D.O. D.O.s are monitored by a special department of the Ministry of Agriculture. The regions are the Upper Ebro, Andalucía, Aragón, Cataluña, Galicia, the Levant, the Centre, and the Duero.

The Upper Ebro region comprises the D.O.s of Navarre and Rioja. Navarre D.O. extends from the banks of the Ebro to the foothills of the Pyrenees. Fifty-nine thousand acres of vineyards are divided into five subzones. Two types of "black" grapes are blended to produce a rich, hearty red wine. Navarre rosés are made from the Garnacha grape, famous for its smooth fruitiness. Rioja wines have been celebrated for more than a century. The secret lies in climate, soil combination, and wine-making know-how. One hundred thousand acres, flanked by two mountain ranges, lie along the course of the Ebro. Several Riojan grape varieties are blended to make full-bodied red wines with 17 percent alcohol. The Viura and Malvasia grapes produce a refreshing fruity white wine. The towns of Haro, Logroño, and Laguardia have wine-tasting *bodegas*, or cellars, open to the public.

Andalucía has four D.O.s: Condado de Huelva, Jerez (or Xeres), Málaga, and Montilla-Moriles. Huelva's 45,000 acres produce a white table wine and two fortified varieties. Amber-colored Condado Palido and darker-hued Condado Viejo have an alcohol content of 14 to 23 percent.

Two important factors in the international success of sherry (wine fortified with brandy) are climate and soil. In the Jerez region there is a perfect balance between Mediterranean and Atlantic climates. The lime-rich spongy soil soaks up and stores moisture. Ninety-five percent of the 57,000 acres of vineyards around Jerez are planted in the white Palomino Fino grape, the remaining 5 percent in Pedro Ximénez and muscatel grapes, yielding sweet dessert wines with an alcohol content of about 20 percent.

In the northern part of the province of Málaga, most of the wine is made from the Pedro Ximénez grape. Muscatel grapes are cultivated on rocky slopes near the Mediterranean. Here a large part of the 30,000 acres furnishes grapes for the table and raisin markets. The remainder are made into a sweet dessert wine. Another outstanding wine of

Málaga is Lágrima, deep amber in color and very smooth, perhaps because mechanical pressing is never used in its production.

The wines of Montilla-Moriles were known throughout the Roman Empire and were permitted during long years of Moorish domination because of their excellence. This D.O. covers the whole of the southern half of Córdoba province. Pedro Ximénez (possibly of central European origin) is practically the only grape grown. The soil is rich in calcium and lime, the climate is Mediterranean with a few modifications. The area is blessed with 2800 hours of sunshine per year. Six kinds of fortified wines are produced as well as the dry, light Ruedos, which require no aging.

Borja D.O. and Cariñena D.O. are found in Aragón. Winters are bitterly cold, summers hot and dry in Campo de Borja, northwest of Zaragoza. The porous soil is ideal for growing grapes. Garnacha, a hardy "black" grape, rules supreme in over 25,000 acres. Reds and rosés are full-bodied with relatively high alcohol content.

Cariñena's 55,000 acres are south of Zaragoza in softly rolling terrain. After Almería, Cariñena has the lowest amount of rainfall in the country. Garnacha grapes produce a dark, almost purple wine, often more than 14 percent alcohol. Viura and Macadeo grapes produce a white wine called Las Pajarillas.

Alella, Ampurdán, Penedés, Priorato, and Tarragona are the five D.O.s of Cataluña. Alella is tiny, only about 14 acres in prime real estate of Greater Barcelona. The vines here are the only survivors of a once-extensive area decimated by Phylloxera plague (caused by a European aphid) in the late nineteenth century. Alella is a fruity red wine.

Ampurdán is a narrow coastal strip on the Costa Brava. A mixed climate encourages a grape yield necessary for high-quality, light, well-balanced red wines. Equally popular are the rosés, low in alcohol and delicate in taste.

Penedés D.O. is inland, south of Barcelona, and extends a little bit into Tarragona. A mild Mediterranean climate, a yearly rainfall of about 30 inches, and the blending of three varieties of white grapes enable Penedés to turn out some of Spain's finest white wines. In the area around San Sadurni de Noya very good sparkling wines are produced.

Wine making in the Priorato D.O. goes back to the Middle Ages when monks arriving from Provençal in France set up a monastery and planted vineyards. The climate is temperate, drier and cooler than that on the Mediterra-

nean coast. The yield of Priorato's 91,000 acres is the lowest in Spain. Inhabitants of small villages scattered over a
rugged landscape of rocky, steep hillsides carefully tend
their vineyards and are determined to produce a quality
product. The resulting Priorato is a deep red, robust, rich
wine.

Ribeiro and Valdeorras are found in Galicia, the moist,
green northwestern corner of Spain. More than 77,000 acres
of vines, following the course of the Miño River, grow
around the old town of Ribadavia, wine center of Ribeiro.
The soil is granitic and sandy. There are rarely climatic
extremes in Ribeiro. As a result, the white wines are fresh-
tasting, pale with greenish hues, and low in alcohol.

Valdeorras D.O. lies about 100 km east of Orense. Vines
are trained on trellises on the terraced hills. A rather mild
climate, many hours of sunshine, and over 30 inches of
rain are perfect conditions for producing quality wines.
Along the valley of the Sil River, 75,000 acres of vines grow
in slatey soil. The cherry-red wines are light and tart, with
about 12 percent alcohol.

In the Levant region there are five D.O.s: Alicante, Jumilla, Utiel-Requena, Valencia, and Yecla. Alicante's 85,000
acres are planted largely with the "black" Monastrell grape,
able to survive this area of low rainfall. The red wines are
full-bodied and high in alcohol. When aged, they make
marvelous dessert wines.

Jumilla is an area less than 100 km west of Alicante. The
struggle to raise grapes here has been going on since Roman times. The yields are very low. But the vineyards in
Jumilla withstood the Phylloxera plague and remain today
the area with the highest percentage of ungrafted vines
having no need of American rootstock to survive. The
Monastrell grape produces a strong red wine. When mixed
with the Garnacha Tintorera, the result is a purple-red table wine with an alcohol content of between 12 and 14
percent.

Utiel-Requena extends inland from Valencia between the
Turia and Cabriel rivers. Ninety-five percent of the 124,000
acres are planted in the black Bobal grape. Small vines with
compact branches are closely planted and well tended. Red
and rosé wines are densely colored, pleasingly acidic and
moderate in alcohol content.

Valencia is divided into three subzones and the 47,700
acres produce white and red table wines.

The soil around Yecla is poor for all crops but grapes.

The Monastrell grape loves a porous soil high in calcium. An average of 3000 hours of sunshine per year helps to produce a deep red, smooth dry wine. Yecla also markets smaller quantities of whites and rosés.

Almansa, La Mancha, Méntrida, and Valdepeñas make up the Centre, located in the southern half of the great central plateau. Almansa is mostly in Albacete province, extending a bit into Valencia. Vines planted in limestone soil at an altitude of 2300 feet struggle to withstand very little rainfall, a long hot summer, and very cold winters. Red wines of Almansa are deep-colored and full-bodied, with alcohol content often in excess of 14 percent.

La Mancha is the largest single vine-growing area in the world. Driving through even a few of the over one million acres seems a voyage through a sea of vineyards. Here 43 percent of Spain's wine is produced. Sixty-five percent of all the white wine in the country comes from La Mancha's white Airén grape. Huge cooperatives employ whole villages during harvest. In addition to white wine, La Mancha also produces reds and rosés.

The soil of Méntrida, south of the Sierra de Gredos and southwest of Madrid, is slightly acid clay, sandy on the surface. Extreme climates and irregular rainfall along with the properties of the soil account for wine high in alcohol and color. Most of the wines are drunk while young. The reds are fruity and dark, the rosés lighter, with a pleasant aroma and color. Alcoholic contents range from 13 percent to 18 percent.

The wines of Valdepeñas, in the southern half of La Mancha, have been popular with Madrileños since the seventeenth century. Eighty-five percent of the vines are Airén. The remaining 15 percent are the black grapes Cencibel and some Garnacha. The Airén grapes yield white and rosé wines, the Cencibel and Garnacha smooth reds.

The Duero region in Castilla León has two D.O.s: Ribera del Duero and Rueda. Ribera extends along both banks of the Duero River and takes in parts of the provinces of Valladolid, Burgos, Segovia, and Soria. Thirty thousand acres are devoted to the production of red and rosé wines. The grape Tinto del País yields a bright red wine. Rosés are called *claretes* in this D.O. and the *claretes* of Ribera del Duero are among the best in the country.

In Rueda, a local white grape called the Verdejo is used to make pale wines with strong aromas and fresh tastes. The vineyards are found in the south of Valladolid province. Here a system of pruning encourages vines to grow along the ground, as the area receives very little rainfall.

When ordering the house wine, specify white (*blanco*), rosé (*rosado* or *clarete*), or red (*tinto*).

Here is a favorite Spanish toast: "Amor, salud, y dinero, y mucho tiempo para gustarlos," "Love, health, and money and plenty of time to enjoy them!"

Geography and Climate

Spain may be divided into three principal topographic regions: the vast central *meseta*, or plateau, the coastal plains, and the *sierras*, or mountain ranges, which surround and occasionally interrupt the plateau and generally run west–east.

The plateau comprises three-fourths of the land area of Spain. The altitude of this semi-arid plateau varies from 1000 to 6000 feet. It extends from the Cordillera Cantábrica, or Cantabrian Mountains, in the north to the Sierra Morena in the south, from the coastal plains in the east to the border with Portugal in the west. Winters on the plateau are dry and windy. January's average temperature is 41 degrees Fahrenheit. Summers are hot and dusty, with temperatures in July averaging 78 degrees. Yearly rainfall is about 18 inches.

The eastern coastal plain spreads from Barcelona south to the Gulf of Almería, encompassing the parts of the coast called (from north to south) the Costa Brava, the Costa Dorada, the Costa del Azahar, and the Costa Blanca. Streams flowing from the Sierra Nevada to the Mediterranean provide irrigation for the fertile soil. Another coastal plain in southwestern Spain, where the Costa del Sol and the Costa de la Luz are found, has been created by soil carried down mountain slopes. Marshes called Las Marismas are found in the central part of this region, between Cádiz and Huelva. In northern Spain, a narrow land strip extends from the Atlantic and the Bay of Biscay to steep mountains. Rainfall along the eastern and southern coasts averages 14 inches a year while the northern coasts receive 60 inches. Mild winters of 50 degrees and warm 80-degree summers are enjoyed along the eastern and southern coasts. Temperatures are cooler in the north, with January averages of 49 degrees and July averages of 64.

Spain has three primary mountain chains. The Pyrenees, Cantabrian, and Galician mountains form the northern chain; the Sierra de Gata, Sierra de Gredos and Sierra de Guadarrama form the central; and the Sierra Morena and Sierra Nevada form the southern barrier.

Four major rivers rise in the plateau. The Duero and Tajo (Tajo is called Tagus in English) flow southwest through Portugal (where they are known as the Douro and Tejo, respectively) to the Atlantic. The Guadalquivir River flows south through Spain to the Gulf of Cádiz on the Atlantic, which the Guadiana River reaches through Portugal. The Cantabrian Mountains are the source of the Ebro River, which flows southeast to empty into the Mediterranean Sea.

Ten million acres of wheat are under cultivation. Other cereals include rye, oats, barley, corn, and rice. Cotton is grown in the south and along the southern coast. Ninety-two percent of the olives gleaned from five million acres are used in the production of olive oil. Spain is the world's largest producer, processing 350,000 tons annually. Over four million acres of vineyards enable Spain to be the third-largest wine producer among the Mediterranean countries. One-third of the world's supply of cork comes from the trees of Spain. Citrus fruits are another important export.

Suggested Reading

Don Quixote, by Cervantes, completed in 1615, is a satirical novel that has been translated into more languages than any another literary work, except the Bible. *A Stranger in Spain,* by H. V. Morton, is worthwhile reading before and after a trip to Spain (published by Dodd, Mead and Co.). *Or I'll Dress You in Mourning,* by Collins and La Pierre (Simon and Schuster), is a fascinating biography of El Cordobés, the great matador. *Castile for Isabella, Spain for the Sovereigns,* and *Daughter of Spain* make up a trilogy by the popular historical novelist Jean Plaidy (Putnam). *History of the Spanish Civil War,* by Hugh Thomas (Harper and Row), is a scholarly, readable account of the conflict. *The Cypresses Believe in God* is a two-volume historical novel by José María Gironella translated by Harriet de Onís, set in the province of Gerona during years leading to Civil War of 1936 (New York: Alfred A. Knopf, 1955).

Dates in Spanish History

15,000–12,000 B.C. Iberians of undetermined origin left as evidence of their existence on the peninsula paintings in the caves of Altamira, dolmens in Antequera, and talayots in the Balearic Islands.

2000 B.C. Celts from southwestern Germany and eastern France cross the Pyrenees to war, then mix with the Iberians.

1100s B.C. Phoenicians establish colonies.

480 B.C. Carthaginians from Africa invade and conquer peninsula.

400s B.C. Greeks establish colonies. Ruins exist in Ampurias on the Bay of Rosas.

201 B.C. Romans begin invasions.

200 A.D. Christianity spreads throughout Spain.

400. Visigoths enter peninsula as invaders, remain as allies of the last Roman emperors.

573. Visigoths conquer Spain and establish court at Toledo.

mid-600s. Visigoths merge with Hispano-Romans.

711. Moors from Africa invade and conquer peninsula in seven years.

1200s. Christian kingdoms reconquer all lands held by the Moors except Granada—called the Reconquest.

1479. Castilla and Aragón become one kingdom with the marriage of Ferdinand of Aragón to Isabella of Castilla.

1480. Isabella and Ferdinand set up Inquisition to rid Spain of non-Catholics. Inquisition in effect until 1834.

1492. The Catholic monarchs drive Moors from Granada. Columbus (Colón) sails to America and claims it for Spain.

1500s. Spanish empire expands to include the Philippines, most of South America, parts of North America and Africa, Naples and Parma in Italy, the Netherlands, Portugal, Sicily, Sardinia, and the Canary and Balearic islands.

1581. The Netherlands successfully revolt and declare their independence.

1588. England's navy defeats the Spanish armada.

1640. Portuguese drive Spanish from Portugal.

1714. Spain surrenders Naples, Parma, Sardinia, and Milan to Austria.

1808. Napoleon invades and conquers Spain.
1813. Spain and England unite to drive the French from Spain.
1810–24. Spain's American colonies revolt and declare independence.
1898. Cuba, Puerto Rico, and the Philippines lost in the Spanish-American War.
1923. Miguel Primo de Rivera declares himself dictator and rules until 1930.
1936–39. Civil War devastates the land. Franco defeats the Republicans and establishes a dictatorship.
1975. Death of Franco. Juan Carlos I accedes to the throne.
1977. First general elections.
1986. Spain joins European Common Market.

Monarchs of Spain

FERDINAND I, THE GREAT (1035–65). First king of a united Castilla and León, became leader of the Reconquest.

ALFONSO VI (1065–1126). Succeeded his father and took Toledo from the Moors. Adventures of El Cid occurred during his reign.

ALFONSO VII (1126–57). Grandson of Alfonso VI; captured Córdoba in 1144.

ALFONSO VIII (1158–1214). Succeeded his father. Married Eleanor, daughter of King Henry II of England.

ENRIQUE I (1214–17). Son of Alfonso VIII.

FERDINAND III, THE SAINT (1217–52). Nephew of Enrique; called the Saint because of piety and devotion to Reconquest. Ruled wisely, allowing Jews and Muslims to retain laws, customs, and religion.

ALFONSO X, THE WISE (THE LEARNED) (1252–84). Son of Ferdinand. A poet, scholar, student of astronomy, author of Book of Laws, encouraged Arabic studies, attempted to promote merger of Arabic and Christian cultures, established custom of writing documents in Castilian rather than Latin, began development of a navy and endowed departments of medicine and surgery at University of Salamanca.

SANCHO IV (1284–95). Succeeded his father.

FERDINAND IV (1295–1312). Son of Sancho. Captured Gibraltar.

ALFONSO XI (1312–50). Succeeded his father. Had one le-
gitimate son, Pedro, and several illegitimate ones, Enrique the most famous.

PEDRO I, THE CRUEL (1350–69). Called the Cruel because
of numerous murders and assassinations including
Enrique's mother and four brothers. Concluded Treaty
of London with Edward III. Made alliance with English governor of Aquitaine, the Black Prince.

ENRIQUE II, OF TRASTAMARA (1369–79). Proclaimed king of
Castilla in Calahorra. Brought Carmona, loyal to Pedro,
under submission. Killed Pedro.

JUAN I (1379–90). Succeeded his father.

ENRIQUE III (1390–1406). Son of Juan; married Catharine,
daughter of Duke of Lancaster, John of Gaunt, and
granddaughter of Pedro I.

JUAN II (1406–54). Son of Enrique III.

ENRIQUE IV, THE IMPOTENT (1454–74). Son of Juan. Had a
daughter, Juana la Beltraneja, born to second wife.
Nobles thought Juana was fathered by someone else
so they offered crown to Isabella, Enrique's half-sister.
Isabella, refusing the crown as long as he lived, was
eventually recognized as heir by Enrique.

ISABELLA I, THE CATHOLIC (1474–1504). Married Ferdinand
of Aragón and became queen of Castilla at Enrique's
death. Castilla and Aragón united although ruled in-
dependently. Isabella and Ferdinand called the Catholic monarchs (*reyes católicos*) because Inquisition to rid
Spain of all non-Catholics was begun in 1480.

FERDINAND, THE CATHOLIC (1474–1516). After Isabella's
death, Ferdinand entrusted Castilla to the care of Cardinal Cisneros until grandson Carlos was old enough
to rule. Juana, daughter of Ferdinand and Isabella and
the mother of Carlos, was called the Mad because of
derangement after death of husband Philip the Fair.
Lived for 40 years in the confinement of a convent in
Tordesillas.

CARLOS I (1516–56). After death of paternal grandfather
Maximilian, became Carlos V, Holy Roman Emperor,
and ruled over more countries than any other European monarch. He was unsuccessful in attempt to defeat Protestantism in Europe. After abdicating in favor
of his son, he entered monastery at Yuste.

PHILIP II (1556–98). Son of Carlos. Broke power of Turks
in Battle of Lepanto in 1571 under leadership of half-

brother Don Juan. His reign started decline of Spain as world empire. Armada was defeated by England. Was married to Queen Mary I of England.

PHILIP III, THE PIOUS (1598–1621). Succeeded his father and was victorious over German Protestants in Battle of White Mountain. He banished the remaining 100,000 Moriscos (Moors converted to Christianity).

PHILIP IV (1621–65). Son of Philip III. Allowed incompetent favorites to run government. Waged continual wars against the Netherlands and France. After peace with France, his daughter María Teresa married Louis XIV.

CARLOS II (1665–1700). Like his father, he was a weak ruler. Three wars with France resulted in loss of territory, men, money and prestige for Spain. Died with no direct heir.

PHILIP V (1700–46). Chosen by great-uncle Carlos to succeed. Was Duke of Anjou, Louis XIV's grandson. Philip became first of Spanish kings of royal Bourbon family of France. Lost much land to Austria and England. Abdicated in favor of son Luis but returned when Luis died within a few months.

FERDINAND VI (1746–59). Son of Philip and first wife Maria Louisa of Savoy. Intelligent ruler who reformed tax system and promoted construction of roads, shipyards, and public buildings.

CARLOS III (1759–88). Succeeded half-brother and continued projects of previous reign. Many monuments and important buildings date from this period.

CARLOS IV (1788–1808). Son of Carlos III and cousin of Louis XVI. In 1804 Napoleon involved Spain in war with England, resulting in defeat by Lord Nelson in the Battle of Trafalgar in 1805. He was forced to surrender crown to Napoleon.

JOSEPH I (1808–14). Appointed to throne by victorious brother Napoleon. With help from England, Spain forced evacuation of French and Joseph.

FERDINAND VII (1814–33). Son of Carlos IV; returned to claim crown, ruling as absolute monarch. All colonies in North and South America were lost during his reign.

ISABELLA II (1833–68). Daughter of Ferdinand and his fourth wife María Cristina, who ruled as regent after his death. Isabella became queen when she came of age. Don Carlos, brother of Ferdinand, claimed the throne and the conflict flamed into the Carlist Wars, in essence a Civil War. Isabella married her cousin, Don Francisco,

Duke of Cádiz. Marriage was an unhappy one. Reign saw deterioration of royal power. Forced to abdicate, she fled to France.

AMADEO I (1868–73). Spanish Parliament, the Cortes, appointed this duke of Aosta, son of the king of Italy, to the throne. Because of his indifference to problems, he was forced to abdicate.

ESTANISLAO FIGUERAS, PI Y MARGAL, NICOLÁS SALMERÓN, AND EMILIO CASTELAR (1873–74). Served as successive presidents of the First Spanish Republic.

ALFONSO XII (1874–85). Son of Isabella. Returned the Bourbons to the throne. Married to Maria Christina of Habsburg-Lorraine. Their son was born after the death of his father.

ALFONSO XIII (1886–1931). Maria Christina acted as regent for her son from 1885 to 1902. Alfonso ruled as a constitutional monarch. Marriage to Victoria Eugenia of Battenberg, Queen Victoria's niece, produced four sons, two of whom died as youths. The third was disabled. The youngest son was Don Juan, prince of Asturias and count of Barcelona. Alfonso became a voluntary exile but did not abdicate his authority.

MIGUEL PRIMO DE RIVERA (1923–30). In a coup backed by the army and Alfonso, Rivera became head of state and ruled as a dictator until 1930, when he resigned and retired to die in Paris later the same year.

THE SECOND SPANISH REPUBLIC. Struggled through periods of strife until Civil War broke out in 1936.

FRANCISCO FRANCO (1939–75). Emerged from Civil War victorious and became dictator.

JUAN CARLOS (1975–PRESENT). Son of Don Juan and grandson of Alfonso XIII. Proclaimed king by the Cortes.

Parador Príncipe de Viana, Olite.

Paradores, Hotels, and Hosterías Nacionales

Andalucía

ONE-FIFTH OF SPAIN'S POPULATION LIVES IN THIS colorful southern region. The vegetation is subtropical, abundant, and varied thanks to an always springlike climate. Irrigation enables shallow soil to yield olives, citrus fruits, almonds, figs, and wine grapes. World-famous sherry is produced in Andalucía. Almería, Cádiz, Córdoba, Granada, Huelva, Jaén, Málaga, and Sevilla are the provinces of Andalucía.

Ancient civilizations flourished along the coast. Cádiz is the oldest inhabited city of Spain and, along with Málaga, was an important Phoenician port enriched by mineral wealth of the Sierra Morena. Today, picturesque fishing villages of white-washed houses climb the gentle slopes of foothills.

The heart of Andalucía is the valley of the Guadalquivir River. This is Moorish Spain—Sevilla, Córdoba, and Granada, the last Arab stronghold reconquered in 1492 by the Catholic monarchs, Ferdinand and Isabella.

Jaén to the north is called the "Silver Door of Andalucía" because of vast acreage in olive groves and minerals in the subsoil.

Recreational opportunities seem limitless. Coastal areas offer swimming, boating, fishing, golf, and tennis. Skiing is enjoyed 250 days a year in the snow-capped Sierra Nevada. Andalucía's principal forest reserve, luring hunters with an abundance of game, is in mountains near Cazorla.

Parador Nacional de Antequera

ANTEQUERA, MALAGA

*** govt. rating
Regional architecture, 55 rooms
Swimming pool, garden
Opened in 1940
Phone 952/84 02 61

The highway between Granada and Antequera goes through an agricultural area of fields of corn, asparagus, and red peppers. One sees many tobacco barns, made of bricks laid with spaces between them to let in air, which are strung with drying and curing leaves. Whitewashed houses cluster together while large haciendas, encircled with white walls, stand out against the ocher soil.

Northwest of Antequera, Highway N-334 affords views of gently rolling farmlands dotted here and there with white out-buildings. La Roda is a picturesque village of sidewalks lined with orange trees, plants, shrubs, and outdoor cafes inviting the traveler to stop. For miles around La Puebla de Cazalla, olive hills and cereal fields are seen. The skyline of La Puebla has a golden dome atop what appears to be a mosque, but upon closer scrutiny the bell tower and cross are seen attached below the dome. From La Puebla de Cazalla to Marchena (12 km west from La Puebla on N-334 and then 7 km north on N-333), land holdings are separated by prolific hedgerows of giant cactus whose orange, persimmon-shaped fruit may be for sale in the old Arab market in Granada. Close to Carmona on Highway C-339, notice the method of collecting olives. Two ladders are placed against the tree and a canvas to catch fallen fruit is stretched between them.

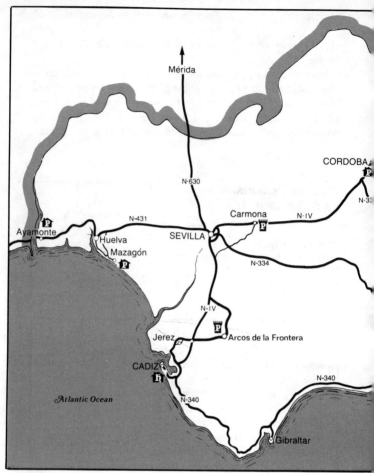

Andalucía

DIRECTIONS: 47 km north of Málaga. The white parador topped with a red tiled roof is located on the western outskirts of Antequera. Parador signs are much in evidence. There is covered parking near a porticoed entrance.

Several large salons of this parador have furniture groupings attractively placed on handsome area rugs from Lorca and Alpujarra. In an ell of one lounge are five green felt-covered game tables with smaller side tables to hold drinks. An atrium luxuriant with green plants is seen from the hallways leading to guest rooms, where twin beds are covered with colorful quilts and flanked by matching night-stands. A low table is shared by two comfortable arm-

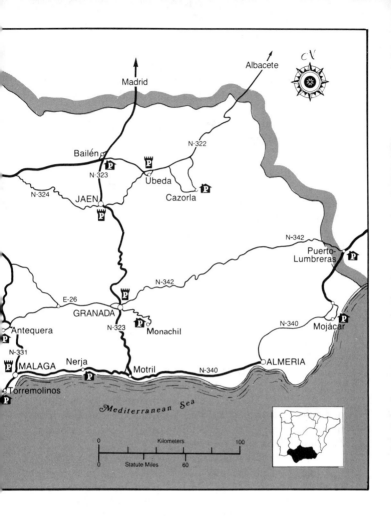

chairs. A desk and minibar are nice additions. Laundry chores are minimized in the large tiled bathroom.

Piped-in classical music enhances food in the upstairs dining room. *Ensalada de aguacates con mariscos* (avocado stuffed with shellfish), *berenjenas rebozadas* (fried eggplant), and *gallina en pepitoria* (chicken stewed in an earthen pot) are recommended. House wines are red and white served in pitchers. Sangria here is delicious.

Antequera, in the heart of a fertile valley, was in existence before the Romans, who called it Anticaria. Things to see and explore include ruins of a Roman fortress, a Moorish castle, sixteenth-century Church of Santa María, the Menga and Viera caves, El Torcal's weirdly shaped rock formations, and Peña de los Enamorados. From this last spot legend says a captive Christian and the Moorish governor's daughter threw themselves into the river below.

Side trips can be made to Málaga (46 km), Ronda (114 km), and Loja (47 km).

Parador Nacional Casa del Corregidor

ARCOS DE LA FRONTERA, CADIZ

*** govt. rating
Regional architecture, 21 rooms
Opened in 1966
Phone 956/70 04 60

DIRECTIONS: 80 km northeast of Cádiz, 93 km south of Sevilla on C-344.

Closed over a year for structural rehabilitation, the parador reopened early in 1986. On the approach, white-washed houses can be seen ascending a hill crested by a well-preserved Moorish castle, owned today by the duke of Arcos. Narrow cobbled streets wind so precariously that in some places signal lights allow cars to go only one way at a time. Signs warn of 7 percent grades.

The parador was rebuilt around the former home of Vicar Gonzalez de Gamaza and had once been a coach house of Jesuits. Although it was named Casa del Corregidor, it is questionable whether it was ever occupied by a *corregidor*, or magistrate. It is said that Charles de Gaulle wrote some of his memoirs while staying at the parador.

From a semicircular terrace, a panoramic view takes in the old castle resting on a steep cliff with the Guadalete River weaving round its base, along with rolling farmland dotted with fruit orchards. The dining room opens onto the terrace and an enclosed patio with decorative grill-work, colorful tiles, and a well surrounded by potted greenery. Lounges radiate from a tiled bar where one wall has a series of plaques depicting a bullfighting folktale.

Interesting parador cuisine includes: *caldillo de perro del Puerto de Santa María* (a soup of fresh fish, onions, and bitter orange juice), *chocos con judías* (squid with white beans), *berenjenas arcenses* (an Arcos delicacy of eggplant, ham, *chorizo*, and bay leaf), and *pez espada a la Molinera de Arcos* (swordfish garnished with lemon). *Tourrón de Cádiz* is a dessert specialty. Wines, of course, are from Jerez, just 31 km to the west.

JEREZ DE LA FRONTERA. On the way to or from Arcos, spend a few hours in Jerez de la Frontera. Vineyards burgeon from one knoll to the other for miles around. This is sherry country and wine enthusiasts will want to visit some of the 350 *bodegas* (wine cellars) open for public tasting.

If you are in the area the last of April or first part of May, you will have a chance to attend the Feria del Caballo, a horse show featuring the superb Andalusian horses used by Vienna's Spanish Riding School.

If you visit around the first of September, you will enjoy the pageantry and exuberance of the annual Wine Festival.

If approaching Arcos de la Frontera from Sevilla, the north-south road that is yellow on the Firestone map is recommended. It is of good quality and furnishes contrasting agricultural scenes. There are few towns on this route, but it is interesting to count the astounding number of private swimming pools. Huge haciendas command fields of wheat, sugarbeets, cotton, and groves of olive trees.

Parador Nacional Costa de la Luz

AYAMONTE, HUELVA

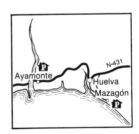

*** govt. rating
Modern, 20 rooms
Swimming pool, garden
Opened in 1966
Phone 955/32 07 00

DIRECTIONS: At the mouth of the Guadiana River, on the border with Portugal.

The view from grounds of the parador seems never-ending as it encompasses the village below and neighboring towns, the Guadiana River, Portugal, and beyond to the

Atlantic Ocean. The modern parador has a striking tiled entry extending in open fashion to the bar and lounges. Several planted areas add warmth and color to the interior. In guest rooms, which have twin beds, there are area rugs on cool tile floors, color-coordinated with bedspreads. Dining room specialties are understandably heavy on seafood. Two to try are *raya en pimentón* (fish with red pepper) and *calamar relleno* (stuffed squid).

When landing by ferry from Vila Real de Santo António, Portugal, look for a sprawling white building on the highest spot. That is the parador. During busy seasons, ferries run every half hour between the Portuguese and Spanish sides of the river. In off season, only one ferry operates and the whole process takes about an hour and a half.

Ayamonte is an ancient city where Phoenicians rested between voyages. Roman historians wrote of Ayamonte as "Esurias." Now it is a fishing port tucked in at the foot of a hill crowned by ruins of an old fortress. The Church of San Francisco, with a unique coffered ceiling, is a national monument worthy of a visit.

Parador Nacional de Bailén

BAILEN, JAEN

*** govt. rating
Modern, 86 rooms
Swimming pool, garden
Opened in 1932
Phone 953/67 01 00

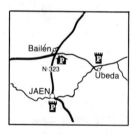

DIRECTIONS: 39 km north of Jaén. On the outskirts of town near the intersection of highways N-IV and N-323.

For those traveling the Madrid–Sevilla or Madrid–Málaga road in the heat of summer, a rest at the air-conditioned parador, a dip in the sparkling pool, or a stroll through a colorful garden may be very appealing. For luncheon have gazpacho or *pipirrana jaenense* (cucumber and tomato salad). Choose an accompanying wine from Valdepeñas, La Mancha, or Montilla-Moriles.

It was on the plains around Bailén that two great battles were fought. During the Reconquest, the Moors met defeat at the hands of Alfonso VIII. In 1808 Spanish troops under General Castaños defeated Napoleon's forces for the first time in the Peninsular War.

Hotel Atlántico
CADIZ

*** govt. rating
Modern, 173 rooms
Swimming pool, gardens
Opened in 1929
Phone 956/21 23 01

DIRECTIONS: Cádiz is reached via a long isthmus. To arrive at Hotel Atlántico, keep straight. At the sign Praia Victoria, bear left and continue along the water. You will see the six-story white cubistic hotel graced by swaying palms on the edge of Parque Genovés.

Hotel Atlántico was the second property acquired by the royal commissioner for tourism. In 1982 it was refurbished and reinaugurated by King Juan Carlos I and Queen Sophia. The entire staff—manager, porter, housekeepers—is friendly and helpful, providing anything but the cold atmosphere experienced in many large hotels. It is difficult to understand why it is rated only three stars by the government.

Ask for a room on the water, the Gulf of Cádiz, that is. Delicious marine air and sounds of lapping waves will lull you to sleep. Guest rooms (with twin beds) are unusually furnished with black, bent, cane-trimmed bedsteads, tables, desk, chairs, and minibar. Small white wool rugs are placed by each bed. The room's own balcony has a white table and two chairs. The bathroom is marble, not tile.

A modern outdoor "cloister" encircles a marble patio and has some cane and rattan furniture. There is a huge pink marble salon between the bar and dining room. Buffet service for all meals enables guests to sample many varieties of traditional Spanish dishes. Alongside a well-stocked salad bar, a large bowl of iced gazpacho waits to be ladled into earthern bowls. An underground garage for guest use is an important adjunct to the hotel.

Although Cádiz is Spain's major shipyard and second-largest naval base (after El Ferrol), the city itself is of a manageable size, conducive to walking. Start out from the hotel and walk all along the sea wall, sometimes climbing steps over older ramparts. Also within walking distance of the hotel is a lovely pedestrian shopping area in the vicinity of Ancha Novena. Enthusiastic walkers can take in the fine arts and archeological museums on Plaza de Mina at

---

Motorists going south from Cádiz can take the coastal road to the southern tip of Spain at Tarifa. Take time to drive to the port, which is only 8 miles from Africa. Leaving the docks, the road through town goes past ivy-covered city walls. Notice a tiled plaque over an archway recounting the gallantry of fort commander Alonso de Guzmán during a battle against the Moors in 1292. The castle, looking down on the waterfront, was built by the Moors and is now an army installation.

There is a turn-off for viewing and photographing El Estrecho, the Strait of Gibraltar. On a foggy day only the tops of Africa's coastal mountains are seen as ships, seemingly strung out in a convoy, glide through the famous passage.

the same outing. Weather permitting, take a cruise of the harbor and stroll along three sides of the port.

Cádiz is the oldest inhabited city in the Western world, though there are few ancient buildings standing as witness. Because it was the wealthiest port in Western Europe, it was repeatedly attacked by pirates and sacked by "gentlemen" pirates like Francis Drake, Essex, and Howard. The city was rebuilt in the early years of the seventeenth century only to be pounded three times in that century by the British. During the Peninsular War, Lord Nelson had the Spanish and French bottled up in the harbor. In October 1805, the fleets escaped and headed south along the coast. However, they were sighted by Nelson off Cape Trafalgar. The ensuing English naval victory assured England's supremacy at sea and destroyed Napoleon's hopes of an invasion, but cost the life of Lord Nelson.

Parador Nacional Alcázar del Rey Don Pedro

CARMONA, SEVILLA

**** govt. rating
Fourteenth-century castle/fortress,
    59 rooms
Garden, elevator, swimming pool
Opened in 1976
Phone 954/14 10 10

DIRECTIONS: 33 km east of Sevilla.

The approach to Carmona (from Highway C-339) presents a dramatic picture of an ancient city circling a ridge topped by a fourteenth-century fortified castle, *alcázar*. The parador, built within old protective walls, is an architectural triumph, a successful blend of old and new. Lounges are numerous and elegant. Guest rooms are fitted out with dark wood and leather furniture, and colorful woven drapes, spreads, and rugs. Rooms lead onto balconies looking down on the Carbones River as it snakes along through endless plains extending to the horizon. A stunning blue-tiled swimming pool lies down the hill, about 100 feet below the parador.

In the regal dining room, sparkling crystal lamps hang from a vaulted ceiling. Among items on the menu is *huevos escalfados indiana*, not a dish from Indiana but one using India's curry to season poached eggs resting on a bed of rice. *Pechuga de pollo a la parrilla* is roast chicken garnished with french fries, mushrooms, carrots, and squash. *Buñuelos*, cream-filled puffs dusted with powdered sugar, make a satisfying dessert.

A circular fountain is set in a courtyard edged with twentieth-century Mudejar columns. Around the lip of the fountain are these words:

> Oh sweet and cleansing water, crystal clear as the source of this fountain, the architect has placed you here in order to erase from memory blood shed in the most cruel of wars between princes, sons of the same king.

The *alcázar* was enlarged by Pedro and was a favorite residence until his death, brought about by step-brother Enrique of Trastamara, who succeeded him. Although Pedro has been labeled "the Cruel" and "the Justicer," history does not bear out the titles. He appears to have been a psychotic womanizer who unsuccessfully pursued his father's mistress, Leonor de Guzmán, mother of Enrique. Pedro's one "true love" may have been María de Padilla, who bore him four children. During his frequent absences, he kept her a virtual prisoner in a nunnery in Palencia. One of the nuns, beautiful María Coronel, caught his fickle wandering eye. To really discourage him from attempting to dishonor her, María disfigured her face with boiling oil. (Her remains are preserved in the Convent of Santa Inés in Sevilla.)

Pick up a map of Carmona at the parador desk and begin a walking tour of one of Spain's national monument cities. Julius Caesar and Cervantes wrote of Carmona. A Roman phrase sings

As the morning star
Shines at daybreak
So in Andalucía
Shines Carmona.

This sentiment appears on Carmona's coat of arms. An Iberian city of prominence, it was on the Roman road Via Augustus. The gates of the town at the roads to Sevilla and Córdoba are of Roman construction. Nineteenth-century excavations revealed a necropolis containing hundreds of burial chambers cut into stone hillsides. After the defeat of the Moors by Fernando III in 1247, Carmona was repopulated and granted its own laws. Land was distributed among Christian settlers by Fernando's son, Alfonso X the Wise. The entire city of Carmona merits fame because of its mansions, churches, convents, and palaces.

Nearby Sevilla is not to be missed, though motorists ought to consider making the trip by bus, as traffic in Sevilla is simply impossible. Walk down from the parador to the main square, Saint Ferdinand's. Buses leave from the Bar Parada across the street from the green Teatro every hour. At the end of the line in Sevilla, the bus stops at a large bus area within easy walking distance of Plaza d'España. Buses return to Carmona at 3, 5, 6, and 6:30 P.M.

Parador Nacional del Adelantado

CAZORLA, JAEN

*** govt. rating
Modern, 34 rooms
Garden
Opened in 1965
Phone 953/72 10 75

DIRECTIONS: 104 km east of Jaén via C-328, 28 km southeast of Cazorla.

For those who like untamed mountain scenery and who don't mind a difficult drive, Parador Nacional del Adelantado will be just the ticket. From the village of Cazorla, the road climbs 28 curly, slow kilometers up into the Sierra de Segura.

The parador is a simple, comfortable, unpretentious mountain lodge. The surroundings in the lush forest reserve teem with deer, wild boar, and ibex. The source of the mighty Guadalquivir River lies in the mountains near Cazorla. Popular sports here are hunting and fishing.

Enjoy eating in the gracious rustic dining room. Local dishes to try include *truchas en salsa de almendras estilo Cazorla* (trout cooked in an almond sauce), and venison prepared two ways: *chuleta de venado en adobo* (chops in a sauce) and *venado al horno* (roast venison). Rabbit also appears on the menu as *conejo en salsa de monte*. A ham omelette, *tortilla serrana*, is also served. Wines offered by the parador are hearty ones: Valdepeñas, La Mancha, Montilla-Moriles, Jumilla, and Yecla.

The landscape en route to the parador is worth the effort. Thousands of hills sprout puffs of olive trees, so continuous they could be a chenille bedspread for Paul Bunyan in this, the largest olive-producing area in Spain. Minuscule pueblos present a striking scene of white houses embellished with strings of red peppers hanging from the eaves. In autumn sudden splashes of orange from shrubs and accents of gold from slender poplars make one wish for talent and a palette. The town of Cazorla itself is quite dramatic, as its pristine dwellings ascend almost to the ruins of an Arab stronghold.

Parador Nacional La Arruzafa

CORDOBA

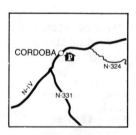

**** govt. rating
Modern, 83 rooms
Swimming pool, tennis, elevator, garden
Opened in 1960
Phone 957/27 59 00

Arruzafa is an Arabic word meaning "garden of palm trees." Córdoba's parador does not have such a garden but is so named because it was built on the site once occupied by a country mansion of Abdu'r-Rahman I (765 A.D.), who planted the first palm trees in Europe. The parador is located in a hilly section north of the Guadalquivir River, 3 km from the center of town.

Flowers cascade from guest room balconies that face the city. Furnishings are Castilian in style—carved dark woods with metal and leather trim. Piped-in music in guest and public rooms adds to the gracious ambience (each room has on/off and volume controls). Lounges are plentiful and attractively spacious.

Outdoor terrace dining is enjoyed during warm weather. Menus in the popular dining room list two cold soups. *Gazpacho de almendras* is almond-flavored, Córdoba's version of the Spanish classic. *Salmorejo* is a heartier soup of lean meat, garlic, and olive oil. Two other specialties to try are *huevos espárragos* (an egg and asparagus dish) and *rabo de toro a la cordobesa* (oxtail stew). Montilla-Moriles are excellent regional wines served at the parador.

Córdoba is of ancient origin and was Rome's capital of southern Spain. However, it attained its full glory under the Arabs, when it became the court of the Caliphs of the West. From the eighth to the eleventh centuries, Muslim, Jewish, and Christian societies lived in harmony, each culture making rich contributions in art, science, and philosophy. In astonishing contrast to most of Europe, Córdoba had a population of 500,000, with 300 mosques and more than twice that many inns and public baths. One of the tenth-century rulers had a library of nearly half a million books. Córdoba's offspring include Seneca, Averroës, Maimonides, Manolete the Matador, and his later counterpart El Cordobés.

There is much to see in Córdoba. Take a cab from the parador to the Puente Romano (Roman bridge), still carrying traffic over the Guadalquivir River. Start your walking tour here. Córdoba's most famous edifice is the Mezquita, Great Mosque, begun in 785 by Abdu'r-Rahman I. Succeeding Arab rulers made additions, with El Hakam II contributing what is considered a masterpiece of Moorish architecture, the exquisite *mihrab*, where the Koran was guarded. Four chapels of the *mihrab* are embellished with Byzantine mosaics, dazzling polychromatic pillars, and gold capitals. Imagine six acres of 850 columns joined by striped, scalloped, arabesque arches! After Ferdinand's victory over the Moors, the northern part of the mosque was converted into a cathedral, a chore that took two centuries.

Across the Roman Bridge is La Calahorra Tower, now used to house the Museum of the History of Córdoba—as intriguing to see the building as the contents.

The *alcázar* (castle) was built on Moorish ruins by Alfonso XI in 1328. Alterations and additions were made by ensuing monarchs. Ferdinand and Isabella lived in the *alcázar* periodically during their campaign to reconquer Granada, and received Columbus there before his first voyage to America. Boabdil, the last Moorish king of Granada, was imprisoned within the palace-fortress. Now, beautiful gardens extend to the Guadalquivir.

Continue to the Plaza del Potro, Córdoba's city center in the sixteenth century. A stone fountain is capped with a small statue of a *potro* (colt). On the square is the Posada del Potro, an inn frequented by Cervantes. In another building on the plaza are the Museo de Bellas Artes (fine arts) and Museo de Julio Romero de Torres, dedicated to a well-known Córdoban artist.

On another day, taxi to the Plaza de Maimonides and stroll through the nearby fourteenth-century synagogue, one of only three still standing in Spain (Toledo possessing the other two). From the plaza, walk through arches to enter a courtyard leading to the Municipal Art and Bullfighting Museum. Many famous matadors were born in the Santa María section of Córdoba. Their portraits, sculptures, artifacts, and personal effects are on display. One wall holds the hide, ear, and tail of the bull that fatally gored Manolete in 1947.

Do make the effort to visit the Archeological Museum, containing some of the most important finds in Spain. The fine building housing the antiquities is the delightful Páez Palace, a Renaissance mansion located on Plaza de Jerónimo Páez.

Eight kilometers west of Córdoba are the ruins of Medina Azahara, a city built in the tenth century by Abdu'r-Rahman III in honor of his favorite wife, the beautiful Zoraida. Enough remains to give one the idea of how grand the city was before it was destroyed in the eleventh century by Berbers.

Before leaving Córdoba, take time to wander through the *callejas* (narrow alleyways), whose walls hold pots of colorful blooms, for a lasting impression of the timeless city.

Parador Nacional San Francisco

GRANADA

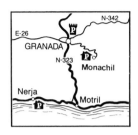

**** govt. rating
Sixteenth-century convent,
35 rooms
Garden
Opened in 1945
Phone 958/22 14 93

DIRECTIONS: Upon entering Granada, motorists should follow signs reading The Alhambra. Should you become discouraged with hectic traffic, hail a cab and ask the driver to lead you to the parador. When you arrive, after unloading baggage, park your car in a covered area provided by the parador at 300 pesetas a day and leave it until you're ready to depart Granada.

Spain's most popular parador rests on the grounds of the Alhambra. On this site Yusuf I of Granada rebuilt a Moorish palace and mosque between 1332 and 1354. After the fall of the city, Ferdinand and Isabella ordered the Arab remains converted into a Franciscan convent. The reconstructed parador retains a portion of the chapel where Isabella's body was interred until transferred to the royal chapel down in the city. A charming tiled patio, leading to guest rooms, remains from convent days. The parador rooms and hallways hold antique Spanish furniture. The products of Granadan artisans add much to the overall decor: engravings, portraits, El Greco reproductions, carpets, woven drapes and spreads, embroideries, and iron and copper wares.

Menu suggestions include *tournedos Rossini* (a continental rather than Spanish dish), *pollo a la alpujarreña* (delicious chicken, though heavy on garlic), and *tortilla a la Sacromonte*, an unusual omelette of the region. The following ingredients are prepared before mixing with eggs in the omelette pan: calves' brains and sweetbreads fried in a batter, fried lamb or veal kidneys, diced fried ham, and potatoes and boiled peas. The authentic Sacromonte is cooked just enough so that the eggs are still white but not raw. In addition to Montilla-Moriles, Valdepeñas, Málaga, and La Mancha wines, the parador offers as its house wine a good *rosado* bottled by the Marqués de Cáceres bodega.

Reservations at the parador must be made months in advance. If you are unsuccessful, try for one of Hotel Alhambra Palace's 135 rooms. It is within walking distance of the Alhambra and is the last word in nineteenth-century Moorish style.

TOURING GRANADA. Do a little homework before you embark on your tour of the Alhambra. Purchase an explanatory guidebook with map (available in shops a short walk from the parador). Washington Irving's *The Alhambra* can also be purchased. The U.S. author, famous for "The Legend of Sleepy Hollow" and the characters Rip Van Winkle and Ichabod Crane, came to Granada on a diplomatic mission in 1829. You will visit the room in which he lived while writing his tales.

The Alhambra is a series of palaces begun in 1238 and added to by subsequent Arab rulers. The Generalife, whose entrance is near the parador, consists of the exotically beautiful gardens and fountains of the Moorish kings. The Alcazaba was their fortress, the most important remaining structure being the Torre de la Vega, tower of the plains. The bell of this watch tower warned of approaching danger and also signaled times for nightly irrigation. It was from this tower that the banner of Castilla was flown on January 2, 1492, announcing the victory of Ferdinand and Isabella. Be sure to notice an inscription in marble. These lines are by the poet Francisco de Icaza:

> Give him alms, woman, for there is nothing in life, nothing, so sad as to be blind in Granada.

The view from the Torre de la Vega encompasses the snow-capped Sierra Nevada, the Generalife, the city below and the plain beyond, and the Alhambra itself.

Also on the grounds is a Renaissance castle built by Carlos V. Today it houses the Archeological and Fine Arts Museum.

You will want to explore the city of Granada. Take a bus down the hill from the parador. Get off on the corner of Angel Ganivet across from the Victoria Hotel. Walk one block right from that corner, three blocks left, and you will be in the vicinity of the cathedral. (Get your return bus in front of the restaurant of the Hotel Guadalupe.) In the cathedral, locate coin boxes and deposit a few pesetas to automatically illuminate sections of the ornate church. The Capilla Real (royal chapel) is adjacent to the cathedral. The chapel was built expressly to hold the magnificent Carrara marble tombs of Ferdinand, Isabella, daughter Juana the Mad, and son-in-law Philip the Fair. In the sacristy, look for Isabella's jeweled crown and scepter and Ferdinand's sword.

A fascinating area very nearby is the Alcaicería, once an Arab silk market, now crowded with tiny shops selling Granadan handcrafts.

Parador Nacional Castillo Santa Catalina

JAEN

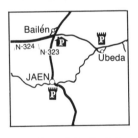

**** govt. rating
Thirteenth-century castle-fortress, 43 rooms
Swimming pool, elevator
Opened in 1965
Phone 953/26 44 11

DIRECTIONS: 97 km north of Granada. Approaching Jaén, look for castle ramparts on the highest hill. To reach the proper ascent, go past the cathedral and turn right at the dead end.

As the road inches up the hill to the parador, views of the castle are marvelous. The ultimate panorama is reached at the top: Old city buildings yield to new, olive groves stretch for miles through the lush valley of the Guadalquivir, and the whole is encompassed by the Sierra Morena extending to the lofty Sierra Nevada. From guest room balconies, one can spend hours reveling in 180 degrees of the sight.

The parador was built alongside thirteenth-century remains in a medieval castle style. Ornate metal and crystal chandeliers hang from vaulted ceilings in public rooms. Furniture is suitably heavy Castilian. Canopied beds in guest rooms rest on elevated platforms. The parador boasts a *taberna* where snacks and sandwiches can be ordered. The dining room is commodious enough to handle tour busloads as well as overnight visitors. Two specialties of the house are *pipirrana* (a cucumber and tomato salad) and *espinacas al estilo de Jaén* (a spinach dish). Valdepeñas wines are favorites here.

Jaén is a city of ancient origin. The Romans called it Aurigis, a name based on their reverence of its extensive silver mines. Jaén was one of the first cities in Andalucía to be captured by the Moors, who called it Geen (caravan route), for it was the crossroads between Castilla and Andalucía.

Arab ruler Alhamar ordered construction of a castle-fortress, and under its lofty protection Jaén lived peacefully for several centuries. In 1246 the *alcázar* was taken by Christian troops of Ferdinand III, the Saint, on Santa Catalina's Day. He extended and improved the fortifications, enabling Jaén to withstand almost two centuries of Arab assaults.

Visitors today can stroll along the grassy former parade ground, which is rimmed by defensive towers, peer into the Torre del Homenaje (castle keep), and linger in the Santa Catalina Chapel, built in the thirteenth and fourteenth centuries.

Parador Nacional Gibralfaro

MALAGA

*** govt. rating
Regional architecture, 12 rooms
Opened in 1948
Phone 952/22 19 02

DIRECTIONS: Directional signs reading Gibralfaro tell motorists they're on the right track to the parador, for it stands on Mount Gibralfaro near ruins of a fortress rebuilt on Phoenician foundations by the Moors.

The present parador was extended and enlarged from an old inn built long ago on the site. The split-level three-story building retains the character of the older structure.

Outdoor dining terrace and guest room balconies look down on the Plaza de Toros, the busy harbor, and the Mediterranean; on clear days, Gibraltar may be seen over 100 km away. It is extremely difficult to secure a reservation here because of the small number of rooms. But the trip up the hill should be made for the view and a meal in the dining room, justly deserving of its reputation for fine cuisine. Three entrees to consider are *rape a la malagueña* (grilled fish seasoned with garlic), *cocktail de gambas y nueces* (shrimp cocktail with nuts), *pez espada parrilla* (grilled swordfish), and *pechuga de pollo Villaroy* (fried breast of chicken). With any of these, choose Valdepeñas wine. After your *tortilla noruega* (baked Alaska), sip one of the dessert wines of Málaga relished since days of the Romans.

The Moors called their fortress Jebelfaro because of a tall lighthouse (*faro*) that served not only to guide ships but to warn of pirate presence. It took the troops of Ferdinand and Isabella 40 days to wrest the fortress from the Arabs. To commemorate the victory in 1487, the Catholic monarchs granted the new Christian city a coat of arms bearing the outline of Gibralfaro castle.

A minibus departs the parador every hour and a half for the cathedral down on Calle Molina Lario. Buses leave the cathedral stop every hour for the return uphill. This is an easy, convenient way to visit the Renaissance cathedral, built between the sixteenth and eighteenth centuries, the former Moorish fortress, or *alcazaba*, and the Archeological Museum on its grounds.

Parador Nacional Cristóbal Colón

MAZAGON, HUELVA

*** govt. rating
Modern, 20 rooms
Swimming pool, tennis court, gardens
Opened in 1968
Phone 955/37 60 00

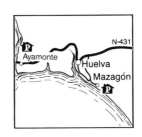

DIRECTIONS: 23 km southeast of Huelva to Mazagón, then another 3 km southeast of Mazagón.

On a bluff overlooking the Gulf of Cádiz, with an aromatic pine grove as a backdrop, the parador offers opportunities for relaxation and exploration of Christopher Columbus (Cristóbal Colón) territory. Guest rooms have patio-balconies leading to grounds planted with flowers and shrubs and continuing to the swimming pool. A footpath leads down to a sandy beach where tides deposit myriad seashells. Seventy-degree air in late October is wonderful.

Public rooms, including the bar and dining room, are attractive. The menu lists typical Andalusian dishes but also features seafood of several varieties. Three suggestions are: *pargo encebollado* (seabream with onions), *rape a la marinera* (angler fish stew using *rape*, pronounced RAH-pay), and *choquitos rellenos* (a kind of squid more like shellfish in flavor served with peppers). A nice dry white wine to order is from nearby La Palma del Condado. Two dessert specialties are *tortas de Moguer* (a layer cake) and *tocinillos de Aracena* (an egg yolk and sugar confection).

Places that Columbus knew include the Monastery of La Rábida (20 km from the parador), Palos de la Frontera (10 km), and Moguer (28 km). La Rábida, according to tradition, has quite a history. First the site held a Phoenician

---

A vast national park of dunes and salt marshes known as Coto de Doñana lies 24 km south of Parador Cristóbal Colón, beyond the town of Torre de la Higuera. The park serves as winter shelter for migratory birds of Europe and Africa. To book seats on a Land Rover for an approximately 80-km tour of Coto de Doñana, telephone 955/43 04 32 and make reservations. You may reach an answering service, so if you are hesitant in Spanish, ask one of the parador staff members to make the call. There are two trips a day, one in the morning and another in the afternoon. Times vary with the seasons. The price is 1250 pesetas per person. Situated at El Acebuche (which may not appear on national maps but does on regional ones), the park headquarters has a reception/information/interpretive center, rest rooms, lunch rooms, picnic areas, a bar, and gift shop. If you do not care to take the land rover trip, you can walk to five observation points. For more information (in Spanish), write to Ministerio de Agricultura, Instituto Nacional para la Conservación de la Naturaleza, Parque Nacional de Doñana, Huelva, Spain.

altar to the god Baal, then a Roman temple to the goddess Proserpina, next a Muslim *rápita*, where ascetics prayed, followed by buildings of the Knights Templar, and finally, in the beginning of the fifteenth century, a Franciscan convent. Here Columbus talked at great length with Fra Juan Pérez, eventually persuading him to present to the Catholic monarchs Columbus's dream of finding a new route to the Indies. Visitors are shown the room where Columbus held his conversations and the chapel where he and his crew prayed prior to the first voyage.

You must use your imagination to picture Columbus setting off from Palos de la Frontera because the harbor is now silted over. (Cortés also departed Palos in 1528.) The edict of Ferdinand and Isabella ordering preparation for Columbus's voyage, including conscription of local seamen and construction of three caravels, was read by the mayor of Palos in the public square before the Church of San Jorge.

In Moguer, fourteenth-century Santa Clara Convent Church saw Columbus spend a night in prayer upon his return from the first voyage.

Parador Nacional Reyes Católicos

MOJACAR, ALMERIA

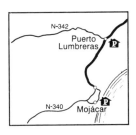

**** govt. rating
Modern, 98 rooms
Swimming pool, garden
Opened in 1966
Phone 951/47 82 50

DIRECTIONS: On the coast 90 km northeast of Almería, a few km off Highway N-340. Follow signs out of Mojácar to Garrucha to reach the parador, almost 3 km down the hill on the beach.

Mojácar's white houses seem to perch precariously on rocky heights. According to Pliny, Mojácar or Murgis Acra (high mountain) marked the boundary of Bética, the Roman name for Andalucía. The narrow winding streets have an Old World feeling.

The two-story white cubistic building of the parador encompasses an extensive brick terrace broken by wells of brilliant petunias and geraniums. There is a children's playground near the oversized pool that faces the Mediterranean. Public rooms with congenial furniture groupings flow one into another. Each of the 98 guest rooms has a balcony admitting the sounds and gentle breezes of the sea. In the upstairs dining room, with 180-degree marine views, fish plays a dominant role. The *fritura* (platter of fried fish) is highly recommended. The *zarzuela* (fish stew) is likewise excellent. For dessert, try the *tarta de manzana* (apple tart). Enjoy *blanco, rosado,* or *tinto* wines bottled for the paradores by the *bodegas* of Rioja.

Don't fail to notice the antique apothecary chest in a room off the reception hall.

If you arrive in the afternoon, try to catch the return of fishing boats into the harbor of Garrucha, just 3 km north of Mojácar.

If traveling east to Mojácar from the Costa del Sol around lunch time, stop at the Club de Mar restaurant on the coast route at the western outskirts of Almería. From the club terrace, look back to the city's alcazaba, an eighth-century Arab fortress whose high ruddy walls dominate the old town, and ahead to the harbor. You may be treated to a sideshow watching the ferry Ciudad de Santa Cruz de la Palma *depart.*

Just north of Almería, along Highway N-340, the land may remind some visitors of the mountains around Palm Springs, California, with verdant orange trees thriving on flat stretches. Then from Benahadux to Tabernas come 12 miles of desert land where scenes from Lawrence of Arabia *were filmed. The town of Sorbas is particularly picturesque, as old homes cling to a cliff very like those of Cuenca.*

Parador Nacional de Nerja

NERJA, MALAGA

**** govt. rating
Modern, 60 rooms
Swimming pool, tennis court,
   gardens, elevator
Opened in 1965
Phone 952/52 00 50

DIRECTIONS: 50 km east of Málaga on N-340. Motorists departing Málaga should stay in the right-hand lane and follow signs to Almería.

Much of the area west of Nerja is taken up with truck gardens, with some tiny plots still being tilled by oxen and plow. Whole sections of hillsides are covered with plastic greenhouses. At strategic points along the coast stand remains of *torres,* watchtowers built by local residents after the Reconquest as lookouts for Barbary pirates, who continued raids until the eighteenth century.

The parador consists of a two-story original building and, at right angles, a one-story addition. All rooms in the older building have balconies overlooking gardens, swimming pool, and the Mediterranean. The newer guest rooms lead onto patios. Terraces and courtyards are paved with pebbles painted black and white and laid in checkerboard fashion. Exotic flowers bloom among orange trees and frame a blue-tiled fountain in the center of a courtyard. Off the bar-lounge, a sunken dining room and salon are separated by an open-sided buffet holding colorful ceramic ware of the region. To the far right of the grounds if facing the Mediterranean is an elevator down to the Burriana beach.

Dinner is served at a welcome, unusual 8 P.M. rather than the customary later hour. Specialites include *fritura de pescado* (variety of deep-fried fish), *cocktail de aguacates con gambas* (shrimp in avocado halves), *pez espada a la naranja* (swordfish in orange sauce), and *langostinos a la plancha* (grilled jumbo prawns). Málaga, Montilla-Moriles, and Condado de Huelva wines are served.

It was Alfonso XII who suggested Nerja as the site for a

parador. He was intrigued with the area and especially with a prowlike promontory extending out over the Mediterranean. He called it the Balcón de Europa, balcony of Europe.

The parador is a good healthy walk from the older part of town near the Balcón. Those driving might want to leave their car in a large parking lot near the city hall and then stroll through the narrow streets full of interesting shops. Have lunch at the Rey Alfonso restaurant. Walk down steps of the palm tree–edged promenade of the Balcón to the very tip. Enjoy a delicious chef's salad and a bottle of wine, and bask in the marvelous vista of waves emanating from a placid sapphire sea, crashing ashore beneath you.

A trip to the Cuevas de Nerja, 3 km east of Nerja and off the road to Motril, is highly recommended. The spectacular caves were discovered in 1959. Rooms of limestone formations have been dramatically lighted. A well-maintained footpath leads to a climax in the Hall of Cataclysm, where ceilings reach a height of 60 meters. One wishes for a Bach fugue performed on a thunderous pipe organ rather than the mild, pleasant music played in the caves. Festivals of dance and music are held annually.

SEVILLA

There are four main sights to see in Sevilla: the *alcázar*, the Barrio of Santa Cruz, the cathedral, and Giralda tower.

The *alcázar* is a magnificent palace built on orders of Pedro the Cruel in the fourteenth century. He employed Mozarabic artisans (Muslims converted to Christianity), who created a Mudejar masterpiece of slender columns joined by keyhole-shaped arches, ornate gold-leafed ceilings, intricate wall tracery, and lavish use of brilliant *azulejos* (painted tiles). The *alcázar* is reminiscent of Granada's Alhambra. A walk through terraced gardens lush with flowers, shrubs, fruit trees, and reflecting pools leads, by way of a covered passage, to the enchanting old Santa Cruz Barrio (neighborhood). Amble leisurely through the twisted alleyways and delight in the flower-adorned patios and tiny squares shaded by orange trees.

Sevilla's cathedral is the largest in Spain, third-largest in Europe after Rome's Saint Peter's and London's Saint Paul's. Early in the fifteenth century, the largest mosque in Sevilla was demolished and work proceeded on the cathedral until completion in the sixteenth century. The Gothic church is incredibly rich inside and out. Columbus is buried here, say church officials, although there are some who say he was buried in what is now the Dominican Republic. But whoever is buried in the ornate tomb borne by four kings, it is worth a look.

The Giralda is Sevilla's favorite monument. Built as a Muslim minaret on Roman foundations in 1184, it soars 322 feet into the skies. In the mid-sixteenth century, a belfry with 25 bells was constructed and the whole crowned by a large statue representing Faith serving as a weather vane, or *giraldillo*.

Parador Nacional Condestable Dávalos

UBEDA, JAEN

*** govt. rating
Sixteenth-century palace, 25 rooms
Opened in 1930
Phone 953/75 03 45

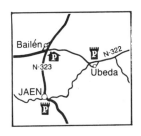

DIRECTIONS: 40 km east of Bailén on N-322.

Situated on Plaza de Vásquez Molina, the parador began life as a palace belonging to Don Fernando Ortega Salido, dean of Málaga, who was known as Dean Ortega. Although built in the sixteenth century, it was totally renovated in the seventeenth. Restorative maintenance was done on the parador in 1942 and again in 1977. At the top of a grand staircase, second-floor guest rooms lead off glass-enclosed galleries overlooking a charming courtyard. The rooms are large with tile-decorated floors. The baths are also unusually large. Antique furniture completes the timeless atmosphere.

Fresh flowers grace tables in the ell-shaped dining room. This is partridge country and *perdiz* appears on the parador menu as *perdiz estofada o en escabeche* (stewed or pickled). If that doesn't appeal, try *chuletillas de cordero* (lamb chops). For dessert *leche frita* is suggested. Literally fried milk, the sweet is actually a very thick custard that is sliced when congealed, dipped in bread crumbs, fried quickly in

butter, then dusted with sugar and spices. Very tasty. Valdepeñas, La Mancha, and Montilla-Moriles wines are
served.

Ubeda was one of the first towns taken from the Moors.
Thus the architecture in this monumental city is not Moorish but Italian Renaissance. The parador shares the plaza
with other remarkable buildings such as seventeenth-century Church of Santa María, sixteenth-century Church of
El Salvador, Palacio Vázquez de Molina, called Las Ca-
denas and now the city hall, and the palace of El Marqués
de Mancera, once viceroy of Peru. There is a tourist office
across the plaza from the parador. Calle Valencia is a street
of craft studios luring the shopper.

The parador was named Condestable Dávalos as a tribute to Ruy López de Dávalos, a warrior captured by the
Moors of Granada. After he won favor with the Arab king,
he was set free. The off again/on again favorite of Juan II
was given the honorary title Condestable, High Constable.
Notice the portrait of him over the fireplace in the dining
room.

Just 9 km to the west is Baeza, which along with Ubeda
was designated an exemplary city during the International
Year of Architecture in 1975 by the Council of Europe.
Aristocratic mansions, public buildings, and churches range
from Romanesque to Renaissance.

Parador Nacional de Sierra Nevada

MONACHIL, GRANADA

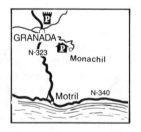

*** govt. rating
Modern, 32 rooms
Tennis, garage
Opened in 1966
Phone 958/48 02 00

DIRECTIONS: 35 km southeast of Granada. Driving out of Granada,
follow signs for Motril. Eventually Highway GR-420 to Sierra Nevada will appear.

At 8125 feet above sea level, the parador accommodates
winter sports enthusiasts, who can enjoy skiing from November to May. Built of rustic stone with pine trim, the
parador is a skier's dream. Guest rooms are large, pleas-

ant, and functional. Lounges focus on fireplaces to gather round after an invigorating day on the slopes. Cuisine in the beamed dining room is typical of the region of Granada, such as *tortilla a la Sacromonte* (that unusual omelette described under Granada's parador), *conejo asado en pobre* (roast rabbit), and dishes featuring the famous Trévelez hams. For dessert, try *piononos de Santa Fe* (a confection of sugar, egg yolks, and white wine). Montilla-Moriles, Málaga, and Valdepeñas wines are served.

Scenery en route to the parador on the Granada–Veleta highway, the highest in Europe, is spectacular. The parador is in the upper part of the Sol y Nieve (sun and snow) winter sports area, where there are a touted 250 days of sunshine a year. Among facilities at the parador are two cable cars, several ski lifts, and four chair lifts.

Parador Nacional del Golf
TORREMOLINOS, MALAGA

**** govt. rating
Modern, 40 rooms
Swimming pool, tennis, golf
   course, gardens
Opened in 1956
Phone 952/38 12 55

DIRECTIONS: 14 km southwest of Málaga on N-340. If approaching the parador from Málaga, go past the *aeropuerto* (airport) and keep in the right-hand lane for a special turn, then take the overpass to the parador, which is on the other side of the highway. If coming from the west, just past La Colina, a huge apartment devel-

opment on the right, get in the right-hand lane, go 3 km, and turn right off the highway.

Even though the town of Torremolinos is hectic and touristy, the parador is away from it all, a perfect place to spend a few days of relaxation. A circular swimming pool, set in a broad expanse of lawns, separates two wings of guest rooms. Lounges, bar, TV room, and dining room face the pool, part of the golf course, and the Mediterranean. Guest rooms open onto balconies. Don't be alarmed when you hear a "zap" noise. This is the mosquito catcher doing its job. You may need a repellent lotion to sit out on your balcony. We found that Autan, sold in supermarkets and pharmacies, worked well. Much of the 18-hole, par 72 golf course designed by Robert Trent Jones goes along the beach.

Cuisine in the airy dining room is typical Andalusian, featuring gazpacho, *fritura de pescado* (delicious variety of fried fish), and *pollo asado* (roast chicken). A pleasing *rosado* comes from the Marqués de Cáceres bodega.

When golf, swimming, and tennis begin to pall, indulge in some sightseeing. Casares is a village down the coast said to have been named by Julius Caesar, who came for therapeutic mineral baths. It is a classic Andalusian village, where whitewashed houses are stacked block-fashion on sides of a steep hill topped with what's left of Moorish fortifications. (Drive southwest from Torremolinos about 100 km and at San Luis go northwest 14 km to Casares.) If you hurry you may still be able to enjoy the lovely marina at Estepona, 74 km southwest of Torremolinos on the coast road. It has not yet reached the calamitous stage of wall-to-wall people and yachts that has been the fate of Puerto Banús. Lunch at an outside cafe and revel in the sights, peace, and air that is balmy even in late November.

A full day should be allowed for a trip to Ronda, 106 km to the west of Torremolinos, but also reached by heading down the coast. Fifty-five of those kilometers are through mountainous terrain. This is one of the oldest cities in Spain, with evidence that the Greeks lived in the area. During Roman tenure, it was an important trading center. Later it served as the capital of a minor Moorish kingdom. A natural fortress, it perches on top of soaring rocky cliffs over El Tajo, a ravine over 700 feet deep. Count on an hour and a half for a stroll through La Ciudad, the old town.

Aragón

ONCE A TINY KINGDOM LYING AT THE BASE OF THE
Pyrenees, Aragón developed steadily, due to commercial
acuity and monetarily advantageous royal marriages. Its
domain stretched from France to Murcia and included the
Balearic Islands, Naples, and Sicily. In the early sixteenth
century, hoping to secure an English alliance against France,
Catherine of Aragón, daughter of Ferdinand and Isabella,
was married to Arthur, prince of Wales, and later to Henry
VIII.

Today the provinces of Huesca, Zaragoza, and Teruel
make up Aragón, extending from the Pyrenees in the north
to the Levant in the south, from Navarra in the west to
Cataluña in the east. The climate of Aragón is continental,
with pleasant springs and autumns, warm summers, and
cold winters.

The Upper Aragonese Pyrenees are thickly forested, re-
lieved by steep-sided valleys. In Ordesa National Park,
dominated by 11,000-foot Monte Perdido, many species of

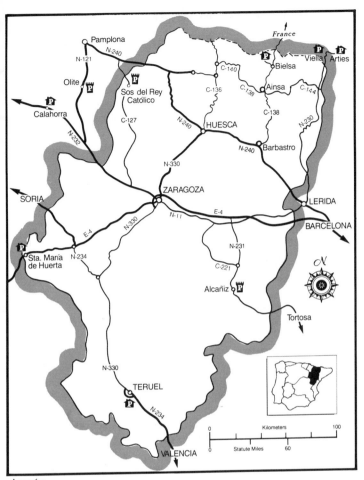

Aragón

wild game and fowl abound. Tumbling cascades are created by the Arazas River as it flows from east to west.

Other rivers enrich the farmland of Huesca. Zaragoza's fertile plains, rimmed by the Moncayo mountains and Sierra del Maestrazgo, are watered by the Ebro River. Wheat fields and olives flourish despite sections of bleak moors and harsh rocky land. Vineyards in the area provide grapes for a strong red wine high in alcohol content.

The area around Teruel is rather barren, with poor soil. Small mines yield coal, iron, manganese, zinc, and sulphur.

Remnants of Iberian, Roman, Visigothic, and Arabic civilization exist throughout the region. The many monasteries found here give testament to generations of profound religious devotion. A powerful kingdom during the Middle Ages, Aragón's fiercely independent people were linked politically to Castilla after the marriage of Ferdinand of Aragón to Isabella.

Mountain hiking and skiing, hunting, and fishing are the popular sports in Aragón.

Parador Nacional La Concordia

ALCANIZ, TERUEL

*** govt. rating
Twelfth-century castle, 12 rooms
Elevator
Opened in 1968
Phone 974/83 04 00

DIRECTIONS: 132 km southeast of Zaragoza on N-232.

Parador La Concordia is a castle on a hilltop. Centuries-old houses cluster around the base of the hill while modern highrises edge the environs. The late twelfth-century castle-convent was given to the Order of Calatrava by Alfonso II. In 1728, Prince Philip converted part of the castle into an Aragón-style palace. It was this section that was reconditioned into a parador in 1968. In addition to the 12 guest rooms, there is a lounge, a library, a bar, and a dining room. The rest remains as it was.

Guest rooms are furnished with twin beds, two occasional chairs, a coffee table, desk, and minibar. Ceilings are 12 feet high and walls three feet thick. The decor has a castle motif. From windows the view is of rooftops of the medieval town, terraced garden plots, a stream tumbling over a weir, and a patchwork of farms stretching to the horizon. The dramatic dining room has a lofty beamed ceiling and a fireplace large enough to have roasted meat for an entire entourage of knights. Walls are hung with heraldic banners of bygone kings of Aragón.

Three Aragonese entrees are *pollo al chilindrón* (chicken with red peppers, onions, and tomato sauce), *cordero a la pastora* (a lamb dish), and *arroz a la aragoñesa* (rice with rabbit). Hearty regional wines are Cariñena, Campo de Borja, Campo de Tarragona, and Priorato. Cap the meal with *torta de almendrados,* an almond tart.

A tiled plaque in the parador tells the story that Martin the Humane, king of Aragón, Cataluña, Valencia, and Mallorca, died in 1410, leaving no direct descendant. Noblemen of the kingdom met to discuss the rights of the pretenders. For two years, members of parliament met with ambassadors from Castilla, France, Sicily, and the Vatican. In 1412 they agreed upon a king and signed a *concordia* naming Fernando I king of Aragón. Fernando was the grandfather of Ferdinand the Catholic.

Parador Nacional Monte Perdido
BIELSA, HUESCA

*** govt. rating
Modern, 16 rooms
Gardens
Opened in 1968
Phone 974/50 10 11

DIRECTIONS: 74 km northwest of Lérida to Barbastro on C-240; 102 km north of Barbastro to Bielsa on C-138; 14 km west of Bielsa to parador.

The rugged four-story stone parador sits at the western end of the Valle de Piñeta. Tumbling Cinca River has its genesis here and is audible and visible from the parador. The music of cowbells fills the air as cattle graze on the verdant meadows nearby. Anglers and hunters frequent the parador, trout and *sarría* (wild mountain goat) being the main prey. In the reception hall is a stuffed mounted *sarría* with sweet and wistful eyes.

A comfortable lounge is furnished with leather furniture. Focal points are the TV and fireplace. A bar and game room are also available to guests. Suggested menu items are: *chuletillas de ternasco belsetana* (succulent lamb chops) and *pastela de la casa* (white three-layered cake). The house wine is a hearty Somontano from Huesca *bodegas*.

In late September, the waterfall Cola de Caballo (horse's tail) is seen against distant mountain slopes as only a thread of water streaming from three levels. It is glorious in spring.

Heat at the parador was welcome in late September—no need to wait for certain dates in October arbitrarily set by some power that be, regardless of temperatures.

The parador is one of three in the eastern mountains of Spain. The roads are adequate. We were glad to be traveling them in autumn. In heavy summer traffic, one might be a bit apprehensive sharing roads with no center stripe. Traveling between Bielsa and the parador at Viella, you will encounter Congosto de Ventanillo 3 km south of Castejón de Sos on C-139. The Congosto is a dramatic narrow gorge whose rocky walls reach heights of 1000 feet. The Esera River froths over boulders of many different sizes. Lacy trees cling to the gorge's damp sides.

The drive between the paradores of Bielsa and Viella took about five hours including lunch and three sheep stops—to allow sheep to clear the road.

Parador Nacional Fernando de Aragón

SOS DEL REY CATOLICO,
ZARAGOZA

*** govt. rating
Regional architecture, 66 rooms
Elevator, garden
Opened in 1975
Phone 948/88 80 11

DIRECTIONS: 58 km southeast of Pamplona on C-127.

Ferdinand the Catholic was born in the Sada Palace in Sos, now undergoing restoration to its medieval glory. The parador was built on a hill near the few remaining walls that once encircled Ferdinand's domain. It is a fine example of a new building in harmony with surrounding structures four or five centuries old.

Guest rooms are richly appointed with crystal and brass lighting fixtures. Draperies and bedspreads are of colorful woven material. An outside terrace leads off the dining room. Here one can sit and sip while reveling in the Aragonese countryside by day and the brilliant heavens by night. A consistently good choice for lunch is *espárragos* (asparagus), excellent long white plump spears served cold with two sauces: mayonnaise and a tomato relish.

Walk down from the parador through winding streets where balconies overflow with vivid geraniums and impatiens. There is much bustle in town as workers refit crumbling masonry and re-stucco old walls.

Parador Nacional de Teruel
TERUEL

*** govt. rating
Modern, 40 rooms
Elevator, garden
Opened in 1956
Phone 974/60 25 53

DIRECTIONS: 2 km from the northern outskirts of the city of Teruel, on N-234/N-330.

Situated 3000 feet above sea level and overlooking the city, the handsome parador has a Mudejar arched entry leading into the reception hall. Polished marble floors, warm dark woods, and potted greenery give the parador the aura of a country mansion. Cuisine is typically Aragonese: *pollo al chilindrón* (chicken prepared with pimientos, onions, and tomatoes), *magras al estilo de Aragón* (a dish featuring ham slices), and *castellar* (veal stew). As a wine accompaniment, select a full-bodied Cariñena *tinto*. Desserts include *suspiros de monja* (nun's sighs), a meringue and almond concoction.

TOURING TERUEL. There is a wealth of Mudejar architecture to be seen in Teruel. Here Christians, Jews, and Moslems lived in harmony until the last mosque was closed and all Moors expelled in 1502. Of the five Mudejar towers, two are outstanding: those adorning the Church of El Salvador and the Church of San Martín. The sizable Los Arcos, a bridge-aqueduct, was built in the sixteenth century.

In addition to the many buildings with Arabic touches, Teruel is also noted as the City of Lovers. Legend says that in 1217 Isabel Seguras and Diego Marcilla, friends from childhood, wanted to marry. But the fortunes of Diego's family had dwindled, whereas Isabel's father had become the wealthiest man in town. Señor Seguras would not consent to the marriage. However, the persuasive Diego got him to agree that if he went away and returned a successful man within five years, he and Isabel could be wed. So Diego went out into the world to seek his fortune.

When at the end of five years there was no word from Diego, Señor Seguras pressed Isabel into marriage with a very rich man from a nearby town. Just as the marriage vows had been completed in the Church of San Pedro, Diego, having achieved his monetary goal, appeared to claim Isabel. But he was one day late. Broken-hearted Diego begged Isabel for a kiss to sustain him when he must leave her forever. But newly married Isabel refused, whereupon Diego, prone with grief, died at her feet. On the following day, Isabel, clad in her wedding gown, once more entered the Church of San Pedro, this time to attend Diego's funeral. While kneeling before his bier, she collapsed and died.

The townspeople were so distraught over the deaths of the lovers that they insisted Isabel and Diego be buried side by side in the church. Three hundred years later during restorative repairs to San Pedro, the two graves were uncovered. The bodies were removed to a nearby chapel and interred in a mausoleum designed by Juan de Avalos. The sculpted figures of Isabel and Diego lie atop marble caskets decorated with their family shields. Their hands reach out to each other. Through grilles on the elaborate lighted tombs may be seen the skeletal remains of the lovers.

Asturias

COASTAL ASTURIAS HAS BROAD BEACHES, SE-
cluded coves and estuaries emptying into the Bay of Biscay. Abrupt rocky cliffs form the shoreline. Inland Asturias is a symphony of green meadows, woodlands, and
forests framed by gray slopes of the Picos de Europa. Small
farms, apple orchards, and lush pastureland contribute to
the region's agriculture. Large coal fields and iron and steel
works make Asturias the richest mining basin in Spain.
Essentially a seafaring people, Asturians operate fishing
fleets along the coast. The region is bounded on the north
by the Bay of Biscay, on the west by Galicia, on the south
by the Cantabrian Mountains, and on the east by the
province of Santander; there is one province, Oviedo.

Caves in Asturias served as home to people in prehistoric times. In 772 A.D. King Pelayo, leader of the rugged
Asturs, defeated the Moors at the Battle of Covadonga,
the first victory of the Reconquest in Spain. Roman bridges
and more than sixty Romanesque buildings are to be seen

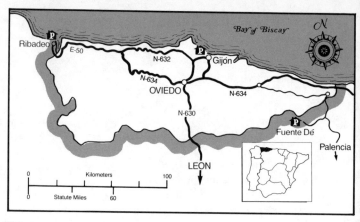

Asturias

in Asturias. Today, small villages preserve ancient dialects and old forms of folk dancing and music.

The *horreo*, or family granary is a typical structure seen throughout Asturias. The square building is encircled by a porch and is built on concrete pilings to discourage rodents. Strands of onions, corn, and even laundry hang to dry from its eaves. They are so traditional that many of today's houses have gaily decorated *horreos* on the grounds.

Parador Nacional Molino Viejo

GIJON, OVIEDO

**** govt. rating
Modern, 40 rooms
Garden
Opened in 1967, remodeled in 1985
Phone 985/37 05 11

DIRECTIONS: 28 km north of Oviedo via the *autopista*.

Molino Viejo means "old windmill"—the parador once saw life as one of a large number of windmills in Gijón between the fifteenth and eighteenth centuries. The mills were driven by springs, streams, and even the tidal flow of the sea. The ancient water course is still preserved on parador grounds. The parador is located in a far corner of one of Spain's loveliest parks, that of Isabel the Catholic. Have an apéritif in the bar overlooking a small island alive with fowl activity—black and white swans nesting and tending their young.

The attractive dining room serves cuisine *a la asturiana*. Try *fabada asturiana* (a hearty white bean stew seasoned with corned beef and chorizo sausages). *Arroz con leche* (chilled rice custard sprinkled with cinnamon) is a dessert specialty. Wines are Ribeiros and Valdeorras from Galicia. For an unusual treat, ask to be shown the room reserved for drinking the famous *sidra* (cider) from Asturias.

Gijón is of surprising size and hums with commerce. Its harbor experiences very low tides and as a result fishing boats and large vessels swaying gently at high tide are marooned on mud flats at low tide.

Be alert when driving through nearby rural areas for you will see pairs of oxen with leather shields over their heads and intricately tooled fringe hanging before their eyes. You may wonder at the hardiness of farm women who work alongside men. Using pitchforks, they spear and heave incredible loads of hay up into waiting horse- or donkey-driven carts. Notice that their wooden shoes have three wooden cleats on the bottom, perhaps to give better footing on hillsides.

Castilla La Mancha

CASTILLA NUEVA AND MURCIA, TWO ANCIENT RE-
gions distinct in geography and history, have been com-
bined to form the new Castilla La Mancha. Diverse landscapes are found here in the core of the peninsula,
extending to the Mediterranean Sea. Here are the red earth
and sapphire skies around Toledo, the vineyards and plains
of La Mancha, which saw Cervantes's Don Quixote. Ciudad Encantada is an "enchanted city" of huge masses of
curiously shaped rock transformed over millennia by water,
ice, and snow.

Albacete, Al-Basite (the plain) in Arabic, has an arid climate and miles of flat land conducive to growing cereal
crops. Wooded sectors are broken by undulating fields.
Large tracts of empty land are uninhabited not only because of inhospitable terrain but also because of centuries
of incessant warfare.

Some mines in Murcia are being worked although most
of the mineral wealth was exploited first by the Phoenicians and last by the Arabs. Orange and lemon groves,

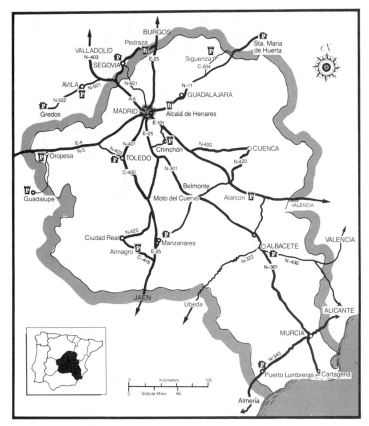

Castilla La Mancha

thriving because of irrigation systems perfected by the Arabs, stretch along the coastal plains while sandy beaches washed by the Mediterranean are broken by occasional rocky outcrops.

This expanded region now includes the provinces of Ciudad Real, Cuenca, Guadalajara, Toledo, Madrid, Albacete, and Murcia.

Parador Nacional
Marqués de Villena
ALARCON, CUENCA

*** govt. rating
Castle, 11 rooms
Elevator, garden
Opened in 1966
Phone 966/33 13 50

DIRECTIONS: 187 km southeast of Madrid, 3 km off N-111.

Named after one of the principal owners of this, the best-preserved castle in Cuenca, the parador has been reconstructed within castle walls. Charming in every respect, the parador invites one to stay in twentieth-century comfort and muse on innumerable vignettes of history experienced by the old citadel. Cuisine is typically Cuencan: *morteruelo* (finely chopped, highly spiced dish of pork liver and bread crumbs), *zarajos* (cured lamb tripe), *cordero en caldereta* (lamb stew), and *gachas de almortas* (a pork dish). A Valdepeñas *tinto* would be an excellent choice of wine for any of these dishes.

Historians say that the fortified castle of Alarcón was the Llercao of Celtiberians, a place lost to the Romans, retaken by a son of Visigoth King Alarico. Later the Arabs built a strong fortress on the site. Alfonso VI captured the castle in 1085, and held it briefly until it was regained by the Moors. Their final capitulation occurred in 1184. Struggles and intrigues continued for centuries until the structure's life as a fortress ended with the Civil War of 1833–40. Its geographic position had foretold its fate, for the land rises dramatically from a rocky base almost completely encircled by a natural moat, the meandering Júcar River.

Much of the ancient construction remains: the vigilant watch tower whose ramparts offer spectacular views of the countryside, lesser towers, and remains of walls and gates. Now it stands in noble serenity, the stillness broken by the bleats of grazing sheep and goats and the tinkling of their bells.

It will take a bit of planning to fully enjoy two of the most well-known attractions in the city of Cuenca. The Museum of Spanish Abstract Art and Mesón Casas Colgadas (a restaurant) are adjacent to one another in fifteenth-century Casas Colgadas, hanging houses. These three linked houses sit precariously atop 600-foot cliffs looking down on a gorge cut by the Huécar River. Phone ahead for luncheon reservations at the restaurant (21 18 22) and time your visit to coincide with museum hours: 11 a.m. to 2 p.m. and 4 to 6 p.m., Saturdays 4 to 10 p.m., closed Mondays. Cuenca is about 97 km from the parador.

Another possible excursion from Parador Marqués de Villena is to Ciudad Encantada, another 37 km beyond Cuenca. Although the rock formations are interesting (perhaps very to a geologist), on a scale of 1 to 10, they receive a Ballard rating of 3.

Parador Nacional de la Mancha

ALBACETE, CASTILLA LA MANCHA

*** govt. rating
Regional architecture, 70 rooms
Gardens, tennis, swimming pool
Opened in 1970
Phone 967/22 94 50

DIRECTIONS: 4 km south of Albacete, off N-430.

Set on the sprawling plains of La Mancha, the parador is suitably decorated in a country motif. Salon walls hold oxen yokes, brilliantly colored blankets, primitive wooden farm implements. Of special interest are double reed baskets carried on backs of donkeys. One lounge has a rustic beamed ceiling and a fireplace bordered by decorative tiles. Guest rooms are large and comfortably furnished, with cool, shining red-tiled floors.

Cuisine is typical of La Mancha, substantial and flavorful. Gazpachos here are flavored with bits of rabbit and partridge. *Pisto* is a mixture of fried vegetables. *Pollo a la magra de Chinchilla* is a chicken specialty of the parador. *Tortilla guisada con caldo* is an omelette topped with a savory sauce. Be sure to order for dessert *flores manchegas*, made with honey. The wine list is long and varied: Almansa, La Mancha, Valdepeñas, Jumilla, Yecla, Valencia, and Alicante. *Cuerva* is a regional drink prepared with wine and sliced peaches.

Hostería Nacional del Estudianté

ALCALA DE HENARES, MADRID

**** govt. rating
Opened in 1930
Phone 91/888 03 30

DIRECTIONS: 46 km east of Madrid on N-11. Perhaps the best way to find the *hostería* is to ask directions to the Oficina de Turismo, tourist office. When you find that, you are just around the corner from the *hostería*. Both are on the Plaza de Cervantes on Calle de los Colegios. Directional Hostería signs are nonexistent in this city of over 100,000 people.

Alcalá is an old and new university town. In a dining hall of the 450-year-old university which was once used by students, the Ministry of Tourism has installed a fine restaurant. You may enjoy traditional Spanish dishes accompanied by the house wine from Argarda. For dessert, try *costrada,* a layered confection of puff pastry and vanilla creme, topped with meringue and sprinkled with almonds.

The birthplace of Cervantes and of Catherine of Aragón (first wife of England's Henry VIII and daughter of Ferdinand and Isabella), Alcalá was also chosen by Cardinal Cisneros as the site of a university in the early sixteenth century. Ask the maitre d' to show you the old lecture hall now used for opening ceremonies of Madrid University. In Cisneros's day, the university was famous for its teaching of languages. In 1520 it published the first polyglot Bible, with parallel texts in Latin, Greek, Hebrew, and Chaldean.

As is often the case with the old cities of Spain, street repair and changes here seem to be constantly in progress. Even with the difficulty of locating the *hostería,* a trip is worthwhile.

Parador Nacional de Almagro

ALMAGRO, CIUDAD REAL

**** govt. rating
Sixteenth-century convent, 55
  rooms
Swimming pool, gardens
Opened in 1979
Phone 926/86 01 00

DIRECTIONS: 23 km east of Ciudad Real on C-415. The route to the parador through town is well marked and easy to follow.

Built in 1596 as a convent for Franciscan monks, the parador extends around 14 courtyards so that all guest rooms have garden views. The furniture is of dark wood and

bedsteads are carved. As Almagro has an important lace industry, beds are made with lace coverlets. Public rooms are spacious, with decorative ceramic ware as accents. The bar, also called a cafeteria, is built over a cellar *bodega* believed to be part of the original building. In a locked section of the *bodega*, wines are stored and hams hung to cure from rafters. Sandwiches made of crusty bread, ham, and famous *queso manchego* (cheese of La Mancha) can be ordered in the bar.

The parador menu offers *cordero lechal al horno* (roast lamb), *perdiz entera a las uvas* (partridge with grapes), and *bonito fresco al vino de Valdepeñas* (tunny baked in wine). Vegetables served with the entrees can include a broiled half tomato, purple cabbage, and fried green peppers. If it is in season, be sure to order *berenjenas* (eggplant), an Almagro specialty first introduced by the Moors. Among dessert choices are *crepes a la normanda* (crepes stuffed with applesauce and topped with custard sauce) and *bizcochada de Almagro* (a biscuit or shortcake dusted with nutmeg and floated on thin custard).

In one of the large conference halls of the parador hangs a painting of Christ on the cross, wearing a lace skirt. The crown of thorns is draped on his feet.

TOURING ALMAGRO. Enjoy a walk to town from the parador. On sunny days, *señoras* sit outside their houses and tat lace. Fascinating to see them deftly managing as many as thirty bobbins. The many escutcheoned houses from the 1500s and 1600s lining the streets are evidence of the one-

time splendor of Almagro. Some of the fine ol
stem from the days when the Knights of Calatrava,
military force during the Reconquest, headquartered in ⌐
city.

The *plaza mayor* is unique in Spain. Dating to 1372, when
citizens obtained the right to celebrate fiestas, the plaza
has seen feats of jousting, bullfights, and performances by
strolling musicians and actors. Shops form the ground floor
of two-story buildings, whose arcaded stone columns edge
the elliptical plaza on three sides. Frames of the many-
paned windows are painted a dark bright green. Behind
one of the green gates fronting the plaza is the Corral de
Comedias, open 9 A.M. to 2 P.M. and 4 to 7 P.M. This sixteenth-century theater built around an open courtyard saw
some of the earliest performances of Spanish drama and is
the only one of its era still intact. On August 24, Almagro
celebrates the feast of its patron saint, Bartholomew. Fes-
tivities include performances in the Corral de Comedias.
Wednesday is market day in Almagro.

Almagro was the birthplace of explorer Diego Almagro,
who took many parts of Chile and Peru for Spain. He and
his countryman Francisco Pizarro carried on a bitter running feud climaxed with the murder of Almagro by male
relatives of Pizarro in 1538.

Ciudad Real is not a difficult town to maneuver for a
shopping expedition.

---

*In late October, look for fields of purple flowers outside
Almagro. These are a lavender crocus native to Spain. Their
stigma is saffron, a prime ingredient of* paella. *It takes
250,000 stigmas to make one pound of saffron, explaining
the seasoning's high cost.*

Parador Nacional de Chinchón

CHINCHON, MADRID

**** govt. rating
Convent, 38 rooms
Swimming pool, gardens
Opened in 1982
Phone 91/894 08 36

DIRECTIONS: 51 km southeast of Madrid on C-300.

It was from the friendly staff of Chinchón's parador that we learned the main difference between a convent and monastery in Spain is size: a monastery is bigger. Both institutions house monks. The parador is a former Augustinian monastery of Saint Mary of Paradise, moved to within city limits in the seventeenth century. In 1835, following Mendizabal's Disentail Law secularizing all church property, the monastery was turned into a prison and later served as courthouse. Although a great portion was destroyed by fire in the 1930s, the walls and enough remnants survived to be incorporated into one of Spain's most charming paradors. The reconstruction and restoration took ten years to complete.

Glassed-in cloisters frame a courtyard enhanced by a fountain, shrubs, and flowers. These galleries are used for lounging and as an overflow bar area. The new "antique" furniture is predominantly green with hand-painted floral designs. One large wall is hung with three modern tapestries in a style called "bordado al trapo," according to a local *señora*. They are done by Rosa Cubero, evidently the number one tapestry artist in Spain. Various materials are used to make up designs that are then appliquéd onto a background cloth. The *bordados* are unusual, striking, and colorful. Light snacks may be ordered in the bar-taberna.

Guest rooms are furnished in the same style of green furniture as the public rooms. Windows look out onto gardens of trimmed hedges, rose bushes, and pomegranate and other fruit trees. There are clusters of outdoor tables and chairs for restful lounging. Trilling bird songs complete the utopia.

The dining room is wainscoted with brilliant old Spanish tiles. Menu recommendations are *solomillo a la mostaza de hiervas verdes* (sirloin steak with mustard-herb sauce) and *entrecote de cebón a la brasa* (braised steak). The rioja *blanco, rosado,* and *tinto* wines are bottled especially for the paradores by the Marqués de Cáceres *bodega.*

TOURING CHINCHON. Close to the parador is Chinchón's famous *plaza mayor,* irregular in shape and edged by arcaded galleries of shops topped with three-story houses. On fiesta days, the area is roped off and serves as the *plaza de toros,* where bullfights have been staged since the sixteenth century. (*Corridas* are held on Sundays starting June

1 and ending with the second Sunday in October.) At other times, tables and chairs accommodating various restaurants and bars rim the area. To sit and sip Chinchón's celebrated beverage, anisette, and watch the passing parade, including hucksters selling elaborate hanging garlic concoctions, is a marvelous way to spend an afternoon. The anisette is so powerful that one glass can last a couple of hours. (Suggestion: order your anisette *seco*—the *dulce* is too, too sweet.)

The *plaza mayor*, used as a film set in very early Spanish movies, is almost overshadowed by the great parish church whose altarpiece is said to have been painted by Goya when his brother was parish priest. Buried in a mausoleum in the church is the third duke of Chinchón, Don Diego, close advisor to Philip II.

Ferdinand and Isabella "gave" the town to Andres de Cabrera and Beatriz de Bobadilla as a reward for their defense of the *alcázar* in Segovia. Above the doorway to Chinchón Castle may be seen the coat of arms of the Cabrera-Bobadilla families: a goat, a lion, castles, and eagles. (The castle is not open to the public.)

Chinchón has another claim to fame. When the countess of Chinchón, wife of a seventeenth-century viceroy to Peru, became ill with a fever, she was cured by Indian medicine made from tree bark. She took the miracle medicine back to Europe. Swedish botanist Linnaeus named the bark-bearing tree *chinchona* in honor of the countess. Today we know the medicine as quinine.

MADRID

Every visitor to Spain will want to spend some time in the capital city of Madrid, geographic center of the Iberian Peninsula. At over 2000 feet above sea level, spring and autumn temperatures are ideal, but summers can be very hot and winters very cold.

Many of Madrid's monuments can be seen on your own: the Prado Museum, with over six thousand works of art; the adjacent Botanical Gardens, with thirty thousand species of plants and trees; the Royal Palace; Retiro Park, whose lovely lake is set in 322 acres of lush woodland; and the Convent of Las Descalzas Reales, to name a few.

For other sights, we recommend taking tours because of the distance from central Madrid and the size of the institutions. In this group would be El Escorial, Philip II's incredible palace, monastery, and pantheon; the Valley of the Fallen, dramatic tribute to the Civil War dead; La Granja (11 km away), a Versailles-type palace with splendid tapestries and crystal chandeliers; and Aranjuez, about 50 km south of Madrid, with a vast palace, gardens, and museums.

For those wanting to spend some time exploring Madrid and nearby cities, a stay at Hotel Chamartín in the new Chamartín train complex is suggested. Several of the hotel staff speak English and all are pleasant and helpful to tourists. There is always a long line of available taxis just across the street from the hotel, at the entrance to the station. The station houses a branch of the Spanish National Tourist Office, a *correo* (post office), car rental agencies, and information centers where English is spoken. Travelers can take advantage of Madrid's clean, fast, and efficient Metro system and take side trips by train. The Metro station is beneath the train complex.

From the tourist office, pick up a Metro schedule and a brochure in which the Metro system is superimposed on a map of Madrid. It is very easy to figure out how to reach any place you want to go. The routes and signs are color coded and named according to the stations at either end of the particular line, so the only things you need to know are the stop where you want to get off and the last stop on the line in that direction. And the Metro is very inexpensive: The fifteen-minute ride to Puerto del Sol will cost about 35 pesetas.

Certainly if Avila, Toledo, or Segovia are not on your itinerary, you should schedule day or weekend tours to these fabulous cities, which should not be missed. Arrangements can be made with the Chamartín Hotel to hold the bulk of your luggage in a hotel storage room. The hotel staff can help with tour arrangements. Half-day tours range from 1250 to 1750 pesetas. Day tours, including lunch, start at 4000 pesetas. Of course, you can do these cities on your own by train, but probably not as comprehensively.

Parador Nacional de Manzanares

MANZANARES, CIUDAD REAL

*** govt. rating
Modern, 50 rooms
Swimming pool, elevator, garden
Opened in 1932, since remodeled
  and enlarged
Phone 926/61 04 00

DIRECTIONS: 176 km south of Madrid off N-IV; if coming south, after entering Manzanares, turn right at the intersection of N-IV and C-5. 50 km east of Ciudad Real via N-420 and N-430.

For those who want to linger a while in La Mancha, land of Don Quixote, the parador makes an ideal base. It is a large white building on tree-shaded grounds. Furniture in tile-floored guest rooms includes twin beds, desk with chair, and round cocktail or coffee table with two accompanying chairs. Balconies extend the rooms' views.

Salons are spacious and inviting. In the large bar area, snacks such as grilled ham and cheese sandwiches may be ordered. Meals are served buffet style in a pleasant dining room. Tiles with likenesses of Don Quixote decorate serving tables laden with countless dishes of La Mancha. For 1100 pesetas, choices seem endless: *gachas* (green pea puree with crisp bacon), *galiano* (gazpacho a La Mancha prepared with garlic, rabbit, partridge, ham, rosemary, thyme, and bay leaves), *caldereta* (lamb stew), *cochifrito* (fried lamb or kid). Dessert specialties to try are: *mostillo* (cooked grape must flavored with aniseed, cinnamon, cloves), *arrope* (cooked and whipped honey), *leche frita* (fried custard), or *bizcocho* (sponge cake). Wines are from nearby Valdepeñas.

Manzanares, once the feudal domain of Alvaro de Bazán, is now an important marketing city. In the town center is the fourteenth-century parish Church of Nuestra Señora de la Alla Gracia. The Plaza Mayor bustles with commercial activity.

Campo Criptana, with ten windmills dominating the town, lies 54 km northeast. Three are still working and are called El Infante (king's second son), El Borleta (tiny tassel), and El Sardinero (sardine seller). Each windmill is three stories high, one story for storing sacks of wheat, another for storing flour, and the third for machinery. Three others are now museums. A ballad of the region goes like this:

> To Campo de Criptana
> Waft my sighs
> Land of pretty damsels
> And of windmills.
>
> At the door of the windmill
> I stopped to ponder
> The turns that a millstone gives
> To grind a sack of flour.

On hills above Moto del Cuervo, 36 km northeast of Campo on N-420, there are seven windmills, now idle but picturesque. The whole landscape is planted in cereals, sunflowers (how glorious to see a field in bloom in autumn), olive trees, vineyards as far as the eye can see. Smaller fields of red peppers and green melons offer contrasts. Irrigation is by sprinklers and narrow canals. Belmonte, 14 km northeast of Moto on N-420, has a stunning castle and city walls. This was one of several second-line fortifications constructed along the frontier between Aragón and Castilla. Others in this chain are Alarcón and Sigüenza. If approaching Belmonte from the north, you won't see the castle until the road turns south, but be sure to look back for a view upon departing.

Parador Nacional
Virrey Toledo
OROPESA, TOLEDO

**** govt. rating
Fourteenth-century castle, 44 rooms
Elevator
Opened in 1930
Phone 925/43 00 00

DIRECTIONS: 100 km west of Toledo, off of N-V.

The site of Oropesa's parador is very ancient. Some say Hercules came along in 1716 B.C. and founded a town he called Orospeda, also Comedium Orbis, center of the peninsula.

In any event, the present castle was built during the reign of Pedro I. In 1366, the town, surrounding countryside, and castle were given by Enrique II to Don García Alvarez de Toledo. Don García restored the castle only to have it practically demolished later in the century. Restoration occurred again in 1402 and it is basically this structure that is seen today. The Torre Albarrana, located outside castle walls, remains as an example of a medieval bastion.

Additions made to the castle now house the parador named for a count of Oropesa, Francisco de Toledo, who served as *virrey* (viceroy) to Peru. Guest rooms are rather small, but adequate, with dark wood furniture, upholstered occasional chairs, and woven drapes and bedspreads. Windows look out to a high plateau of vineyards, olive groves, large cereal fields, and grazing land framed by the snow-capped Sierra de Gredos.

Cuisine in the parador dining room includes *perdiz a la toledana* (partridge), *pucherete de Virrey* (a thick soup), *goulash de ciervo* (stewed venison), quiche Lorraine, and *ensalada de pimientos* (red pepper salad). Two suggested desserts are *suspiros de monja* (cream puffs) and *tarte de fraise* (raspberry tart). The house wine is a *tinto* from Gutiérrez *bodega*.

Take a walking tour through the streets of Oropesa and notice centuries-old manor houses bearing family escutcheons.

Just 2 km from Oropesa is the well-known village of Lagartera. Houses are decorated with tile plaques advertising *bordados* (embroideries) for sale.

In Talavera de la Reina, 32 km east of Oropesa, the distinctive blue and yellow ceramic ware seen throughout Spain may be purchased from one of many shops.

Parador Nacional de Puerto Lumbreras

PUERTO LUMBRERAS, MURCIA

*** govt. rating
Modern, 60 rooms
Gardens, elevator
Opened in 1946
Phone 968/40 20 25

DIRECTIONS: 139 km northeast of Almería. 80 km southwest of Murcia.

Fronted by a small grove of orange trees, the parador is right on the main road through town. It is a typically sparkling parador. Common room floors are gray and white marble laid in a checkerboard pattern. Brilliant local ceramics are displayed on the walls and colorful carpets from Lorca lie under clusters of furniture. Guest room bedsteads are black wrought iron with brass trim. Leather occasional chairs and textured matching spreads and drapes complete the room decor.

Menu items are unusual: *pastel de puerros y langostinos* (leek and prawn pie), *suprema de ave salteada salsa estragón* (breast of chicken with tarragon sauce), and *cazuela de mer-*

luza a la sidra (hake in casserole with cider). *Zaragollo* and *mirichones* are dishes of finely chopped vegetables. *Pastel murciano* is a pie filled with meat, slices of sausage, and hardboiled eggs. A dessert favorite is *alfajores,* a biscuit made of almonds, nuts, and honey. House wines are Jumilla *blanco, tinto,* and *rosado.*

There seems to be no rhyme or reason for the *puerto* in the city's name as there is no port or mountain pass anywhere close. It has been an important stopping place for centuries, as it is near the point where the road branches one way to Granada and another to Almería. Emigrants from the area are called swallows because they always return. The soil around Puerto Lumbreras doesn't seem to be good for much except as material for exceptional pottery. Nevertheless, attempts at raising garden vegetables continue. They do raise healthy-looking cactus! Beyond Lorca, cotton and artichokes seem to thrive. In late autumn, overhead arbors droop with large white dessert grapes.

Those travelers who are anticipating a drive through extensive date groves (palmerales) between Murcia and Elche will be greatly disappointed. The palms have been drastically thinned and the air is heavy with smoke and dust around Elche, once known for its vast palmeral.

Parador Nacional Castillo de Sigüenza

SIGUENZA, GUADALAJARA

**** govt. rating
Twelfth-century castle, 77 rooms
Elevator
Opened in 1976
Phone 911/39 01 00

DIRECTIONS: 130 km northeast of Madrid via N-II. At junction with C-204, turn northeast and go 29 km to Sigüenza. Follow Parador signs to the crest of the hill.

As you approach Sigüenza from the south, rosy, terra-cotta-hued medieval buildings lead to a castle on high to the right and a twelfth-century cathedral on the left.

It took 12 years to reconstruct the 77-room parador, opened within walls of a castle built by Visigoths on Roman ruins in the fifth century. In 712 the Moors arrived and fortified it into an *alcazaba*. Reconquered by Fernando I and El Cid, it was secured by Bishop Bernardo de Agén in 1124 and converted into an episcopal palace. Various fortifications were added over the years for it was an important link on the border between Aragón and Castilla.

Some guest room balconies overlook an enclosed patio-garden with fountain and well. Others look down over red roofs of the historic city. Furnishings are regal Castilian. Floors and baths are tiled. The one-time castle dining room is now a vast lounge accommodating two fireplaces, nine chandeliers, ten sofas, sixty occasional chairs, two knightless suits of armor guarding a Fonseca-crested tapestry, and a television. Pots of greenery and brilliant seignorial banners add zest and color to the halls.

The "new" dining room's paneled windows look out to Castilla's red-soiled wheat fields and its infinite succession of rolling hills. The food is exceptional. Try *medallones de solomillo al fino olorosa* (succulent pork in wine sauce). For dessert, order *kiwis con puré de frambuesa* (red raspberry creme puree topped with slices of kiwi). The house wine is a very pleasant *rosado* from Avila.

In addition to the elegant castle-parador, Sigüenza has three other treasures. Walk down through the old streets to the Museo Antigua, whose pride and joy is a painting by Zurbarán. The twelfth-century cathedral has an El Greco and the foremost example of sepulchral art in Spain, the Doncel. Martin de Arce was a favorite *doncel*, or page, of Queen Isabella. When he died at the gates of Granada in one of the first battles of its reconquest, the queen commissioned a statue for his tomb, to be placed in the cathedral of Sigüenza, his hometown. The Doncel, with one ankle crossed over the other, lies atop his tomb. As he casually rests on one elbow, reading a book, a smile lingers on his lips. It is a truly marvelous work of art.

Parador Nacional Conde de Orgaz
TOLEDO

**** govt. rating
Modern, 75 rooms
Elevator
Opened in 1968
Phone 925/22 18 50

DIRECTIONS: 70 km southwest of Madrid on N-401. There are four or five trains daily from Madrid's Atocha station. If driving, allow about an hour and a half because of heavy traffic on N-401. Just before reaching the entrance to the city through Puerta Vieja de Bisagra (also spelled Visagra), bear right, take the road running along the cliff, cross the Tajo River, and continue another kilometer or so up to the parador.

Standing on Cerro del Emperador (emperor's hill) in the suburb of Las Cigarrales, the parador offers a gorgeous view. Its salons and hallways are brightened with colorful ceramics and copperware of the region. Guest room balconies allow visitors to revel in the glory of Toledo. The ever-changing "Velázquez skies" of billowy clouds in blue-violet heavens provide a veritable kaleidoscope for the architectural gems of the ancient city. Equally thrilling at night are lights twinkling to songs of a thousand crickets.

Specialties of the dining room include *perdices a la toledana* (partridge stewed in red wine from Méntrida), *tortilla a la magra* (ham omelette), and *berenjenas rellenas* (stuffed eggplant). *Mazapán de Toledo* (an almond concoction introduced by the Moors) is a favorite dessert. Wines are from Méntrida, La Mancha, Valdepeñas, and Almansa.

Since the parador is popular with domestic as well as foreign guests, reservations need to be made months in advance.

TOURING TOLEDO. Toledo has such wealth and so many monuments that one should spend several days trying to uncover its secrets. Drive down or take a cab from the parador and before entering through Puerta Vieja de Bisagra, stop in the tourist office on Paseo de Madrid for information and a map. Park outside Puerta del Sol and begin a walking tour through a maze of narrow streets where flowers cascade from windows. Stroll from one small square to another. Cervantes called Toledo "Spain's most precious jewel" and visitors who linger in the city will agree.

Purchase a map and guidebook outside the cathedral and become acquainted with the layout. You may want to go through on your own the first time, but on the second, hire an English-speaking guide so as not to miss any of the treasures in this, Spain's richest cathedral. To mention just a few must-sees: the Monstrance of Arfe, said to contain the first gold brought by Columbus from America, is 10 feet high, weighs 450 pounds, and is carried through the streets on Corpus Christi; two volumes of the Bible lavishly illuminated in the thirteenth century; and in the Sacristy, several masterpieces by El Greco, Titian, Rubens, and Bellini.

In addition to taking in all the culture and art in Toledo, visitors will be delighted with many opportunities to purchase the traditional Damascus steel of Toledo. Black steel inlaid with gold, silver, and copper wire appears in countless articles from jewelry to scissors to swords. Try to find a shop where a blacksmith demonstrates the age-old method of forging steel for swords that were sought after for hundreds of years.

In Santo Tomé Church is found perhaps El Greco's most famous painting, *The Burial of Count Orgaz*. The parador takes its name from the count.

Castilla León

THE REGION OF LEÓN NOW JOINS THAT OF CASTILLA La Vieja (Old Castilla) in the new region of Castilla León. The three provinces of León, Salamanca, and Zamora contain highlands, forests, and broad plains through which flow rivers teeming with trout. The Leonese Cantabrian Mountains are rich in big game, including a near-extinct species of bear and the *urogallo,* in addition to the more common roe, chamois, and wild boar.

The area was populated by Iberians, conquered by Hannibal, developed by Romans, ravaged by Moors, and finally united with the kingdom of Castilla in the thirteenth century. It was visited by millions of pilgrims on their way to Santiago de Compostela during the Middle Ages. As a result, the region has an abundance of medieval villages, monasteries, hermitages, churches, and hospitals, and three great universities in Salamanca.

The provinces of Avila, Burgos, Cantabria, La Rioja, Palencia, Segovia, Soria, and Valladolid have such contrasting scenes as lofty pine-covered mountains, highland

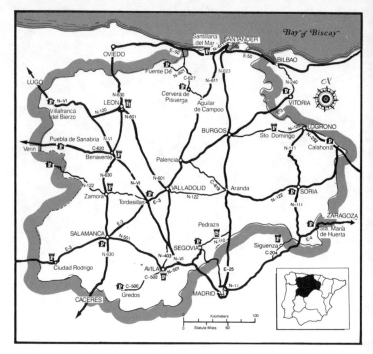

Castilla León

meadows, wheat fields, and lush fertile valleys. Here in Old Castilla is the source of the Duero River.

Here also are remains of prehistoric and ancient civilizations. The whole area is an inexhaustible font for historian, tourist, mountaineer, angler, hunter, and skier.

Today's inhabitants enjoy festivals, delight in bullfights, and maintain those basic qualities of courtesy, dignity, detachment, and self-denial that enabled Castilla to dominate Spanish history.

Try not to shudder at the word bullfight. If you are an enterprising visitor, you will do a little research beforehand to learn the cast of characters and acts of the *corrida*. You will then understand that it is drama, not sport, to the Spaniard. Attend a *corrida* in any city's *plaza de toros*. Witness the pageantry, audience participation, and music. If the proceedings get too bloody, simply turn your head

Parador Nacional
Raimundo de Borgoña
AVILA

*** govt. rating
Fifteenth-century palace, 62 rooms
Elevator, gardens
Opened in 1966
Phone 918/21 13 40

DIRECTIONS: 112 km northwest of Madrid on N-501. There are frequent train departures for Avila from both Atocha and Chamartín stations in Madrid.

The walls of Avila are as awesome today as they surely were 1000 years ago. Entrance to the parador is through the Carmen Gate. Once the fifteenth-century Palace of Benavides (also called Piedras Altas, high stones), the parador was reconstructed near the northern section of the walls. The architects preserved as much as possible of the original granite and limestone building. A few years ago the parador was enlarged so skillfully that it is difficult to distinguish the new from the old. There is much use of *azulejos*, colored tile, climaxing on one long wall of the bar. Guest room windows look out onto gardens and countryside with always a sight of the walls for inspiration.

Dishes of the region are served in the popular dining room. Choices include: *judías del barco de Avila* (kidney beans with *chorizo* sausage), *pucherete teresiano* (stew of vegetables, *chorizo*, and other meats), *ternera asada en su jugo* (veal roasted in its own juice), *chuleta de cordero a la plancha* (grilled lamb chops), and *cochinillo asado estilo arevalo* (roast suckling pig). As a very appropriate dessert in this city of Saint

Teresa, order *yemas de Santa Teresa* (candied egg yolks). Rueda, Méntrida, and Ribera del Duero are the wines offered, with the house wine being riojas bottled for the paradores by the Marqués de Cáceres *bodega*.

Avila is the highest provincial capital in Spain and at an altitude of 3600 feet, it can be quite cool in autumn and spring. Ptolemy called the city Obila; parts of Roman roads, bridges, and stone tablets remain. After the Romans came the Goths, Visigoths, and, in the year 714, the Moors. Reconquered by knights under Count Raimundo de Borgoña, the Ciudad de los Caballeros (city of knights) was restored and, on orders of father-in-law Alfonso IV, was repopulated with Christians from Asturias, Galicia, León, and Burgos.

As Avila was to be a second line of defense, the walls were begun in 1090, making it the first fortified Romanesque city in Europe. It took 3000 laborers (probably captured Moors) nine years to raise walls 10 feet thick, 40 feet high, a mile and a half long. Eighty-eight turrets are spaced along the walls, which form a trapezoid with nine gates.

There is much to see and visit within the walled city. The tourist office is across the street from the entrance to the twelfth-century cathedral. Friday is market day in Avila and it is fun to time a visit to catch all the commercial activity and color.

The royal Monastery of Santo Tomás is located outside the walls to the southeast. Ferdinand and Isabella frequented the monastery during the summer months and their only son, Prince Juan, who died at 19, is buried in the mausoleum.

Parador Nacional Rey Fernando II of León

BENAVENTE, ZAMORA

**** govt. rating
Twelfth-century castle, 27 rooms
Gardens
Opened in 1972
Phone 988/63 03 00

DIRECTIONS: 67 km north of Zamora, via N-630 and N-VI.

Located on a bluff between the Obrigo and Tera rivers, above railroad tracks south of town, the parador consists of two wings added to Torre del Caracol (tower of the snail), the only remaining portion of a castle-fortress built during the reign of Ferdinand II of León (the name is Fernando in Spanish). The square red brick and stone tower has rounded turrets at each corner. Bits and pieces of the castle ruins were used in the entry hall and lounges. One large salon has an ornate, domed, coffered ceiling three stories high. Guest rooms open off the second-floor balcony. Large tapestries on walls depict in brilliant color historical events of Benavente and Zamora. The large bar-lounge is another unusual room, where wall hangings display heraldic banners and coats of arms. A burnished iron chandelier in the center is in the shape of a crown, with cut-out letters spelling Fernando II. Guest rooms are comfortably furnished and have balconies with arched roofs, looking out over a fertile agricultural valley.

On the walls of the dining room, old weapons and artifacts frame a mounted boar's head. The mantel of a fireplace in the center holds colorful regional pottery. The fireplace is flanked by two towering terra-cotta figures, skirted and helmeted warriors from the remote past. Specialties of the dining room include *merluza alancostaza* (a fish stew), *cordero asado* (roast lamb), *dos y pingada* (eggs with pork), *bacalao a la tío* (cod with red peppers), *bacalao a la tranca* (grilled cod), and *presas de ternera zamorana* (spiced slices of veal). Pena Trevinca, Vega de Toro, and El Cubeta are the regional wines served by the parador.

Historians believe that Benavente, known as the town of counts, was on the itinerary of the Roman Antoninus and was known as Brigetio. The castle-fortress was built during the period of "repopulating" following the Reconquest. The town was given a charter in 1167 and in 1176 a parliament was held in the castle. Situated at the junction of roads leading to León and Galicia, Benavente was a booming commercial center during the Middle Ages, as evidenced by the names of two Romanesque churches of the town: San Juan del Mercado (Saint John of the market) and Santa María del Azogue (Saint Mary of the market—*azogue* coming from the Arabic word *souk*). San Juan has the distinction of having over its chancel the first Gothic vault built in Spain. Santa María has five apses with some interesting statues. One is a wooden figure of Christ with human hair and beard, bearing a ponderous cross and clothed in a purple gold-embroidered velvet robe. Another is an early Byzantine Virgin in stone, set in a special niche. Traces of frescoes are still discernible on ceiling and walls.

> *Thousands of private, domestic* bodegas *are seen in the vicinity of Benavente. They are constructed of the native orange soil, of conical shape with a small entry door at the base.*

Parador Nacional
Marco Fabio Quintiliano
CALAHORRA, LA RIOJA

*** govt. rating
Modern, 63 rooms, elevator,
    gardens
Opened in 1975
Phone 941/13 03 58

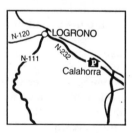

DIRECTIONS: 149 km southeast of Logroño.

Calahorra is a very old town, Calagurris being its Roman name. The parador was named for a famous son, the elocutionist who was born in Calahorra in the first century

A.D. It is located at one end of a mall, on Paseo el Merca-
del. The Paseo borders a park of trees, flower beds, and
statues—Marco Fabio being one, of course. Unusual lamps,
pictures, and artifacts are used with striking effect in guest
and public rooms. There are several furniture groupings
for relaxation and game tables for recreation.

The cuisine of the parador is typical of La Rioja: hearty,
tasty stews, soups, roast pork and lamb, dishes using snails,
tripe, and lamb fries—all liberally flavored with *ajo* (garlic).
Two suggestions: *pimientos rellenos de La Rioja Baja* (stuffed
red peppers) and *acelgas en pepitoria* (silver beets). For dessert, order *biscuit de brandy con pasas* (a brandy biscuit). As
would be expected in one of the principal wine regions of
Spain, the wine list seems endless.

Calahorra is booming, with many new highrise apartment complexes. Thanks to the small truck farms, orchards, and vineyards in the countryside, a canning industry flourishes here. Whirring machinery can be heard
along the Paseo even during siesta hours.

> *Towns in La Rioja that have* bodegas *(wine cellars) open
> for visiting and tasting are Laguardia (11 km northwest of
> Logroño) and Haro (45 km northwest of Logroño). These
> could be day trips from the paradores in Calahorra and
> Santo Domingo de la Calzada.*

Parador Nacional Fuentes Carrionas

CERVERA DE PISUERGA, PALENCIA

*** govt. rating
Modern, 80 rooms
Elevator, gardens
Opened in 1975
Phone 988/87 01 05

DIRECTIONS: 100 km north of Palencia, then 25 km west of Aguilar
de Campóo. The parador is on a hill 3 km beyond the village of
Cervera. From Santander, take N-611 south to Aguilar, then west
to the parador.

Set in high meadows leading to foothills of the Picos de
Europa, the parador is a handsome five-story lodge. Each

room has a balcony providing marvelous 180-degree vistas. Lounges and bar area are suitably decorated with mounted heads of wild game and colorful ceramics.

Still-life paintings of tempting foods hang on paneled walls of the dining room, illuminated by wood and brass chandeliers. Here certainly is the place to order *truchas fritas montañesa* (fried mountain trout) preceded by a bowl of *sopa de ajo burgalesa* (garlic soup). *Leche frita* (fried custard) is a dessert specialty of the parador. Wines include those from Rueda, Ribera del Duero, La Rioja Alta, Navarra, and Campo de Borja.

The landscape between Palencia and Cervera de Pisuerga changes often. The color of the soil determines the color of village buildings. The road northward climbs slowly and steadily to an altitude at Parador Fuentes Carrionas of 3000 feet. Quite a long stretch of the road affords views of the Canal de Castilla bordered by poplars.

Hikers and nature lovers will enjoy seeing all kinds of low-mountain foliage in differing shades of green and brown, punctuated with yellow, blue, and violet wildflowers. Two short drives will reward the camera buff. Follow a narrow road from the parador for a few kilometers to Resoba, an unpaved pueblo of primitive dwellings. Village dogs do not bark at strangers, merely stare with raised eyebrows. Along another nearby road bordering a small lake, muscular, long-horned cows with bells saunter musically and nonchalantly down the middle of the pavement. Completing this pastoral scene are velvety leas dotted with grazing black and white cattle.

Parador Nacional Enrique II

CIUDAD RODRIGO, SALAMANCA

*** govt. rating
Fourteenth-century castle-fortress, 28 rooms
Gardens
Opened in 1931
Phone 923/46 01 50

DIRECTIONS: 89 km southwest of Salamanca on E-3.

Near the banks of the Agueda River, the crenellated keep of the ancient *alcázar* dominates the skyline of Ciudad Rodrigo. A Celtic boar stands guard at the entrance to the ivy-covered parador, which is constructed from portions of a fourteenth-century castle-fortress. In some guest rooms of the original wing, ivy may creep in when windows stand open. Another wing was added in 1957. Rooms are not large, but are comfortable, with essential furniture and the addition of minibars.

The dining room is popular with locals as well as travelers. It is a lunch stop for tour buses. While enjoying fine food, guests look out over the river and parts of the old city. Menu items include *pechuga de pollo villaroi* (chicken fried in batter), *chuletillas de cordero* (lamb chops), *chuletón de ternera* (veal chops), *tostón asado* (roast suckling pig), and *perdiz estofada jardinera* (stewed partridge). *Copa de helado con piña* is a refreshing dessert of chocolate ice cream and slices of pineapple. Viñasierra *blanco* and *tinto* are the regional wines, served by the carafe.

For more than four centuries, Ciudad Rodrigo flourished as a Roman city. It was called Mirobriga; today's inhabitants are called *mirobrigenses*. Pillars, stone tablets, coins, and sarcophagi have been unearthed. Three columns believed to have been part of a Roman temple stand at the entrance to the walled city. During the reign of Alfonso VI in the first part of the twelfth century, Count Don Rodrigo González rebuilt and repopulated the deserted town, which came to be called Ciudad Rodrigo. Ferdinand II of León ordered construction of city walls to reinforce the frontier with Portugal. Originally there were eight entrances through the walls. Seven remain in use today.

When citizens supported Enrique II in struggles with his half-brother, Pedro I, Enrique decreed that Ciudad Rodrigo should have an *alcázar*. The old fortress, on the highest point of the city, has seen many battles, the most famous being that of 1812, when troops under the duke of Wellington drove out the French under Marshal Ney. As a result, Wellington was accorded the titles duke of Ciudad Rogrigo and grandee of Spain.

Ciudad Rodrigo has been proclaimed a national monument—it bustles with commerce and shines with TLC. Tuesday is market day, when farmers and vendors set up stalls to entice buyers. There are several mansions to be seen: fifteenth-century Casa de Montarco, sixteenth-century Casa de los Aguila, and Casa de Marqués de los Altares. The twelfth-century cathedral, founded by Ferdinand II, is a blend of Romanesque, Gothic, and plateresque architectures. Take time to study the choir stalls, carved in the fifteenth century by one Alemán. Instead of religious themes, they are embellished with monkeys, tigers, wild boars, dragons, and flowers. Above the stalls is a statue of Saint Francis of Assisi said to be the oldest in existence. Some say he even posed for it when visiting the city in 1214.

A short drive 29 km west into Portugal furnishes rich material for the photographer. Be sure to turn left off the main road into the walled village of Castelo Mendo to observe ways of life unchanged for hundreds of years.

> *The food specialty of Ciudad Rodrigo is a sausage of bread, pork, and flour, spiced with cumin. Locals are so fond of it they call it* farinato.

Parador Nacional Río Deva

FUENTE DE, CANTABRIA

*** govt. rating
Modern, 78 rooms
Opened in 1966
Phone 942/73 00 01

DIRECTIONS: 133 km southwest of Santander. Take N-634 west,
N-621 south to Potes, and then head west on N-621.

Built of local white stone, this parador lies 3000 feet above
sea level in a natural amphitheater embraced by the Picos
de Europa. Decor and furnishing are comfortably rustic.
Each guest room has a glass-enclosed balcony. On the first
floor, a large sitting room is rimmed with potted greenery.
The main salon has several conversational groupings, a
television center, and game tables.

Flowers bloom in each of the dining room's windows.
Cuisine is Castilian with *cocido labaniego de potes* (a zesty
stew) being the regional specialty. Other dishes to try are
two soups, *sopa montañesa* and *sopa de concorte*, *truchas del
Duero con setas* (Duero trout with mushrooms), and *bacalao
al estilo valle de Liebana* (baked cod). Two dessert delectables are *buñuelos* (crispy fritters) and *puding de nueces* (nut
pudding). Three major wines are offered by the parador:
Rueda, Ribera del Duero, and Rioja Alta. Try the fiery local wine, *chacolí.*

ENVIRONS. Near the parador is an aerial tramway traveling
753 meters up to the Mirador del Cable in only three and
a half minutes. Be sure to take along a sweater even in
summer because it will be cold on top of this part of the
world.

A stay here would ideally be paired with one at Parador
Nacional Fuentes Carrionas in Cervera del Pisuerga. They
are about 85 winding kilometers apart, and Highway
C-627 offers spectacular scenery. Clusters of red-roofed
houses huddle together with splashes of garden flowers
easing the severity. Steep fir-clad mountain slopes alter-
nate with pastures of lush grass. Summits of harsh jagged
rock escarpments are engulfed in misty swirls. Herds of
henna-colored goats are tended vigorously by militant nip-

ping dogs. Munching pink pigs, lambs, and cows get fatter with each mouthful. Clear fast-moving streams break over lichen-covered boulders.

Parador Nacional de Gredos

GREDOS-NAVARREDONDA, AVILA

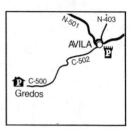

*** govt. rating
Modern, 77 rooms, elevator, gardens
Opened in 1928
Phone 918/34 80 48

DIRECTIONS: 160 km southwest of Avila via C-502 and C-500.

In 1926, King Alfonso XIII personally selected this location in the Sierra de Gredos, at an altitude of 6200 feet, for the first parador. After two years of construction, the building was inaugurated with the king present. A major overhaul and additions were made in 1941.

Guest rooms, large airy salons, bar, and dining rooms are decorated and furnished like a Castilian hunting lodge. A cafeteria allows hunters and anglers flexibility in cuisine and meal times. Dishes are representative of the region and include roast suckling pig and lamb, tender veal, and of course mountain trout prepared several ways. Wines offered are Rueda, Méntrida, Ribera del Duero, and the riojas bottled by the Marqués de Cáceres *bodega*.

Hotel San Marcos

LEON

***** govt. rating
Sixteenth-century monastery, 258 rooms
Hairdresser, parking, children's playroom
Opened in 1965
Phone 23 73 00

DIRECTIONS: The route through León to the San Marcos along the Bernesga River is well marked.

A stay at the San Marcos, possessing all the amenities of a first-class hotel any place in the world, is the luxurious way to relive history.

The original monastery was founded by Augustinian monks in the twelfth century for the purpose of "lodging the poor of Christ" on their way to Santiago. It later became headquarters for the Order of Saint James, those religious soldiers protecting the pilgrims' route. It was demolished in the sixteenth century. The present building, ordered by Ferdinand the Catholic, was built on the site of the previous one. (There is a handsome bust of Ferdinand carved in rich dark wood resting on a long magazine table near the entrance to the bar.)

An excellent example of plateresque architecture is the 328-foot-long façade. It is embellished with medallions, friezes, pilasters, and columns. Medallions depict famous Romans, Spaniards, and biblical heroes: Hercules, Paris, Hector, David, Joseph, Julius Caesar, Octavius, Carlos V (between Augustus and Trajan), Ferdinand I, El Cid, Philip II, and Isabella the Catholic between Judith and Lucretia— just to name a few. Among representations on the friezes are Saint Mark writing the Gospel and Saint James fighting the Moors. Over the Baroque doorway is a *peineta*, an ornate structure in the form of a Spanish *señora's* elaborate coiffure, topped with a statue representing Faith.

Magnificent two-story cloisters built in three stages during the sixteenth, seventeenth, and eighteenth centuries look over formal gardens and are equipped with outdoor furniture for lounging. Public rooms are endless and decorated with tapestries, painting, carvings, and Cuencan carpets.

TOURING LEON. Connected to the hotel is the church, which although emblazoned with a few scallop shells, was never really completed on the outside. The Provincial Archeological Museum is housed on the far side of the church. One of its most valuable treasures is Christ from Carrizo, carved from ivory in the eleventh century.

It is easy to take walking tours of León from the San Marcos. Shops along the boulevard parallel to the river display merchandise at very reasonable prices. The tourist wishes for a large empty suitcase to fill with some of León's goods.

León's roots are ancient. A Roman military city was

founded in 70 A.D. over Iberian ruins. Roman fortification remains form part of the staircase of Saint Isadore Basilica. Then came the Vandals, Suevi, and, in 717, the Moors. The city was completely destroyed by Almansur in the ninth century, but rebuilt and repopulated by Alfonso V. León is proud to claim that it had "24 kings before Castilla had any laws."

In addition to Spanish Renaissance San Marcos, two other buildings must be seen: the Gothic cathedral, and Romanesque Saint Isadore Basilica. The cathedral was begun in the thirteenth century, with construction continuing through the fourteenth century. The stained glass windows rank with those of Chartres, York Minster, and Ste. Chapelle. Documentary evidence indicates that master glassmakers participated in the creation of the windows. Every time period is represented in the work, from the thirteenth century to the present.

Saint Isadore Basilica was built over a ninth-century monastery that had been razed by the Moors. The oldest part dates from 1064, during the reign of Ferdinand I. There are remarkable wall and ceiling frescoes in the Royal Pantheon. In the church's museum are fragments of tenth-century tapestries and a collection of wooden caskets adorned with silver and inlaid with ivory.

Hostería Nacional Pintor Zuloaga

PEDRAZA, SEGOVIA

**** govt. rating
Fifteenth-century mansion
Opened in 1967
Phone 15 and 16

DIRECTIONS: 140 km northeast of Segovia via N-110. Park near the *plaza mayor* (to exit the village, follow blue arrows).

To experience the atmosphere of a timeless Castilian mountain village (population 500), spend a few hours strolling the pathways of Pedraza, whose heyday was the early sixteenth century. Notice the coats of arms on the old buildings. The village castle now belongs to descend-

ants of the painter Ignacio Zuloaga, who lived for some years in Pedraza and whose name the *hostería* honors.

Eventually you will arrive at the *hostería*, once the home of an inquisitor, Escobedo. The last private owners were the Zamarriegos, an illustrious Pedraza family who eventually sold the building to the town hall. Then, for the symbolic sum of 1000 pesetas, the structure was deeded to the Ministry of Tourism for conversion into an *hostería*. The façade of the building is original. There is a main dining room and an attached indoor terrace graced with hanging plants and windows opening to the countryside.

Seated in chairs embellished with hand-carved elongated peppers, you will be served appetizers of garlic olives, slices of *chorizo, morcilla* (blood sausage), melba toast, and a small glass of sherry. The menu is handwritten with a Spanish flourish. Traditional dishes of Segovia are prepared in gourmet fashion. If you have put off trying *bacalao,* try it here. *Bacalao a la madrileña* is cod baked in a tomato-garlic sauce with herbs and mushrooms. *Menestra de verduras* is a delicious concoction of fresh carrots, asparagus, green beans, and cauliflower, flavored with bits of ham and garnished with grated hardboiled egg. Other selections on the menu are *caldereta del pastor con cordero* (shepherd's lamb stew), *cordero lechal asado al horno* (roast baby lamb), *cabrito asado a la serrana* (roast kid), and *cochinillo de Segovia* (suckling pig). *Natillas caseras* (custard) makes a satisfying, not too rich, dessert. We enjoyed Cantosan wine with our meal.

Parador Nacional de Puebla de Sanabria

PUEBLA DE SANABRIA, ZAMORA

*** govt. rating
Modern, 44 rooms
Gardens
Opened in 1945
Phone 988/62 00 01

DIRECTIONS: 111 km northwest of Zamora.

The modern parador blends well with white stone and stucco houses of this attractive foothill village. Some old homes have decorative family crests, others have sagging, timbered, overhanging balconies overflowing with flowers and plants. Because Sanabria Lake is a popular resort for boating activities and there is good fishing in nearby valley streams, the parador was built to accommodate summer guests. Additions in 1985 brought the capacity to 33 double and 5 single rooms.

Some guest rooms have views of the town's distinctive fifteenth-century castle, now housing a library and museum. Others look out to the twelfth-century church. The rooms are small but comfortable.

Menu items in the dining room include *ternera asada en su jugo* (juicy roast veal), *habones a la sanabresa* (large white beans cooked with pork), and *pulpo a la sanabresa* (octopus cooked in olive oil and garlic with peppers). The house wine is a *tinto* from Toro.

Parador Nacional de Salamanca

SALAMANCA

**** govt. rating
Modern, 108 rooms
Swimming pool, gardens, elevator
Opened in 1981
Phone 923/22 87 00

DIRECTIONS: 62 km south of Zamora on N-630.

The large white parador, rather resembling an institution, is different from any other. It sits on a high spot, "hilltop of fairs," so named because every September it was the scene of one of the top livestock fairs in Castilla. One wonders what the natives feel about the parador usurping the site.

The severe building and decor may appeal to modern purists. Each guest room is made larger with a roofed extension with windows, reached by sliding doors. This "gallery" is furnished in bamboo and rattan furniture, while the guest room is more conventional, with matching spreads, drapes, and area rugs. Public rooms are numerous and large. Night views from parador windows, all of which face the city, are spectacular: The monuments of Salamanca beyond the Tormes River glow with a thousand lights.

Try our favorite bill of fare in the dining room, guaranteed to satisfy: *entrecot a la pimienta* (pepper steak served with french fries and assorted fresh vegetables) and *tarta helada al wisky* (chocolate and vanilla ice cream with a thin layer of caramel and liqueur, topped with whipped cream). House wine is bottled especially for the paradores by Marqués de Cáceres *bodega*.

TOURING SALAMANCA. Two plans of action: Either taxi to the Plaza d'España and take a walking tour of all the monuments before eventually crossing the Roman bridge (with its 27 stone arches, built in the first century A.D.) and walking back to the parador, or walk down from the parador, cross the bridge, take in the monuments and end up in the Plaza d'España, then taxiing back to the parador.

Salamanca's *plaza mayor* is one of the finest in Spain. Trapezoidal in shape, it was built in 1720 on orders of Philip V as a reward for the citizens' allegiance during the War of Spanish Succession. The most important city streets start from the plaza's medallioned arches. Rimmed by three-story buildings that are joined at street level by more than one hundred arches and topped with open-work cornices, the pedestrian plaza is the meeting place of anyone who is anyone. Hours can be spent at an outside table at one of many cafes, sipping sherry, eating *tapas* (appetizers) or grilled ham and cheese sandwiches, watching the world of Salamanca stroll by. It's easy to picture bullfights being held in the vast space (they were discontinued in the mid-nineteenth century).

Good examples of plateresque architecture include the façade of the university, the Colegio de los Nobles Ir-

landeses, the Church of San Estéban, Palacio de Monterrey, and Palacio de la Salina. Other buildings to be aware
of and to look for are Museo de Bellas Artes (museum of
fine arts), once the home of Dr. Albarez Abarca, physician
to Isabella the Catholic, and Casa de las Conchas, home of
Dr. Talavera Maldonado, who, because he was a Knight
of Santiago, had the exterior walls of his house plastered
with shells, symbol of pilgrims traveling the road to Santiago de Compostela.

Salamanca has two cathedrals, the old and the new. The
old, founded in the twelfth century by Jerónimo de Peri-
duex, its first bishop and chaplain of El Cid, has a Byzantine statue called *Virgin of the Vega* (fertile valley), the city's
patron saint. The large fortified tower covered with ornamental stone fish scales is Byzantine and called the Torre
de Gallo (rooster tower) because of its weathercock. The
new cathedral was begun in 1513 and was finished more
than 200 years later.

In 1218, Alfonso IX of León founded the first of three
universities in Salamanca. It is the oldest in Spain and one
of the four oldest in Europe. This seat of learning helped
to shape the religious, literary, and scientific life of Europe
during the Renaissance.

The traveler who has alloted only one day to Salamanca
may vow to come back some day, agreeing with Cervantes, who wrote, "Salamanca magically instills the de-
sire to return in all who have enjoyed the peacefulness of
its vitality."

Parador Nacional de Santa María de Huerta

SANTA MARIA DE HUERTA, SORIA

*** govt. rating
Modern, 40 rooms
Gardens
Opened in 1965
Phone 975/32 70 11

DIRECTIONS: 80 km southeast of Soria, off N-II.

The motel-type parador, fronted by a colorful rose garden,
lies on the western outskirts of Santa María. Guest and
public rooms are spaciously comfortable. You may be ser-

enaded by tinkling sheep bells broken by the sharp yips of dogs herding their charges along a country road behind the parador. The dining room faces east for sweeping views of the countryside. Menu features include *trucha ahumada* (smoked trout), *perdiz escabechada* (pickled partridge), *cerdo en salsa de almendras* (pork simmered in almond sauce), *cangrejos de río a la soriana* (river crabs en casserole). For dessert try *buñuelos de San Sturio con nueces* (sweet fritters topped with nuts). Wines offered are Campo de Borja, Rioja Alta and Baja, Cariñena, and Ribera del Duero.

In the village is a twelfth-century Cistercian monastery founded by Alfonso VII and endowed by his son Alfonso VIII. Foundations of the present buildings were laid in 1179.

About 30 km southwest of Santa María de Huerta is the ancient town of Medinaceli, high on a steep bluff. Only a few inhabitants, mostly artists and writers, now live in the town, which boasts a Roman arch, ancient walls, old churches, and houses with emblazoned façades. There is a rambling, well-stocked gift shop of regional and national crafts and art—worth visiting. Upon leaving Medinaceli, before driving down the hill, take time for a panoramic view and consider these words by poet Antonio Machado found on a building plaque in town:

> *But if you climb the height and view the land*
> *From the peaks where the eagle dwells,*
> *You will see sunflowers of crimson and steel,*
> *Leaden plains and silvery hillocks,*
> *Surrounded by violet mountains*
> *With peaks of blushing snow.*

The Cistercians inhabited the monastery until the dissolution in 1835. They returned in 1930 to find the place in a shambles. Restoration began and continues today, helped by contributions coming in from Cistercian orders around the world. There are some interesting frescoed walls, an elaborately decorated seventeenth-century organ, very old Talavera tiles, and tombs of various dukes of Medinaceli. Philip II once spent a night in the monastery and commented upon departure "how inappropriate is so much luxury to the humility and poverty befitting a monastery." The abbot took the royal hint and gave orders for the dismantling of magnificent stained-glass windows that had recently arrived from Flanders.

Parador Nacional Gil Blas

SANTILLANA DEL MAR,
CANTABRIA

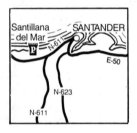

*** govt. rating
Fifteenth-century mansion,
    28 rooms
Gardens
Opened in 1946
Phone 942/81 80 00

DIRECTIONS: 132 km west of Santander, off C-6316.

Once the home of the prosperous Barreda family, the parador faces onto Plaza de Ramón Pelayo. Guest rooms are large and airy, with views from windows set in walls several feet thick. Scenes of village life and the peace of gardens and distant farmlands are visible from the parador. Guest rooms open off large salons decorated and furnished with antiques. A suit of armor stands in a corner of the first-floor staircase. The parador bears the name of a fictitious character in a novel by the French writer Lesage, who had never been to Spain. His hero, Gil Blas of Santillana, wanders through a village in 1715 not remotely resembling the real Santillana.

Fish plays an important part on the parador menu: *zarzuela de pescados* (fish stew) and *calamares o maganos en su tinta santanderina* (squid in its own ink). Other items are *sopa de ajo montañesa* (garlic soup), *potaje campesino* (thick, meat-flavored porridge), and *remojín de la matanza* (pork en casserole). Dessert choices include *quesadas* (cheese cakes), *bizcochos* (sponge cake), and *hojaldres* (pastry puffs). Rioja Alta, Navarra, Ribera del Duero, Campo de Borja, and Rioja Baja comprise the parador wine selection.

Santillana is a village of cobbled streets and plazas where medieval buildings come alive with balconies decked with flowers and laundry, and doorways displaying brilliantly colored ceramic ware for sale. Purchase a guidebook in the lobby of the parador and join the author in a stroll to the twelfth-century collegiate church, the sixteenth-century Monastery of Regina Coeli, and the seventeenth-century Monastery of San Ildefonso, and follow the tour of homes 200 to 500 years old.

> *Parador Nacional Gil Blas is 2 km from the Caves of Altamira, with their famous 15,000-year-old paintings of bison, wild boar, deer, and horses. Unfortunately for those who have never seen these works of art, the caves have been all but closed to the public for some time. Fear that heavy traffic and fluctuation in temperature were harming the paintings led to a drastic restriction in the number of visitors allowed in per day: thirty. If you plan far ahead (say at least three or four months) it is possible to gain admittance. Write to the Director del Centro de Investigación y Museo de Altamira, Santillana del Mar, Cantabria, Spain, and request a date for viewing. Another chance: Upon arrival in Santillana, put your name on the list in the Altamira Museum office for any cancellations or no-shows, wait around, and you may be lucky. While in the Altamira office, pick up a brochure detailing itineraries to nearby picturesque coastal villages.*

Parador Nacional Santo Domingo de la Calzada

SANTO DOMINGO DE LA
CALZADA, LA RIOJA

*** govt. rating
Twelfth-century hospital, 27 rooms
Opened in 1965
Phone 941/34 03 00

DIRECTIONS: 146 km west of Logroño on N-120. The parador faces one side of Plaza del Santo adjacent to the twelfth-century cathedral. You may unload luggage in front of the parador but afterward must park behind the cathedral in the city hall parking lot.

Santo Domingo is another city in Spain's ambitious program of city restoration. Medieval buildings around the cathedral are being rebuilt. You can watch stone masons chisel new blocks by hand, coaxing each to fit perfectly.

Entering the parador is like stepping back in time to the days of pilgrimages to Santiago de Compostela. Saint Dominic (Santo Domingo), using the site of an ancient palace of the kings of Navarra, built the structure to care for those arriving in his village who were in need of medical attention. The main salon is a series of arches with furniture groupings separated by more arches. The center ceiling is of blue and green stained glass. Pots of greenery and comfortable lounge chairs grace spacious stair landings. Guest rooms are large, with a desk, table, and chairs. You may wish for a magical silencer to still clanging church bells that jangle every 15 minutes and toll the correct number of times every hour.

Two specialties of the parador are recommended: *pimientos rellenos* (stuffed mild red peppers) and *solomillo a la parrilla* (tender steak served with french fries and red peppers). The house wine is predictably a rioja.

Replenish your knick-knack supply from some of the many small stores near the parador. If it's time to have a shampoo and set, visit the *señora* in a *peluquería* above the bookstore; she is excellent.

Don't leave Santo Domingo without spending some time

in the cathedral, preferably in the morning so you can hear the cock crow, disturbing the solemnity of the ancient church. The explanation of this oddity is found in the legend that one day several pilgrims on the road to Santiago stopped at a hostel in Santo Domingo. Among them were a couple and their 19-year-old son. The innkeeper's daughter fell in love with the handsome lad, who, unfortunately, spurned her attention. Seeking revenge, she hid a silver cup in the youth's belongings, then announced to all that he was guilty of theft, punishable in those days by death by hanging. Justice was swift and the innocent victim was strung on the gallows. Suddenly, the distraught parents heard their son's voice tell them that he had been saved by Santo Domingo, who had kept his hands under the boy's feet, preventing his falling. The parents rushed immediately to the town magistrate. The official, just sitting down to a meal of roast chicken, scoffed in disbelief, declaring that their son was no more alive than the cock and hen he was about to devour. Whereupon the fowl came to life and flew off the table. The young man was of course released to his parents, to continue on the road to Santiago. And from that day to this, a rooster and hen have occupied a place of honor in a lighted, glassed-in cage across from the tomb of Santo Domingo. For an added touch of realism, a piece of the historic gallows hangs on a wall of the cathedral.

Parador Nacional de Segovia

SEGOVIA

**** govt. rating
Modern, 80 rooms
Elevators, gardens, swimming
  pools, saunas, tennis courts
Opened in 1978
Phone 911/43 04 62

DIRECTIONS: 88 km north of Madrid. If entering Segovia from the south, follow directional signs to Valladolid in order to reach the parador, which is north of the city center and aqueduct.

Standing on the heights of a former estate of almond groves and vineyards, the rosy brick five-story parador sprawls on a natural terrace called Mirador de Lastrilla. Although the interior is concrete and stone, unlike the parador of Salamanca, the austerity is softened by profuse use of greenery in atriums and brick planters. Modern couches and chairs are warmed by colorful pillows and area rugs dot the floor. A large circular indoor swimming pool as well as two on lawns looking beyond to the aqueduct, cathedral, and *alcázar* lure Spaniard and foreigner alike.

Guest rooms are furnished with blond wood furniture, patterned bedspreads and upholstered occasional chairs, and corniced wall draperies opening onto roofed balconies that face the old city.

There are several lounges, TV rooms, and a large bar area. Welcome heat warms public and guest rooms as well as hallways on chilly late autumn days. The parador evidently has clothes dryers (a rarity throughout Spain) because guests' laundry is ready in 24 hours or less, not the customary 48-hour minimum period.

A multilingual maitre d' rules the large semicircular dining room, whose window walls afford a captivating city view. Here is the place to try the region's specialties: *cochinillo asado* (roast suckling pig), *cordero lechal asado* (roast suckling lamb), *judiones del real sitio* (white bean stew flavored with pieces of *chorizo* and *morcilla* sausage), and *sopa de ajo castellana* (garlic soup with an egg sunny-side-up afloat). Wines are Rueda and Ribera del Duero. As an after-dinner drink, try a house specialty, *ponche segoviano*.

TOURING SEGOVIA. The reception clerk will call a cab to take you down to Plaza Azoguejo, spanned by one of the world's best-preserved Roman monuments, the aqueduct (*acueducto romano*) of Segovia. Believed to have been constructed between the second half of the first century A.D. and the early second century, during the reigns of Vespasian and Trajan, the colossus has 118 arches, rises to a height of 96 feet, and is more than half a mile long. It still brings spring water to the city.

Do at least poke your head in to Mesón Cándido, a famous old restaurant very near the aqueduct. It has a unique interior of pebble-patterned floor, strings of red peppers, onions, and garlic hanging to dry from low ceiling rafters, and a brilliant tiled wall behind the bar. If you are desperate for news of home, you can purchase an International Herald Tribune in a kiosk across from Mesón Cándido.

For a walking tour of another part of town, take a no. 1 or no. 2 bus from the plaza and disembark at the *correo* (post office). Information and a map are dispensed at the nearby tourist office. You can explore the cathedral and streets of shops on your own, eventually ending at the *alcázar*. It is wise to hire an English-speaking guide for a private tour through the *alcázar*. On a previous trip, we learned from just such a guide why Isabella is always referred to as the Catholic. "Well of course *all* rulers of Spain have always been Catholic—but Isabella was a *fanatic!*"

The thirteenth-century *alcázar*, rising like a ship's prow on a rocky promontory at the juncture of the Eresma and Clamores rivers, was renovated and enlarged over several centuries. Here in the *alcázar*, Isabella was crowned queen of Castilla in 1474. In the chapel, Philip II was married to his fourth wife, Niece Anne of Austria. Paintings and tapestries adorn the old walls. Splendid suits of armor are on display, including two for young boys learning the rudiments of battle.

SIDE TRIPS FROM SEGOVIA. The parador can be used as a base for touring nearby fifteenth-century Spanish castles: Coca, 48 km northwest; Cuéllar, 57 km northwest; Sepúlveda, 60 km northeast; and Turégano, 30 km north.

Another day's outing could be made to La Granja, 11 km to the south. The lavish eighteenth-century palace is set in extensive gardens festooned with spurting fountains, statues, and urns. If you are lucky, perhaps enough English-speaking tourists will be on hand to warrant a special tour of the fabulous tapestries, objets d'art, and crystal chandeliers.

Parador Nacional Antonio Machado

SORIA

*** govt. rating
Modern, 14 rooms
Opened in 1966
Phone 975/21 34 45

DIRECTIONS: 225 km northeast of Madrid.

Antonio Machado was a poet from Sevilla who wrote thus of Soria:

Silvery heights,
Gray hillsides, ruddy outcrops,
There where the Duero traces its crossbow arc
    round Soria: dark oak groves,
Rough screes, bare ridges,
White lanes and riverside poplars;
Evenings in martial, mystical Soria.

From a hilltop park once the domain of a mighty castle, the expansive windows of the parador lounge afford wonderful views of the Duero River and the eleventh- and twelfth-century buildings of the city. Guest and public rooms are furnished and decorated in Castilian motif: red-tiled floors, leather furniture studded with brass, pottery vases and urns.

Cuisine is likewise Castilian: roast meats, oven-baked trout, crabs, partridge, quail, with *ternera a la plancha* (grilled veal) being a house specialty. Other choices are *jamón asado con pasas* (roast ham with raisins), *bacalao a la soriana* (cod), *judías del Burgo de Osma* (green beans flavored with ham), and *chuletas de cordero forestal* (lamb chops). Wines are from Campo de Borja, Rioja Alta and Baja, Navarra, and Ribera de Duero.

The perceptive traveler will want to make a pilgrimage to Numancia, 7 km north of Soria. Although little remains of the city save a few rows of stones indicating the layout of the streets, it is awesome to stand where Celtiberians withstood a lengthy siege by forces of Scipio's Roman legions. Finally, in 134 B.C., when they could no longer hold out, they set fire to their city and each committed suicide rather than surrender. Their act remains a symbol of bravery to the Spaniards of today.

Parador Nacional de Tordesillas

TORDESILLAS, VALLADOLID

*** govt. rating
Modern, 73 rooms
Swimming pool, gardens
Opened in 1958
Phone 983/77 00 51

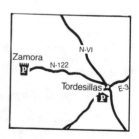

DIRECTIONS: 30 km southwest of Valladolid on N-620; 1 km south of Tordesillas.

This delightful, one-story building rambles in a secluded pine grove. Guest rooms are large and attractively decorated. The wall at one end of the dining room has a stunning tapestry depicting the voyage of Columbus. He stands in the prow of the *Santa María*. The *Niña* and *Pinta* follow, with a Spanish castle on the right and the unknown "Indian" cliffs on the left.

Traditional Castilian dishes are served, along with a few specialties: *besugo castellana* (bream), *merluza al ajo blanco* (white fish seasoned with garlic), *conejo a la cazadora* (wild rabbit), and *lechazo de Tordesillas* (roast suckling pig with various seasonings). *Bizcocho de Medina del Campo* is the house sponge cake. Choose from Rueda, Ribera del Duero, Valdeorras, or Méntrida wines.

TORDESILLAS AND ENVIRONS. There is much to see in the vicinity. First there is Tordesillas, where Spain and Portugal divided the New World with the Treaty of Tordesillas. Santa Clara castle-convent was the prison for Juana the Mad for 44 years and was a favorite residence of Pedro I.

Valladolid has many buildings of interest: the home where Columbus died and an adjacent museum; the National Museum of Polychrome Sculpture; the Church of Santiago, with three Goyas on display; the home of Cervantes; and the cathedral begun by famed architect Herrera and finished in the eighteenth century.

Valladolid saw the marriage of Ferdinand and Isabella and was the capital of Spain under Philip II and Philip III. Because of its importance in earlier years, there are several castle-fortresses in the area. From Tordesillas, one can visit La Mota in Medina del Campo 23 km south, Peñafiel 85 km east on N-122, and Torrelobatón 15 km north on C-611. Fuensaldaña's castle is 6 km north of Valladolid off a local road.

En route from Tordesillas to Valladolid is the spectacular Simancas castle. Until the ninth century a Moorish palace, it was rebuilt in the thirteenth century after its conquest by Alfonso III. Three hundred years later, Philip II decided it should house the General Archives of the Realm. Its 52 rooms hold more than thirty million priceless documents. Although closed to the general public, researchers may gain entrance upon request.

Parador Nacional Villafranca del Bierzo

VILLAFRANCA DEL BIERZO, LEON

*** govt. rating
Modern, 40 rooms
Gardens
Opened in 1959
Phone 987/54 01 75

DIRECTIONS: 135 km west of León; on the eastern edge of town.

Gardens and a parking area front the modern, white, three-story parador. The guest rooms are comfortable, with a desk and chair, twin beds, minibar, and occasional chairs. Striped matching bedspreads and drapes in various tones of brown add warmth to the rooms. The many pots of greenery in halls and on landings give a gracious atmosphere to the parador.

The dining room is quite attractive, with brick partitions and ornate black wrought iron chandeliers. Small flower arrangements are on each table. Perhaps you will be fortunate enough to be served by Señora Duvi, an ebullient Spanish Thelma Ritter. Menu items consist of traditional dishes of the region such as *trucha con unto* (a trout concoction), *pulpo a la barciana* (featuring octopus), and for dessert *suspiros de monje* (monk's sighs, a cream puff sweet). Here is as good a place as any to order *sopa de cebolla*. You can specify whether you want the onion soup with egg (*con huevo*) or without (*sin*).

Villafranca was founded by French pilgrims traveling the way to Santiago de Compostela in the eleventh century. Sometimes called the promised land, Villafranca is situated between two mountain passes in lower Bierzo country, half Galician and half Castilian. Old winding village streets are lined with mansions. There is a sixteenth-century castle with rounded towers at each of its four corners. It is now the property of the counts of Pena Ramiro. Worthy of a visit is the twelfth-century Romanesque Church of Santiago, where, it is said, sick pilgrims received medical aid. San Francisco Monastery has a Romanesque doorway, Gothic paintings, and sixteenth-century choir stalls.

Along Highway N-VI from Astorga to Ponferrada, heading north to Villafranca, a series of coal mines is visible. Village buildings have slate roofs. N-VI is an excellent, fast road.

Traveling north from Villafranca, one climbs barren hills reminiscent of England's Pennines. Watch for oxen with fur pelts draped over their heads.

Parador Nacional Condes de Alba y Aliste

ZAMORA

**** govt. rating
Fifteenth-century palace, 27 rooms
Gardens, swimming pool
Opened in 1968
Phone 988/51 44 97

DIRECTIONS: 62 km north of Salamanca.

In 1459 the first count of Alba and Aliste built a palace over ruins of an Arab *alcazaba*. The magnificence of a Renaissance cloister and Lombard carving on the grand staircase have been preserved in the parador conversion. The two-story cloisters are glassed-in galleries with clusters of furniture and potted greenery. Guest rooms are large and comfortably furnished and have minibars. Tapestries, heraldic banners, and suits of armor astride armored steeds complete the fifteenth-century palace atmosphere. A terrace for outside lounging and dining looks over a large swimming pool set in a broad expanse of lawn.

Dining room entrees include *bacalao a la tranca* (grilled cod), *cabrito asado serrana* (roast kid), *ternera a la toresana* (sauteed veal), and *dos y pingada* (eggs with pork). Two dessert specialties are *remojo zamorano borracho* (sweet crusty type of biscuit with liqueur sauce) and *natillas almendradas* (custard with almonds). With any of the above entrees, be daring and order the favorite wine from nearby Toro, Sangre de Toro, literally bull's blood, a strong *tinto* often 16 percent alcohol.

Iberians, Celts, Carthaginians, and Romans had days of glory in Zamora, situated on banks of the River Duero. In a plaza across from the parador is a statue of famous guerrilla leader Viriatus, known as the terror of Rome because he was victor in eight battles. He fought with a lance that had eight attached red streamers. This formed what later became the banner of Zamora. After the Battle of Toro in 1476, Ferdinand the Catholic rewarded the locals for gallantry by adding an emerald streamer to the emblem.

There are many Romanesque civic buildings and churches to see in Zamora. Called the pearl of the twelfth century, the cathedral was founded and endowed by Alfonso VII in 1135. The most outstanding feature is the cupola of the dome and four smaller corner cupolas all roofed with overlapping stones, giving a fish-scaly effect. Of special interest in the cathedral museum are priceless tapestries, given in 1608 by the sixth count of Alba and Aliste. Some of them depict the exploits of Hannibal and the epic of Troy. There are large manuscripts written on calf skin, a marble statue of the Virgin by Bartolomé de Ordóñez, and a silver monstrance, constructed in 1515 in Toledo, weighing 450 pounds.

Cataluña

CATALUÑA, SITUATED IN THE NORTHEASTERN COR-
ner of Spain, owes its wealth to agriculture, industry, and
tourism. Vineyards and olive groves thrive on plains and
in fertile valleys. Rice and orange groves prosper in the
Ebro River delta near Tortosa. Orchards inland around
Tarragona provide important dried fruit commodities. Cataluña's provinces are Barcelona, Gerona, Lérida, and Tarragona. Catuluña is bounded by France on the north, Aragón on the west, the Mediterranean on the east, and
Valencia on the south.

Barcelona, Spain's major port and a lively city, has developed into a rich industrial center, with textile, metal-
lurgical, and chemical production.

Tourism has grown dramatically. Resorts on the rug-
gedly beautiful Costa Brava of Gerona province and on the
more gentle Costa Dorada south of there continue to
mushroom.

Cataluña has always been involved in trade, although
its vulnerable location opened it to invasion by the Greeks

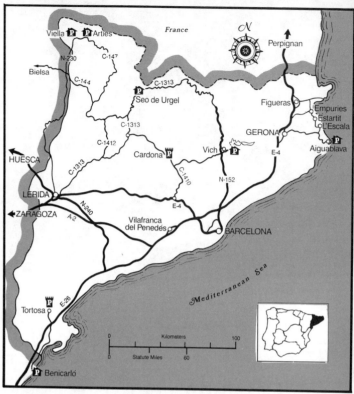

Cataluña

in the sixth century B.C., by the Carthaginians in the third century B.C., by the Romans, and by the Arabs. Charlemagne freed Cataluña from the Moors only to annex it to his own empire. Thus Cataluña came under French influence and was at odds with Castilla for centuries. Even today relations with Madrid are sometimes strained.

During the Middle Ages a fund of literature written in Catalán evolved. With the death of Franco, Cataluña has more say in its affairs and Catalán is once more being used in spoken as well as written communications.

Cataláns are individualistic, hardworking, and energetic. They are hospitable and clever, maintaining *seny*, the Catalán word for common sense and a realistic approach to life.

Parador Nacional
Costa Brava

AIGUABLAVA-BAGUR, GERONA

**** govt. rating
Modern, 87 rooms
Swimming pool, elevator, gardens,
  beach
Opened in 1966
Phone 972/62 21 62

DIRECTIONS: 50 km east of Gerona. Roads along the Costa Brava
are very winding but of adequate quality. To reach Aiguablava,
leave the Barcelona–La Junquera Autopista at Exit 10, with the
sign reading Gerona Norte; when you reach Bagur, you are 8 km
from the parador.

Perched on high cliffs overlooking the Mediterranean Sea,
forested mountains, and a small bay, the parador is an
ideal base for two or three days of exploring in the area.
Guest and public rooms are spacious and decorated in warm
modern motif. All rooms have balconies with spectacular
sea views.

Catalán cuisine is the order of the day at the parador:
escudella i carn d'olla (savory stew of sausage, green beans,
and meat balls, made with bread crumbs, eggs, and spices),
suquet de peix (fish stew with potatoes or rice, tomatoes,
onions, garlic, and parsley), *pollo al ast* (barbecued chicken),
and *zarzuela marinera* (fish and seafood stew). For dessert
try *creme catalana* (custard with crystallized sugar topping)
or *plátanos a la catalana* (a banana confection). Any of the
Catalán wines are excellent: Alella, Ampurdán, Penedés,
Priorato, or Tarragona. Try a different one at each meal.

Bagur's castle bastion and defense towers are visible for
miles. Of feudal origin, the castle was held by the Cruílles
de Peratallada family from the fourteenth to the eighteenth century. The castle was destroyed in the fifteenth
century, reconstructed in the seventeenth, and occupied
by the French during the Peninsular War. Bagur clusters
in a semicircle around the foot of the crowned hill. Defense towers were erected as lookouts against pirates.

Eleven kilometers northwest of the parador is Pals, with
two drawing cards: a well-restored medieval barrio and an
alluring 18-hole par 73 golf course. Palafrugell, just southwest of the parador, has shops offering quality merchandise, and its fifteenth-century Church of San Martín has
outstanding paintings and lovely stained glass windows.

La Bisbal, 23 km west, is an important Catalán ceramics town; its main street is lined with shops selling pottery from local as well as other artisans. The Greek and Roman ruins at Empúries lie 30 km north of Aiguablava. Several nearby seaside villages have sandy beaches luring swimmers and sun lovers. Estartit, L'Escala, and Llafranch are particularly inviting.

Figueres is a bustling little metropolis about 60 km northwest of the parador. Tiled shopping streets reserved for pedestrians radiate from a center *ramblas* edged by outdoor cafes. Salvador Dalí was born in Figueres and a museum is named in his honor. Two of the finest restaurants in this part of Spain are the Ampurdán (phone 50 05 62), 1.5 km north on N-II, and Mas Pau (phone 50 08 62), 5 km southwest on C-260. In both establishments, Catalán dining reaches its zenith.

Catalán appears throughout Cataluña, including on road signs; many place names are different in Catalán and Spanish. Usually Spanish is also given, but not always. Catalán is a language with roots in archaic French and archaic Spanish. Some examples of Catalán words and their Spanish equivalents:

Catalán	Spanish
sortida	*salida*
obert	*abierto*
Girona	*Gerona*
Empúries	*Ampurias*
Figueres	*Figueras*
avinguda	*avenida*
Léida	*Lérida*
praça	*plaza*
carrer	*carretera*

Parador Nacional
Don Gaspar de Portolá
ARTIES, LERIDA

**** govt. rating
Modern, 40 rooms
Elevator
Opened in 1967
Phone 973/64 08 01

DIRECTIONS: 168 km north of Lérida via N-230.

Until a few years ago, Arties's main tourist accommodation was an *hostería nacional*. Now Parador Don Gaspar de Portolá adjoins the *hostería*, a seventeenth-century towered building, birthplace of the explorer of Northern California and founder of the San Diego mission. The *hostería* is open in winter only, when skiers descend on the area.

The parador has two expansive lounges with focal fireplaces. A bar extends from one of them. Both areas have plenty of sofas, easy chairs, and game tables. Wall decor consists of mounted deer heads, antlers, stuffed pheasant, and other wild fowl, and even a wild boar's head. Each guest room holds twin beds, desk, minibar, occasional chairs, and coffee table. Windows look out over the village, framed by the towering Pyrenees.

Window sills holding pots of colorful flowers, heavy ornate wrought iron chandeliers, and a stained glass wall are features of the dining room. Cuisine is Catalán and continental, with a French flair (Toulouse is a mere 160 km distant). One specialty to try is a stew a la Arán, made with beans, potatoes and other vegetables, sausage, and ham.

An excellent wine choice would be a sparkling Penedés. In addition to *creme catalana,* the parador features *crepes de Valle de Arán* (crepes filled with fruit and topped with *natillas,* a cream custard).

When skiers register at the parador, they are given room keys and smaller keys for two lockers for skis and shoes. The slopes are 5 km away at Baquerra. An added convenience in winter is an underground garage accommodating 40 cars.

Arties is a medieval mountain village of somber granite homes with gray slate steep-sloped roofs. It boasts a twelfth-century Catalán church.

BARCELONA

Barcelona is an easy city to tour without a car. The hub of the city is Plaza de Cataluña, so take a cab or the Metro there and start a walking tour of Las Ramblas (Rambles in Catalán), one of the most famous thoroughfares in the world. Once the route of a mountain stream, Las Ramblas, bordered on each side by car traffic, is a broad pedestrian avenue edged by cafes with outdoor dining, flower stalls, kiosks, bird markets, and countless other stalls selling literally soup to nuts. Take several hours to reach the port dominated by a towering statue of Columbus (you can rent chairs from vendors along the way to have a rest and watch the crowd). A replica of the *Santa María* is moored near Columbus. Locate an aerial tramway to take you to the top of Montjuich for lunch at an open-air restaurant. Sup, sip, and drink in spectacular views of the harbor, city, and Mediterranean. After lunch, take the funicular down and cover the opposite side of Las Ramblas. A full day's working pleasure.

On another day, once more start at Plaza de Cataluña but head a bit east down Avinguda del Portal de L'Angel to arrive at the cathedral and Gothic Quarter (Barrio Gótico or Barri Gótic). The cathedral is an excellent example of Mediterranean Gothic erected in the fourteenth century. On the previous day's outing, you have made sure to locate a tourist office for information and a map of things to see in the Gothic Quarter. So called because of its many buildings from the thirteenth to the fifteenth centuries, the quarter and its fascinating labyrinth of alleyways can easily consume a full day. Admirers of Picasso should not miss the world-class Museu Picasso at Carrer de Montcada 15.

By now you may be ready to be shepherded and cosseted. Arrange at your hotel desk for a tour to the monastery of Montserrat outside the city, and another tour of Barcelona to take in various landmarks, including two on Montjuich, the Museum of Catalán Art and the Pueblo Español. Erected for the International Exposition in 1929, the Spanish village contains homes representative of every type of regional Spanish architecture and culture. Stroll through the streets and around squares where artisans are at work turning out handcrafts, on display and for sale.

Parador Nacional Duques de Cardona

CARDONA, BARCELONA

**** govt. rating
Tenth-century castle, 65 rooms
Elevator
Opened in 1976
Phone 93/869 12 75

DIRECTIONS: 95 km northwest of Barcelona on C-1410. If heading north from Manresa, beware that the sign may not read Cardona; follow signs reading Solsona. The parador is visible for miles, since it is on the highest spot.

Once the fortress of Admiral and High Constable of Aragón Don Ramón Folch, duke of Cardona, the parador is
the ultimate in castles. Many of the ancient buildings, additions, and rebuildings from many centuries have been
incorporated into the parador. There are portions of a stately
Gothic cloister, a ducal patio, an aged cistern, the Church
of San Vicente (first erected in 981, then enlarged in 1020),
and the Torre de la Minyona. According to legend, the
tower was the fateful prison for beautiful Adales, daughter
of Viscount Folch. When it was discovered that she had
fallen in love with a Moorish leader and had adopted his
religion, her brothers confined her to the tower, where she
died within a year.

Numerous salons, a bar-cafeteria, cellar *bodega*, and dining room have a castle aura, with beamed ceilings broken
by series of pointed arches, heraldic tapestries framed by
tall wrought iron torch receptacles. The view from guest
rooms seems endless.

The parador menu offers some unusual Catalán dishes:
langostinos hervidos o plancha (boiled or grilled prawns), *lomo
de cerdo ahumada con ensalada* (loin of smoked pork with
salad), and *espinacas a la Catalán* (spinach with raisins). *Soufle
Alaska* (baked Alaska) is the piece de resistance. *Blancos,
tintos,* and *rosados* from the Manresa *bodega* are the house
wines served by the carafe.

The geographic location of Cardona is fantastic. The
Cardoner River flows through a fertile valley floor. The
castle-fortress looms from the summit of a cone-shaped
mountain of salt. According to history, the site had been
assaulted by Charlemagne, Wilfred the Hairy, and Almansur the Moor, and has played strategic roles in Spain's
succeeding conflicts. During the Civil War of 1936–39 it
sustained severe damage.

The mountain of salt was an important advantage to all
who held it. According to the Carta Puebla, a constitution
handed down by the Count of Barcelona in 986, inhabitants of the area could have salt for their own use every
Thursday if they donated one day's work a week to maintenance of the castle's fortification and if they promised to
defend the count against all enemies.

Puente del Diablo, an arch of a Roman bridge, is visible
from the parador. Across this bridge spanning the Cardoner River, medieval pilgrims journeyed to Santiago de
Compostela and to Montserrat. Fifty kilometers to the south

of the parador, Montserrat was founded as a monastery in the eleventh century by Abbot Oliva. It was constructed on a hazardous ledge of strangely serrated mountain peaks whose outlines may be seen from the parador on a clear day. The church has been rebuilt because it was completely destroyed in the nineteenth century. The Escolania, one of Europe's foremost boys' choirs, can be heard daily at 11 A.M., at 1 P.M., and again at vespers at 7 P.M.

Parador Nacional de Seo de Urgel

SEO DE URGEL, LERIDA

*** govt. rating
Modern, 84 rooms
Swimming pool, elevator
Opened in 1979
Phone 973/35 20 00

DIRECTIONS: 6 km south of Andorra on C-1313. Be aware that Madrid and the Spanish National Tourist Office use the above spelling although Catalán prevails in this northern frontier city of Cataluña: Le Seu d'Urgell (literally the cathedral of the city of Urgell). When on the outskirts of town, follow directions to the Seu, which is across the square from a now-defunct church-monastery. Next to the ex-monastery is the modern stone parador, on Carrer Sant Domenec.

The parador's unusually high glass-roofed lounge, incorporating ancient cloisters, is a virtual greenhouse of cascading plants. Guest rooms are comfortable and rather incongruously furnished with white cubistic plastic furniture and carpeted with a jigsaw-patterned rubber matting. An indoor swimming pool is heated by rays of the sun coming through the glass ceiling. The staff is very friendly and eager to help. A big plus for the parador is a locked underground garage.

Dinner is served at 9 P.M. in a glass-domed dining room. The airy effect is nice during the day but a bit cool on autumn nights. Cuisine is Catalán, with the season's yields of fruits and vegetables determining the *menú del día*. Dishes to look for include *cazuela* (potatoes garnished with salt pork, snails, tomato, and onion), *perdiz con coles* (partridge with brussels sprouts), *arroz de jueves lardero* (rice with pork), and *parillada de pescado y marisco* (various kinds of fried fish,

> *For mountain scenery, take the secondary road west from Seo de Urgel (Le Seu d'Urgell in Catalán) to Sort. This route appears only on regional maps. The 78 km will take about an hour and a half to drive in second and third gears. Small villages of seven or eight houses are seen every few kilometers. If the soil is red, the houses are red. All roofs in this area of Spain are charcoal-gray slate. In autumn, mountains seem dusted with powdered sugar. At Sort, take C-147 north. You will reach the acme of this route at Puerto de la Bonaigua (puerto means pass). This is not an easy route, but the road is adequate and the scenery rewarding. It is probably wise not to try it later than October 1, as we found several inches of snow along the road and at the top in the last week of September.*

from tiny octopus, squid, and shrimp to lobster). House wines are riojas, although Priorato, Penedés, and Ampurdán may also be ordered.

Seu d'Urgell was a city of prince-bishops and has been a bishopric since 527. For over 700 years, the duties of the archbishop have included joint rulership of the country of Andorra. The first documents written in Catalán appeared here in the thirteenth century.

The cobbled arcaded streets are narrow, and balconies burgeon with flowers. Stroll through the twelfth-century Romanesque cathedral and be sure not to miss the treasure of the diocesan museum. A copy of Saint John's commentary on Apocalypse was handwritten and illuminated by the priest Beatus of Liébana Monastery in the eighth century.

Parador Nacional Castillo de la Zuda

TORTOSA, TARRAGONA

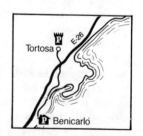

**** govt. rating
Tenth-century castle, 82 rooms
Elevator, swimming pool, gardens
Opened in 1976
Phone 977/44 44 50

DIRECTIONS: 80 km southwest of Tarragona. Upon entering Tortosa from the south, motorists will be going parallel to the Ebro

River; just past the War Memorial sculpture in the midst of the river, turn right for the ascent to the parador.

An inscription by the poet Al-Gaziri hangs near the reception desk of the parador:

> At the summit of a stark height,
> Where no one could hope to find comfortable refuge,
> The ravens squawk and perch on the summit,
> And on it you can hear the winds blowing.
> Those who have climbed it once in their life
> Often complain of having felt their hearts weaken.

It is not all that bad today but you may want to walk up after an excursion down in the town, because taxi fare is about US$3.50 one way.

The advantage of the rocky mass was known by Celtiberians, Romans, Moors, and Castilian kings. The Moors destroyed Roman walls and built the Castle of Zuda (meaning water wheel or well) on a former acropolis in the time of Abd al-Rahman III, in 944. In the Middle Ages it was converted into a royal residence and served as the seat of law courts. But when the Ministry of Tourism began conversion into a parador, not much was left to start with. (Be sure to notice aerial before and after shots of the site on display.)

Once again, parador architects have done a masterful job of blending old with new. One wall, windows, and a fireplace of the dining room are of original Arab construction. Series of salons separated by pointed archways are furnished with furniture groupings set on rich Cuencan area carpets. Paintings, antique engravings, sculpture, and ceramic ware beautify the parador. Guest room balconies look down on the Ebro River and the old walled section of town. Two mounted artifacts to look for are a stone bracket possibly of Greek origin and a funeral plaque dated 349 Arabic era, 961 Christian era, honoring the death of an Arab ruler whose tomb used to be on site, but has recently been on loan to a museum. Roman columns, unearthed on the location, enhance the front façade of the parador. The original *zuda* has a grilled cover and is found in a garden area in front of the parador.

The dining room opens at 8 P.M. and offers specialties gleaned from the Ebro delta: *anguilas* (eels), *ancas de rana* (frog legs), and *langostinos* (prawns). Fish dishes are prepared with *romesco,* a sauce of tomatoes, garlic, olive oil, peppers, ground hazelnuts, and Priorato wine. *Colcotada* is a savory concoction of meat and sausages. *Pollo en xanfaina* is a chicken goulash. Two desserts to try are *garrofetes del papa* (delicate pastries named for Papa Luna, Benedict III, who lived in Tortosa periodically) and *pastissets de Tortosa,* an almond confection inherited from the Arabs.

First populated by Iberians, who called the area Dertosa, it was later captured by Scipio Africanus Major in the third century B.C. Julius Caesar gave it the important status of *municipio* and Octavius bestowed the full rank of *colonia* with the title Dertosa Julia Augusta. The Moors invaded in 778 and held Tortosa until its reconquest in 1148 by Count Ramón Berenguer IV.

At the foot of the parador hill is one of the most beautiful Catalán Gothic cathedrals of Spain, begun in the middle of the fourteenth century on consecrated ground previously occupied by a Roman temple and an Arab mosque. One can also visit Santa Clara Convent, built in the first half of the thirteenth century, the College of San Luis, founded in 1544 by Carlos V for educating young Moors, and the fourteenth-century Lonja (market exchange). In the Museu-Archivo Municipal is a medieval code of laws written and compiled on 300 parchments in 1272, known as Libre de les Costums.

The modernistic metal sculpture rising out of the river is a memorial to the dead who fell during the Battle of the Ebro in 1938. The Republicans, under siege in trenches for four months, lost thousands of men before surrendering to Nationalist forces.

Traveling north on the *autopista* from Tortosa, just after the sign to Tarragona appears, motorists encounter a ter-

rific view of a two-tiered Roman aqueduct, and a camera
turn-off on the right.

---

*Vilafranca del Penedés (population 21,366) is a delightful
city with a very worthwhile wine museum, 47 km northeast of Tarragona on Highway N-340. Vilafranca is the
market capital of an area where more than 50 percent of
cultivated land is vineyard. Park wherever you find a slot
and start walking, following the locals. If it is Saturday,
their destination will be Praça de Vila, the town square,
for it will be market day. Upon entering the* praça, *you
will find the museum a couple of short blocks to the right,
across from the Basilica of Saint Mary.*

*Situated in a thirteenth-century palace built by Jaime II,
a king of Aragón, the museum has outstanding dioramas
presenting the history of the wine industry from Celtiberian times. There are also art, archeological, geological, and
stone carving sections of the museum. At the end of your
visit, you will be treated to a jigger glass of regional wine
and may retain the glass as a souvenir. The town itself is
very appealing, with unusual street lights and tiled street
plaques.*

Parador Nacional de Vich

VICH, BARCELONA

**** govt. rating
Modern, 31 rooms
Swimming pool, elevator, tennis,
   gardens
Opened in 1972
Phone 93/888 72 11

DIRECTIONS: 80 km north of Barcelona. If traveling to the parador
from the Barcelona–La Junquera Autopista, take the Granollers
exit and 2 km west of Granollers, join N-152 north. The parador
is 14 km east of Vich. If traveling to Vich from the parador at
Cardona, to the west, make an abrupt left turn off of C-1410 immediately past the shopping district of Suria. When you come to
Balsareny, turn right to Avinyo. Just past the big gas station, turn
left at the first street, then left again at signs reading 33 kms to
Vic. It is a difficult but scenic drive through reforested hills inter-
rupted by cultivated fields of red soil.

Parador de Vich (Vic in Catalán, and pronounced BEEK) is built of white stone, roofed in red tile in the style of a *masía*, a typical Catalán farmhouse with arched windows, doorways, and open galleried balconies. One enters through an enclosed courtyard made inviting by a profusion of potted plants. The two-story reception salon is quite large and is dramatically decorated with modern murals of headless Roman statues and a ceiling of colored glass. Guest rooms lead off the upstairs mezzanine. They are carpeted, furnished in warm wood tones, and have windows taking in Embalse (lake) de Sau, edged by forested cliffs.

Unique dining room lighting fixtures, each consisting of three "yoked" crystal and brass globes, extend the length of the ceiling. An appealing harvest scene is painted on the end wall. Two luncheon items worth ordering are *ensalada catalana* (Catalán salad of mild fish chunks garnished with tomatoes, asparagus, and lettuce) and *huevos escalfados soubise* (poached eggs on two sausages covered with a kind of Hollandaise sauce). Recommended dinner entrees are *cazuela de lomo y butifarra con haba* (casserole of pork, sausage, and white beans) and *chuletón de ternera a la brasa* (braised rib of beef served with french fries, mushrooms, and crisp fried eggplant). House wines are a Penedés *blanco* and a Priorato *tinto*.

Parador Nacional Valle de Arán

VIELLA, LERIDA

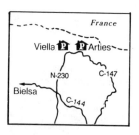

*** govt. rating
Modern, 135 rooms
Swimming pool, elevator, gardens
Opened in 1966
Phone 973/64 01 00

DIRECTIONS: 164 km north of Lérida on N-230. When entering Viella from the southeast, don't despair if Parador signs do not appear. Tunel (tunnel) signs do, indicating the tunnel under the Puerto de Viella, just south of Viella. Moreover, the parador, a white four-story rectangle fronted by a round slate-coned extension, is visible from below. Continue through town until you come to a five-point intersection. Go past the large Pirelli gas station on the right and up the hill for 2 km.

The windows of the parador's semicircular lounge allow unimpeded vistas of mountain grandeur. Guest rooms have

balconies for viewing well-kept grounds, swimming pool, children's play yard, snow-capped peaks, tumbling streams, and near and distant villages. Furnishings are comfortable, with twin beds, desk, leather chairs, minibar, and commodious two-sink baths.

The cuisine is so recognized that the parador is a lunch stop for tour buses. Serving guests are red-jacketed waiters with white napkins draped over left arms, and a multilingual maitre d'. Some suggested entrees are *rodaballo poche salsa holandesa* (poached turbot with Hollandaise sauce), *lomo de cerdo braseado con peras* (braised pork fillet with pears), *truchas a la parador* (fresh-caught mountain trout), and *escalopes de ternera con champiñon* (veal in mushroom sauce). A festive dessert to order is *plátanos flambeados a la catalana* (flambéed bananas). A large variety of Spanish wines is available.

Take time to explore Viella. Go through a thirteenth-century doorway of the parish church for a look at Mig Arán Christ. Protected in a glass display case is the head and upper torso of a twelfth-century wooden sculpture of the descent from the cross. The beard and hair are elaborately curled on an elongated haughty version of Christ.

The six kilometers separating Arties and Viella reveal numerous villages of stone houses clustered round the distinctive square-towered slate-roofed churches of the Valle de Arán. Although a part of Spain since the thirteenth century, the valley remained isolated until the second quarter of this century. In 1925 the first road for autos (now C-147) was built through Puerto (pass) de la Bonaigua. A tunnel giving Viella access to Lérida was completed in 1948. The 6-km tunnel is bumpy and drippy, allowing only 25 to 30 km per hour. The road south of the tunnel is excellent.

If heading for the parador in Bielsa to the west, be alert after passing through Vilaller. We missed the C-144 turn-off to Castejón because of a sea of sheep suddenly appearing round a bend—an estimated 3000 of them! It took four shepherds and as many dogs about 20 minutes to herd them off the road. Traveling south from Castejón on C-139, you will pass through Congosto de Ventanillo, a spectacular gorge.

Extremadura

THE NAME EXTREMADURA, DATING FROM THE DAYS
of the Reconquest, means "beyond the River Duero." Bordered on the north by the Sierra de Gredos, on the west
by Portugal, on the south by the Sierra Morena, and on
the east by Castilla La Mancha, the region had been isolated geographically from the political and economic life of
Spain before new developments in transportation and
communication. The two provinces of Extremadura are
Badajoz and Cáceres.

Life has been harsh in Extremadura. The soil was thin
and unproductive after centuries of grazing and trampling
by immense herds of sheep. But, beginning in 1950, the
government encouraged new methods of crop production
and stock raising. Vast land holdings were broken up into
parcels of 10 to 12 acres to entice workers back to farming.
A series of dams was constructed to provide irrigation. Re-
forestation is still underway. High-yield tobacco and cotton are grown. Power stations are still being built to allow
for the development of food processing plants. New vil-

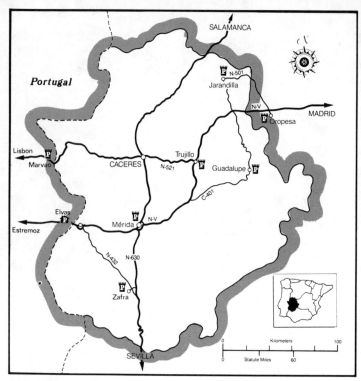

Extremadura

lages sprang up. All of these measures were taken in the hope of stopping the traditional emigration of Extremadurans.

It was from this land that hardy, determined adventurers, conquistadors, left to seek riches and fame in the New World. Their names are familiar: Cortés, Pizarro, Orellana, Balboa, Hernando de Soto, and Pedro de Valdivia. The wealth acquired by conquering the nations of the Americas built many lavish mansions that still stand in the towns and cities of this region.

Parador Nacional Zurbarán

GUADALUPE, CACERES

*** govt. rating
Sixteenth-century hospital-convent,
   40 rooms
Gardens, swimming pool, elevator
Opened in 1965
Phone 927/36 70 75

DIRECTIONS: 129 km east of Cáceres.

The parador was reconstructed from a sixteenth-century
hospital built to care for pilgrims from all over Spain and
Europe who came to pay homage to the shrine of the Virgin of Guadalupe. The two-story, square structure envel-
ops a courtyard planted with citrus trees. Mudejar archways on both floors overlook the patio. Public rooms with
rough-hewn timbered ceilings extend one to another, separated only by round arches. Ancient maps, engravings,
tile plaques, and low copper-covered braziers once used to
hold hot coals for warmth add decorative touches to the
parador. Comfortable guest rooms face onto the gardens
and swimming pool. A large painting by Zurbarán hangs
in one of the salons.

Specialties of the dining room include *potaje de espinacas*
(spinach soup), *migas extremeñas* (bread crumbs fried with
crisp bacon bits), *pollo a la padre Pedro* (chicken), *truchas al
moje Zurbarán* (trout), *cordero asado conquistador* (roast lamb),
sopa de arroz cacereña (rice soup), *pincho mudéjar* (skewered
lamb), sausages and ham from nearby Montánchez, and
for dessert, *puding de Castañas* (chestnut pudding). Mon-
tánchez, Cañamero, and Pitarra are the principal wines offered by the parador.

According to tradition, Saint Gregory brought a statue
of the Virgin said to have been carved by Saint Luke to
Sevilla from Rome. Anticipating the Moorish invasion, a
group of priests buried the statue in a field near a stream
in Guadalupe in 711. Toward the end of the thirteenth
century, a young shepherd, Gil Cordero, discovered the
600-year-old carving miraculously preserved. Installed in a
small shrine, it soon began drawing pilgrims from all over
the country. When Alfonso XI, after invoking the aid of
the Virgin, was victorious in the Battle of Salado against
the Moors in 1340, he ordered a church built to house the

statue. From then to now, Our Lady of Guadalupe has drawn enthusiastic pilgrims.

In 1389 Saint Jerome ordered construction of a monastery. Father Fernando Yáñez supervised the building of a Mudejar cloister, a library, and a capitulary chamber (monastery office). Due to increasing numbers of pilgrims, several inns and hospitals were erected. The great wealth of the monastery, coming from gifts of kings and noblemen, enabled it to build colleges and schools open to laymen as well as to religious orders.

It was in the monastery that Ferdinand and Isabella gave final sailing instructions to Columbus before he embarked for the New World. An ardent devotee himself, Columbus spread the religious fervor that made the Virgin of Guadalupe queen of the Hispanic world.

The monastery was abandoned in 1835, to be taken over in the early twentieth century by the Franciscan order. Some of the riches to be seen are paintings of the life of Saint Jerome by Zurbarán (1598–1664), a large assortment of miniature prayer books, great illuminated manuscripts from the fifteenth to seventeenth centuries, and the most varied and valuable collection of embroidered clerical vestments in Europe.

In the church, the Virgin sits on a throne in a special chapel called the Camarín. Don't miss her fantastic wardrobe and jeweled crown, on display in the adjacent reliquary cabinet.

Village life centers around a large fountain facing the church. It is wonderfully entertaining to sit at an outside table sipping local wine and watching all the activity. On Sundays, exuberant wedding parties add even more color.

If you are unable to obtain a room at the parador, try for one of the monastery's 38 (phone 927/36 70 00).

Parador Nacional Carlos V

JARANDILLA DE LA VERA,
CACERES

*** govt. rating
Fourteenth-century castle, 43 rooms
Gardens, swimming pool
Opened in 1966
Phone 927/56 01 17

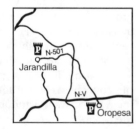

DIRECTIONS: 133 km northeast of Cáceres via N-630 and C-501. Cars are parked outside the original walls.

When Enrique III gave the town of Oropesa to Don Alvarez de Toledo, he also included Jarandilla. Don Alvarez's descendants built a castle-fortress in the last years of the fourteenth century. This castle has been restructured into Parador Carlos V. The two-story square building has four towers at the corners, two round and two square. The entrance, embellished overhead with the coat of arms of Carlos V, leads into a large courtyard, the *patio de armas*, once used for mustering troops. In the center, the one-time cistern is now a reflecting pool glittering with visitors' coins. On vine-covered walls may be seen the shields of the Alvarezes of Toledo, the counts of Oropesa, and the marquises of Jarandilla.

The parador is decorated with paintings, old weapons, colorful ceramic ware and brilliant tapestries. Old banisters, risers, and foot-wide baseboards of patterned tile, open-beamed ceilings, and burnished wrought iron chandeliers lend Old World charm to public rooms. History buffs may want to book the Royal Suite, once occupied overnight by Charles de Gaulle, just one of many illustrious guests of the parador.

A few menu items to consider are *perdiz estofada con salsa* (stewed partridge), *merluza a la cazuela* (hake en casserole), *caldereta de cordero* (lamb stew), *cochifrito extremeño* (roast suckling pig), and *aguacate y gambas* (prawn and avocado cocktail). For dessert, *manzanas asadas* (baked apples) is a good choice. House wine is a *tinto* from Robles *bodega*.

Carlos V, wearying of his demanding life, abdicated in 1555 in favor of his son Philip II and ordered construction of a monastery at Yuste, 12 km west of the parador. While awaiting completion of his final resting place, Carlos lived for two years in the castle that is now the parador. His illegitimate son Don Juan, victor in the Battle of Lepanto against the Turks, grew up in Cuacos, 10 km from Jarandilla.

The Hieronymite monastery at Yuste is open to the public. A few of the interesting things to be seen are the refectory with Mudejar tiles, Gothic and plateresque patios, and Carlos's private rooms, with furniture, paintings, and arms on display.

The region of La Vera is enriched by the Tiétar River and is dotted with hundreds of brick tobacco barns set among fields of red peppers and tobacco. Large cork forests are found south of Talayuela.

Parador Nacional Via de la Plata

MERIDA, BADAJOZ

**** govt. rating
Sixteenth-century convent,
  50 rooms
Gardens
Opened in 1933
Phone 924/31 38 00

DIRECTIONS: 64 km east of Badajoz via C-530 or N-V. Traffic is a headache in the growing city of Mérida. The parador administrator says it is difficult to keep a city map up to date and Parador directional signs in place because of almost constant rerouting and one-way street conversions. The parador is in the southwestern part of the old city, not too far from the Guadiana River. It is near the intersection of two major streets, Calvario and Yagüe, and faces the Plaza Queipo de Llano. Look for white ornate chimneys on a red roof topped with storks' nests.

The square, white, two-story building encompasses a courtyard of rounded arches resting on ancient columns, some Visigothic, others with Arabic inscriptions. The site had been used as a palace housing Roman Pretorian Guards and as a residence of the Visigothic governor. The Military Order of Santiago constructed and reconstructed ruins into a monastery in the sixteenth century. Intricate grillwork separates two sections of the former chapel, now converted into a stunning lounge for guests. Decorative accents include mounted acanthus column capitals of bygone eras, huge ceramic urns, four-basined copper braziers, and an abundance of potted greenery. Guest rooms with woven, fringed spreads and drapes, colorful area rugs, upholstered occasional chairs, desk, and minibar overlook parador gardens.

The dining room is very popular with native as well as foreign guests. Entrees include dishes from clams to partridge stew with specialties being *cochinillo asado emeritense* (roast suckling pig), *chuletas de cordero a la pobre* (lamb cutlets with potatoes), *zorongollo extremeño* (a salad featuring roasted red peppers), *tencas escabechabas* (pickled Extremaduran lake fish), *pollo a la padre Pedro* (roast stuffed chicken). Two dessert delectables are *pastel de kiwis y fresas* (kiwi and strawberry cake) and *repápalos con leche* (custard-filled fritters dusted with cinnamon). The wine cellar is well-stocked and the wine list is extensive. Regional choices would be a Catalina Arroyo *blanco* or Trampal or Lar de Barros *tinto*, all from Almendralejo, a large wine center 27 km south of Mérida.

TOURING MERIDA. The parador gets its name because Mérida was one of the oldest settlements along the Camino de la Plata (silver road; *via* is Latin), the old Roman road. The colony was founded on the north bank of the Guadiana River in 25 B.C. by Emperor Octavius as a colony to reward veterans, *emeriti*, who had fought so hard to bring the western part of Iberia under Roman domination. Its name was Emeritus Augustus and it accommodated 50,000 inhabitants. It was soon to become capital of Lusitania, as the Roman center in Spain was called. Excavations over the years have revealed a hippodrome, or circus, where chariot races and mock naval battles were staged for 30,000 spectators. In an amphitheater built in 8 B.C., promoters arranged gladiatorial programs (men against men, men against lions, lions against lions) for capacity crowds of 15,000 enthralled fans. Near one of the entrances into the arena, you can see slots through which spectators fed lion or gladiator. These grisly games were finally halted by Emperor Honorio in 404.

Agrippa and sons Caius and Lucius donated an outdoor theater in 16 B.C. Gardens, Corinthian columns, and marble arches were added by later emperors to enhance nightly performances. The theater seated 5000. Today, during the last week of June and first two weeks of July, classical drama is presented in this great Roman monument.

Trajan's Arch of Triumph stands near the Plaza d'España. You may drive or walk across the Roman bridge over the Guadiana River. This bridge, with 60 supporting arches, is 2575 feet long, 14-1/2 feet wide, and 39 feet high. The Milagros aqueduct is one of three remaining in the area.

Excavations on the site of an Arab *alcazaba* built in 835 reveal that the fortress was constructed on top of Roman ruins. Colorful mosaics have been reassembled. For an eerie experience, go down into the *aljibe*, a cavernlike cistern of Roman origin.

On a walking tour of Mérida, be sure to enter the *mercado*, town market, to see the bountiful and unusual produce.

Interesting side trips may be made to castles at Medellín, 40 km east, and Alburquerque, 80 km northwest.

Because Mérida has some of the best-preserved Roman ruins outside of Rome, it is a very popular tourist stop, and reservations at Parador Via de la Plata are necessary months in advance.

Parador Nacional
de Trujillo

TRUJILLO, CACERES

**** govt. rating
Sixteenth-century convent,
   46 rooms
Gardens, swimming pool, bar-
   cafeteria
Opened in 1984
Phone 927/32 13 50

DIRECTIONS: 47 km east of Cáceres via N-521. The parador is on
the eastern outskirts of town.

Trujillo's parador is the newest in the network. Part of the
parador was reconstructed from a sixteenth-century Franciscan convent. A new section was built of the same granite as the original. The old part has a courtyard planted in
orange and lemon trees, while the new has a courtyard
filled with a swimming pool. Canopied beds and light pine
furniture give each guest room a pleasant, airy feeling. Large
baths have floors of white marble and walls of white tile.
Twentieth-century paintings in the style of Zurbarán, austere, white-robed religious figures, hang in one salon. Rosa
Cubero's *bordados al trapo* (tapestries) decorate walls of the
TV lounge. In one, King Ferdinand III the Sàint, after invoking the aid of the Virgin, wins a great victory before
the walls of Trujillo. Another recounts how the shepherd

Gil Cordero discovered a statue of the Virgin in Guadal-upe. A third tells how a man who prayed long and hard and was always faithful to the Virgin won such favor that he could subdue a brave bull with only his hands.

Breakfast is served in the refectory, former dining hall of the convent, while lunch and dinner are served in the *comedor*, a large domed room. A wall at one end is covered with a mural composed of blue and white painted tiles.

Highly recommended entrees are *chuleta de añojo* (veal chops with red peppers) and *entrecot al Oporto* (steak with assorted vegetables). With either, order *cazuela de setas guisadas* (casserole of huge mushrooms). If you like, spec-ify you want the mushrooms *junto*, with your entree, not as a separate course. *Tarta del convento* is two layers of chocolate cake with a custard filling. Choose from Mon-tánchez, Cañamero, and Pitarra wines.

TOURING TRUJILLO. Known to the Romans as Turgalium, in later centuries Trujillo has been called the cradle of con-quistadors because of its famous sons: Francisco Pizarro, conqueror of Peru; García de Peredes, founder of the city of Trujillo in Venezuela; Orellana, first European to see the Amazon; Chaves, founder of Santa Cruz in Bolivia; Bartolomé de las Casas, one of the first European settlers of Mexico.

Francisco Pizarro, abandoned by his unwed mother on church steps, won fame as the conqueror of Peru. In the process, he extorted $10 million from Incan chief Ata-hualpa before murdering him. He fought bitterly with fel-low Spanish explorer Almagro, who was eventually mur-dered by Francisco's brother Hernando. A few years later, followers of Almagro avenged his death by eliminating Francisco right in his own palace.

Trujillo's *plaza mayor*, irregular in shape, is one of the most interesting in Spain. It is surrounded by classic buildings built on different levels, all connected by flights of stairs. Palacio de la Conquista was built by Hernando Pizarro, who saved the Spanish exchequer from bank-ruptcy by bringing back from Peru vast quantities of gold. The Gothic Church of San Martín has a Renaissance fa-çade. Seventeenth-century Dukes of San Carlos Palace is now a convent open to visitors. The tourist office is tucked in one corner of the plaza. An equestrian statue of Fran-cisco Pizarro (twin to the one in Lima and sculpted by

American artists) is given a place of eminence. The plaza is spectacularly lit at night.

In fifteenth-century Santa María de Mayor Church are two stone seats beneath a rose window. There Ferdinand and Isabella sat during mass when visiting Trujillo. Pizarro is supposed to be buried in sixteenth-century San Jerónimo Convent, but citizens of Lima may dispute that claim. A castle rules Trujillo from on high. Built on Roman fortifications by the Arabs, who reinforced the structure with four towers, it was strengthened further by cylindrical towers after the Reconquest.

Thursday is market day in Trujillo.

Several side trips can be taken from Trujillo: Guadalupe, 80 km east; Cáceres, 47 km west; and Mérida, 90 km southwest.

Parador Nacional Hernán Cortés

ZAFRA, BADAJOZ

*** govt. rating
Fifteenth-century castle, 28 rooms
Gardens, swimming pool
Opened in 1968
Phone 924/55 02 00

DIRECTIONS: 67 km southeast of Badajoz via N-432; 145 km north of Sevilla via N-630. Parador directional signs may not be posted on the outskirts of Zafra, but the round crenellated towers are easily seen and will point the way. Follow signs to Centro Urbano and you will then begin seeing the Parador sign.

Like other parador structures in Extremadura, the old castle is square, with round towers at each corner, a larger one at the back (now overlooking a swimming pool), two extra towers at the front entrance, and one extra on each side, for a total of nine towers in all. Over the main doorway to the castle, notice the Lorenzo family coat of arms with five fig leaves. Potted geraniums form a border around a magnificent courtyard said to have been designed by Escorial architect Juan de Herrera. Grass is planted alongside marble paths leading to a center fountain. Three-arched two-story galleries frame the patio. A splendid staircase leads to second-floor guest rooms. Several examples of the distinctive tinwork forming candelabra and mirrors are seen throughout the parador. Two rooms of special interest are the Gold Room, whose red and blue Mudejar coffered ceiling has a frieze of fleur-de-lis and coats of arms, and the chapel, with a gilt, octagonal Gothic dome.

Three entrees to try are *entrecot con champiñones* (steak with mushrooms), *judías verdes salteadas con tomate* (green beans with tomatoes), and *tortilla de jamón* (ham omelette). For dessert, order *brazo de gitano* (literally Gypsy's arm, a cake roll filled with custard). Wines are from the Zafra cooperative, as well as Montánchez, Cañamero, and Pitarro.

Today's castle-parador was built in 1437 on top of Moorish *alcazaba* ruins, which in turn were probably on top of Roman ruins on top of Celtiberian ruins. Inscriptions on Roman tombstones say the area was called Contributa Julia. Under the Moors, it was first a hard-pressed frontier called Sajra (high place among crags) and later became a thriving Arab market center. Today, approaching from the north, one sees extensive fairgrounds with permanent exhibition halls, attesting to Zafra's importance in southwestern Spain. The most famous fair is that of Saint Michael, held October 3–8.

The recaptured castle and surrounding little town were assigned by victor Fernando III to the Order of Santiago. In the late fourteenth century, a new royal grant made it the property of Don Gómez Suárez de Figueroa, ancestor of the counts, later dukes of Fería, who greatly enlarged the town and rebuilt the castle and walls. The parador was named for the conqueror of Mexico, who was a protégé of the dukes of Fería and who lived in the castle prior to his departure for the New World.

Stroll through the interesting streets radiating from the parador. Two squares to locate are Plaza Grande, where bullfights and other festivals are held, and Plaza Chica, scene of the town market. In the sixteenth-century Collegiate Church of the Purification are several Zurbaráns, one being a seven-foot canvas depicting Saint Ildefonso receiving the chasuble from the blessed Virgin.

Galicia

GALICIA IS A REGION OF GREAT BEAUTY AND CAP-
tivating sights. It is often rainy, drizzly, and foggy but in
October it can be wonderfully sunny.

La Coruña, Lugo, Orense, and Pontevedra are the four
provinces of this northwestern region. Northern shores are
washed by the Bay of Biscay, western coasts by the Atlantic Ocean. *Rías,* or estuaries, are the most distinctive physical features, created when rivers widen in their gradual
flow through valleys to merge with waters of the Atlantic.
The Rías Altas, upper estuaries, occur in Lugo and La Coruña, the Rías Bajas, lower estuaries, in Pontevedra. In
addition to providing spectacular scenery, the *rías* furnish
much of the fish consumed in Spain.

In the interior are classic examples of *minifundios,* tiny
parcels of walled-in land, some of which have been owned
and tilled by generations of the same family. Others be-
long to absentee landlords who continue to exact payment
and privilege from tenant farmers. Holdings may consist
of a single tree, a small pine grove, or a dilapidated mill.

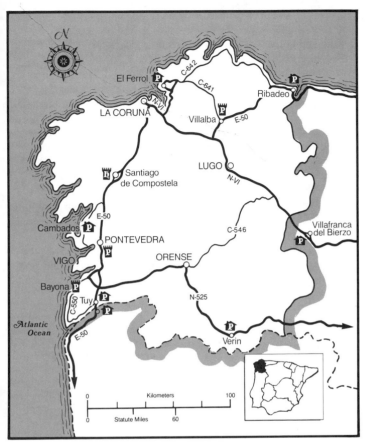

Galicia

Larger tracts vary from two-thirds of an acre to 125 acres. This extraordinary subdivision of land has impeded development of more productive agriculture. It has also been the cause of the perennial emigration of young men. During their absence, the land is worked by the old and the children.

Celts began arriving in Galicia in the sixth century B.C. Despite periods of Roman, Visigothic, and Moorish domination, Galicia is essentially a Celtic land where many speak Gallego, a dialect closer to Portuguese than to Spanish.

Along the coast and in the hills, houses, barns, and *horreos* (granaries) are built of stone and roofed with slate. Celtic crosses top communal *horreos*. Galician *horreos* closely resemble the Portuguese *espigueiros*. Austere granite shrines depicting Calvary themes are seen roadside throughout the region.

Strabo, the Greek geographer writing in the first century B.C., described Galician customs, some of which according to anthropologists are preserved in more remote districts today.

Leather fringed head coverings, protection against flies, are worn by yoked cows and oxen as they pull plows or large-wheeled carts. Three-legged black iron kettles, *potes*, once used for cooking, now serve as flower pots. *Sellos*, wooden buckets banded with brass strips, wider at the bottom than at the top, were originally containers for water, but are now decorative receptacles for umbrellas, flowers, or cigarette butts. The bagpipe, *gaita*, remains the traditional musical instrument of Galicia. Village women, balancing incredible loads on their heads, are fascinating to behold.

Parador Nacional Conde de Gondomar

BAYONA, PONTEVEDRA

**** govt. rating
Modern, within castle walls,
    128 rooms
Swimming pool, tennis courts,
    gardens
Opened in 1966
Phone 986/35 50 00

DIRECTIONS: 18 km southwest of Vigo.

The parador is constructed in the style of a Galician *pazo*, or manor house, with open pillared galleries, balconied windows, stone wall escutcheons, and square crenellated towers. The building lies within the 45-acre confines of a fortress known as Monte Real. It is everything one dreams of a parador being: large, richly furnished guest rooms, spacious lounges and salons equipped with Spanish Renaissance and Galician Baroque furniture, valuable tapestries embroidered with heraldic banners, Cuencan carpets, oils, watercolors, and sketches on Galician themes, broad terraces opening onto luxuriant lawns, a fountained courtyard, groves of pine and eucalyptus, and walls three kilo-

meters in length, from whose heights are awe-inspiring views of sapphire inlets along the Ría de Vigo.

Lobster tanks and an old still used for making Aguardiente, a very powerful clear liqueur ("muy fuerte," according to the waiter), are unusual conversation pieces in the dining room. Fish and seafood are prominent on the menu: *espaguetis con almejas* (spaghetti with clams), *zarzuela de pescado* (fish stew), *rodaballo parrilla maitre d'hotel* (grilled turbot), *crema de ostras* (oyster bisque), *langosta* (lobster), *langostinos* (large prawns), and various *empanadas* (pies filled with meat or fish). *Ternera asada castellana* is delicious roast beef served with potatoes, peas, artichokes, and carrots. Dessert choices include *tarta de almendras* (almond cake), *copa de helado melba* (ice cream like U.S. homemade, with fresh peaches), and *tocinillo de cielo* (two mounds of flan swimming in a dark caramel sauce). Wines are red and white Ribeiros and a sparkling El Rosal.

Geography has had a lot to do with the history of this peninsula, connected to the mainland by a narrow isthmus. Its position commands countless coves and harbors protected from storms by the Cíes Islands. Long before the advent of the Romans, "the rock," as the lofty fortified spot was called, had been surrounded by walls. In the second century B.C., tribal leader Viriatus, headquartering on Monte Real, overwhelmed Roman troops led by Serviliano. Monte Real has seen such historic conquerors as Julius Caesar in 60 A.D., Visigoth King Recaredo in 587, Saracen Almansur in 997, and Alfonso V in 1027. It was involved in wars between Pedro I and half-brother Enrique of Trastamara. John of Gaunt, duke of Lancaster, inherited the fortress from Pedro and occupied it in 1388. In 1474, it was captured by the forces of King Afonso V of Portugal. In 1493 Captain Pinzón of the *Pinta* entered Bayona harbor with the first news of the discovery of the New World. Sir Frances Drake was repulsed in attempts to land in 1585. Napoleon's army conquered the rock in 1809 but it was retaken one month later by Galician General Francheschi. In 1843, the guns of Monte Real were silenced forever. The Ministry of Tourism purchased the property from heirs of Don Angel Benrinana in 1963. The parador was named for the count who was once made perpetual governor of Monte Real.

There are many coastal villages to explore as well as the town of Bayona (Baiona, according to signs in Gallego). A stay of several days in one of the world's most beautiful hotels would not be misspent.

Parador Nacional del Albariño

CAMBADOS, PONTEVEDRA

*** govt. rating
Regional architecture, 63 rooms
Elevator, gardens
Opened in 1966
Phone 986/54 22 50

DIRECTIONS: 35 km northwest of Pontevedra; 50 km southwest of Santiago de Compostela.

Facing the Ría de Arosa, the parador was built on the site of an ancestral *pazo* of the Bazán family. Parklike grounds are planted with palms and sycamores. The two-story building surrounds a courtyard with a fountain in the center. Roomy lounges, guest rooms, and an inviting bar area make a stay here very pleasant.

There are several menu choices of fish and seafood, including *vieras a la gallego* (scallops), *pez espada plancha* (grilled swordfish), and *ostras de Cambados* (oysters on the half shell). If you would like catsup, ask for *salsa de tomate*. Tabasco sauce rests on the sideboard. Two Galician traditions can be sampled: *caldo gallego* (white bean soup flavored with sausage, ham, and chopped greens) and *lacón con grelos* (pork shoulder with turnip greens). You may also choose a lobster or spider crab from the tanks in the dining room to be prepared for your meal. Wines are from Ribeiro and Valdeorras. Do try the regional dry white wine, produced in limited quantities, for which the parador is named, El Albariño.

A local legend says that Satan, when trying to tempt Christ, stated, "I will give you all the world except Cambados, Fefiñanes, and San Tomé." All three are part of this area controlled at various times by the Knights Templar, Order of Holy Sepulchre, and Order of the Hospital; they even found their way into the vast estate of the House of Alba. On a walking tour of Cambados, locate the Plaza de Fefiñanes. The square is bordered on one side by arcaded houses and shops, on another by a seventeenth-century church, and on the other two by the sumptuous *pazo* of the Fefiñanes. Other important *pazos* to see are the Pazo de Figueroa and the Pazo de Montesacro. Near the beach is twelfth-century San Saturnino Tower, which began life as a Roman lighthouse and was later turned into a lookout to guard against the French.

Cambados harbor scenes are intriguing. Seaweed is harvested at low tide and carried off in tractor-driven wagons. Along the waterfront as many as ten young women can be seen sitting and mending fishing nets. Others shovel crushed ice on crates of fish as they are offloaded from the shallow water. Attend the fish auction and learn that clams, the big catch in Cambados, bring 60 to 70 pesetas a kilo, which comes out to about 20 U.S. cents a pound.

ENVIRONS. Short trips into the countryside offer good examples of *minifundios* as grape arbors supported by concrete posts, corn patches, and tiny plots of garden vegetables crowd together so as not to waste one inch of land. Ría de Arosa is dotted with many fishing shacks or rafts. From these, lines are lowered so mussels can attach themselves. Periodically, fishermen go out to harvest their crop.

Many breathtaking views of water, beaches, and islands may be had by driving along the coast to Sanjenjo, 20 km south of Cambados. En route is La Toja, lying west of Cambados at the tip of an island reached by a causeway. Wander through beautiful grounds of the five-star Gran Hotel, reminiscent of San Diego's Hotel del Coronado.

> *Buildings overlaid with seashells will be seen in this sector of Galicia. Legend says that during the days of the Reconquest a nobleman, forced to swim a ría, emerged from the water covered with shells. Thus the shell became a symbol for thousands of pilgrims making their way to Santiago de Compostela.*

Parador Nacional del Ferrol

EL FERROL, LA CORUNA

*** govt. rating
Regional architecture, 39 rooms
Opened in 1960
Phone 981/35 34 00

DIRECTIONS: 67 km northeast of La Coruña.

Adjacent to buildings of a naval base, the parador is a sailor's delight because of many nautical items. Armillary sphere chandeliers hang in the reception hall. Clocks are helm wheels. Guest room windows look out to the harbor. Should you be fortunate enough to be at the parador during afternoon rehearsals of the navy's symphonic band, stroll across the parking lot to a bench in the park and listen to superb music, performed in an arched portico of an administrative building. At sundown when drums roll and trumpets sound, watch the flag ceremony. Bagpipes are much in evidence. Toy shops in El Ferrol sell boy dolls wearing kilts and holding bagpipes.

Be sure to order the culinary specialty of the parador, *sopa de ferrolana*, a delicious soup of onions, parsley, garlic, tomatoes, octopus, and mussels. Other specialties to try are *empanada* (meat or fish pastry) and *lacón con grelos* (pork shoulder with turnip greens). For a sweet, try *cocadas de Pontedeume* (a coconut dessert).

While at the parador, travel to La Coruña, on the other side of Ría de Betanzos, to see the Tower of Hercules, a Roman lighthouse. Built in the second century, it still acts as a beacon for ships approaching the hazardous coast. Go the easy way—by bus, which departs several blocks from the parador at Plaza d'España. You will enjoy the rural scenes en route on the hour-long bus ride. The *estación de autobuses* is on the outskirts of La Coruña, so take a cab or bus into the central city. From the city park, buses depart for the Tower of Hercules. Buses return to El Ferrol every hour.

Parador Nacional Casa del Barón

PONTEVEDRA

*** govt. rating
Sixteenth-century mansion,
    47 rooms
Elevator, gardens
Opened in 1955
Phone 986/85 58 00

DIRECTIONS: On the western edge of the city, about two blocks from the Lérez River. It is very difficult to find because of narrow one-way streets and a dearth of Parador signs. Look for the typical square white stone crenellated *pazo* (mansion) tower on Calle Maceda. Easier to ask a cab to take or lead you. When giving the request, make sure you say "parador nacional," not just "parador." Parking is just through the stone gates.

The restored and modified Pazo de Maceda houses the parador. The three-story mansion bears elongated wood-paneled windows, a columned gallery in the center of the third floor, and a stone escutcheon over the doorway. From the entry hall, a massive stone staircase leads to second-floor guest rooms. To the right of the entry, a spacious salon furnished with sofas, chairs, and game tables ex-

tends to an outside terrace overlooking gardens. An intimate timbered bar is found through the entry archway.

Cuisine is Galician, with a few selections being *pulpo estilo Feira* (octopus Galician style), *vieras al horno Rías Bajas* (pilgrim scallops Galician style), and *jamón fresco asado* (fresh roast ham). Two desserts are tempting: *tarta de Santiago* (almond cake) and *filloas de manzana* (apple pancakes). Ribeiro *blanco* and *tinto* are the house wines.

Believed to be the site of a Roman villa (and some say Roman stones were used in construction), Pazo de Maceda was completely rebuilt in the sixteenth century and enlarged with added features in the eighteenth century by the Count of Maceda. After the death of the owner, marquis of Figueroa, in battle against the French in 1808, the *pazo* fell into disuse and disrepair. From time to time it served as a school, granary, and Masonic lodge. The palace was acquired eventually by the barons of Casa Goda, whose last lord, Don Eduardo de Cea y Naharro, restored and refurnished it. After his death in 1955, it reverted to the town council, which ceded it to the Ministry of Tourism.

Parador Nacional de Ribadeo

RIBADEO, LUGO

*** govt. rating
Modern, 47 rooms
Gardens, elevator
Opened in 1958
Phone 982/11 08 25

DIRECTIONS: 156 km west of Gijón. On the southern outskirts of Ribadeo, on the Santander–La Coruña highway.

The parador is at first glance deceiving. It appears to be a one-story building, though the floor one enters on is actually the fourth floor of a building that rambles down the hill. Ask for a room *alto,* high up, so you can see portions of the Asturian and Galician coastlines and small freighters and fishing vessels tied to docks below the parador. Guest rooms are large and all have balconies.

In one corner of the dining room are tanks holding live lobsters and crabs to be chosen as entrees by diners. *Vieras* (scallops), *ostras* (oysters), *langosta* (lobster), *cangrejo* (crab), *merluza a la gallega* (sweet white fish), *empanada de raya* (pastry stuffed with eel), and *lacón con grelos* (pork with turnip greens) appear on the parador menu. *Filloas* (fritter-pancakes) are a popular dessert. Wines are *blancos, tintos,* and *rosados* from Ribeiro and Valdeorras.

The town of Ribadeo is only a little over a century old. It has developed into a major commercial port because of its location at the mouth of the Eo River on the Cantabrian coast.

Hotel Reyes Católicos

PLAZA D'ESPANA 1
SANTIAGO DE COMPOSTELA,
LA CORUNA

***** govt. rating
Fifteenth-century hospital,
   157 rooms
Phone 58 22 00

The building was erected on orders of Ferdinand and Isabella in the fifteenth century as an inn and hospital to care for pilgrims arriving at their destination after a long, trying journey. The luxury hotel is located on the vast Plaza d'España, facing the cathedral, whose spires can be seen for miles. Splurge and spend a minimum of two days and nights here absorbing the color of twentieth-century Santiago and the important role it played in Spanish history beginning in the Middle Ages.

The building was constructed in the shape of a hollow cross, so there are four courtyards bordered by columned

galleries. Significant additions and embellishments were added in the seventeenth and eighteenth centuries. Guest and public rooms are furnished for comfort, with a sense of timelessness. In addition to an elegant restaurant, the hotel has a large cafeteria opening off an equally large bar-lounge. One can while away a few hours ensconced in one of the plush salon sofas, served periodically by a red-coated waiter bearing glasses of sherry and small dishes of potato chips, ripe garlicky olives, *cacahuetes* (peanuts), and *almendras* (almonds). There is usually an art exhibition in one of the large rooms off the lobby. There is a hairdresser and garage parking for guests.

TOURING SANTIAGO DE COMPOSTELA. Santiago is exciting. The old streets lined with tiny bars and restaurants teem with university students scurrying from one school to another. Every few blocks is a charming little square. One could spend a whole day ambling along, stopping to appreciate emblazoned façades of mansions, convents, and churches, pausing now and then to sample some of the food and wine specialties of Galicia.

According to tradition, James the Apostle came to Spain to convert inhabitants to Christianity. After preaching throughout the country for seven years, he returned to Palestine, where he was beheaded by Herod. His followers fled to Spain with his body, burying it near his original landing place near the mouth of the Ulla River. His grave went unnoticed and forgotten for several hundred years. Early in the ninth century, a bright star appeared to shepherds and guided them to his tomb. Some years later, in 844, a group of Spaniards was attacking a Moorish stronghold near Logroño, when suddenly a knight mounted on a magnificent steed charged across the battlefield. Legend says that the soldiers recognized him as Saint James and thereafter he was termed Matamore, or Moor slayer. In this way Saint James, Santiago, became the patron saint of the Reconquest.

Alfonso II founded a church and monastery on the site of the tomb. These formed the nucleus around which Santiago de Compostela evolved. Santiago became one of the three most important shrines in the medieval world, after Rome and Jerusalem. Most Europeans traveled through France along routes protected by Benedictine and Cistercian monks and the Knights Templar of Spain. Others came by ship along the Atlantic Coast. Their universal costume consisted of a long heavy cape, sandals, and a broad-brimmed hat turned up in front and studded with scallop shells. They carried a tall walking staff to the top of which a gourd carrying water was attached. Estimates of the number of pilgrims in those days range from 500,000 to a million a year. Towns with hospitals and inns grew up along the Camino de Santiago. The pilgrims had a decided influence on medieval architecture, literature, art, thought, sociology, and economy.

After a few centuries, religious fervor cooled and when in 1589 Francis Drake attacked La Coruña, the bishop of Compostela removed the bones (relics) of Saint James from the cathedral. But he forgot where he put them and they remained misplaced for nearly 300 years, until rediscovery in 1879. The relics were acknowledged by the pope and pilgrimages resumed, to continue today.

Purchase a guidebook to the monuments of Santiago at the hotel desk. The cathedral was built on the same site as the original church erected over the apostle's tomb and was completed over a period of 300 years, from the eleventh to the thirteenth centuries. Excavations in 1946 under the nave revealed not only earlier foundations but also a Roman necropolis substantiating a claim that the name Compostela derived from the Latin word for cemetery and not as previously thought from Campus Stellae, field of the star. The Door of Glory is aptly named. Wondrously carved between 1168 and 1188 by one Mateo, the granite statues of saints and apostles are incredibly animated; one agrees with the Spanish poet Rosalía de Castro: "Saints and apostles, see! It seems that their lips move, that they are talking quietly to each other. Are they alive? Are they made of stone? those lifelike countenances—those marvelous robes—those eyes so full of life?" It is a moving sight to watch today's pilgrims, young and old, stop before the Door of Glory, and with bowed heads, place their hands in grooves where millions of pious wayfarers have paused to give thanks for their safe arrival at the shrine of Santiago.

Those visiting Santiago de Compostela should be aware that July 25 is the Feast of Saint James and as a consequence, the city is jammed with people. When July 25 falls on a Sunday, Holy Year is declared and the influx of visitors lasts throughout the year.

Parador Nacional San Telmo

TUY, PONTEVEDRA

*** govt. rating
Regional architecture, 16 rooms
Swimming pool, gardens
Opened in 1968
Phone 986/60 03 09

DIRECTIONS: 30 km southeast of Vigo, on the border with Portugal, on the west bank of the Miño River. The parador is 1 km north of Tuy's city center.

The parador is constructed of native beige stone with warm pine trim. Notice a typical Galician granite Calvary before continuing along the driveway to the columned portico entry to the parador. Many plants of various types and textures add charm to the lounges and reception hall. The bar area opens onto a terrace for outside dining and relaxation. From public and guest rooms there are incomparable views of ancient Tuy topped with a cathedral-fortress, a lush serene countryside, and across the river, the Portuguese township of Valença do Minho.

Specialties of the parador dining room are *lamprese a la tudensa* (lamprey, or large eel, en casserole), *sopa de ostras* (oyster soup), *empanada de anguila del Miño* (pastry stuffed with eel from the Miño), *vieras gratinadas* (scallops with cheese), and *nabos glaseados* (glazed turnips). Two dessert favorites are *filloas rellenas* (crepelike pancakes filled with fruit or custard) and *tarta de almendra* (almond cake). Ribeiro and Valdeorras wines are featured on the parador wine list.

According to legend, Tuy was founded by Diomedes, son of Homer's Tydeus. Much evidence of archaic settlements has been discovered. Tuy gained in importance under Roman rule. Visigothic King Witiza had his court in Tuy and here King Pelayo was born. The dominant feature of the city is the cathedral-fortress built in 1170 but not used as a church until the thirteenth century. In a chapel of the cathedral lies the tomb of Saint Telmo, a Portuguese Dominican who lived and died in Tuy in 1240 and for whom the parador is named.

The quaint fishing village of Laguardia lies 25 km southwest of the parador. Drive north from Laguardia a kilometer or two to observe the sea splashing dramatically over black lava rocks.

The international bridge linking Spain and Portugal is a short distance from Parador San Telmo. The traveler needs to plan ahead and be aware of difficulties that may arise in crossing the border. First of all, escudos are not accepted in Spain nor are pesetas accepted in Portugal. The border bank can be a hassle, especially on holidays and weekends, when Spaniards flock to Portugal for shopping bargains. Traffic can be held up for as long as three hours.

Parador Nacional Monterrey

VERIN, ORENSE

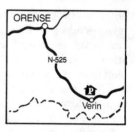

*** govt. rating
Regional architecture, 23 rooms
Swimming pool, gardens
Opened in 1967
Phone 988/41 00 75

DIRECTIONS: 67 km southeast of Orense via N-525; 6 km west of Verin.

Parador Monterrey, similar in style to Tuy's parador, sits on a high knoll overlooking a valley of vineyards. Floor-to-ceiling windows of the salon, bar, and dining room afford views of the well-kept grounds, gardens, and distant mountains. A gleaming knightless suit of armor and a shiny copper still grace the entry hall. The portico and terrace are lined with *potes* (kettles) of brilliant geraniums.

Gastronomic selections may be made from *pote gallego* (Galician soup), *pulpo estilo isla* (octopus), *empanada de vieras* (pastry filled with scallops), *anguilas guisadas a la Miñota* (stewed eel), *sopa de nueces* (ground nuts in a soup base), *pierna de cabrito a la orensana* (roast leg of kid), and *ternera estilo Feira* (roast veal). The perfect dessert would be *filloas de manzana* (apple pancakes). As a change of pace, order a Rueda *blanco,* a fairly strong dry white wine.

Castillo de Monterrey, a twelfth-century castle-fortress, crowns the summit of a hill behind the parador. The towering site served prehistoric civilizations. Within the confines of the castle are ruins of a monastery that housed Jesuit scholars, the Hospital of Pilgrims, whose façade bears a date of 1390, and the Church of Santa María de Gracia, mentioned in documents of 1274 and still a place of worship today. The unoccupied castle's grounds are maintained by the government and are open to visitors. A caretaker living in a cottage near the church will open it for you. Inside, look for two statues: a wooden figure of Christ draped in a goat's skin, complete with head and hooves, and, to one side of the altar, Mary with human hair, clothed in blue and white satin robes. Make the effort to climb 70 feet to the top of Torre del Homenaje (tower of honor) for a splendid panoramic vista.

According to tradition, the castle witnessed struggles between Pedro I and his half-brother, Enrique. After the death of Pedro, Monterrey was assaulted and conquered

by troops of Portuguese King Fernando I led by Fernando
de Castro in 1369. It served as a prison for political enemies of Castilian kings in the last part of the fourteenth
century. During the succeeding two centuries, because of
its strategic position on the Portuguese frontier, the fortress was controlled by various noblemen. In the eighteenth century, Monterrey came under the ducal power of
the House of Alba.

Parador Nacional
Condes de Villalba
VILLALBA, LUGO

*** govt. rating
Thirteenth-century castle, 6 rooms
Elevator, gardens
Opened in 1967
Phone 982/51 00 11

DIRECTIONS: 36 km north of Lugo.

Twentieth-century Villalba has grown up around the octagonal Andrade Tower, all that remains of a once-pow-
erful castle-fortress. An aerial photo shows how the village
has developed in circular fashion around the tower. Enter
via a drawbridge over a dry moat, into an entry hall two
stories high. Banners are painted on the walls; one praises

Fernán de Andrade, victor over the French in Italy at the time of the second count, which would date it about the beginning of the fifteenth century.

There are only six rooms in the parador, two on each of the three floors. The rooms are very large, with furniture placed in front of fireplaces. It's eerie to look out a window set in walls eight feet thick. Baths have two sinks, white marble floors, and white tiled walls. Even though you may not be able to get a reservation at the parador, you would enjoy a stop for lunch. Located in the heart of Lugo Province amid gentle farmlands and broad valleys, Villalba is a bustling, prosperous town.

The dining room is downstairs. From large wrought iron chandeliers dangle black metal letters spelling out the name of the parador. On the walls are mounted antlers attached to polished marblelike skulls. Two excellent luncheon choices would be *caldo gallego* (Galician soup of potatoes, dried beans, salt pork, sausage, and Galician cabbage) and *melón con jamón* (sweet melons with thinly sliced ham, a little stronger than prosciutto). Dinner entrees include *pastelón de pollo* (chicken pie), *caldeirada de pescado* (fish stew), *capón de Villalba* (the town is famous for its capons), *pollo estofado* (chicken stewed in tomato sauce), and *brocheta de ternera* (brochette of veal). *Torta de manzana* (apple torte) is a good dessert choice. The house wine is a dry *blanco* from the local cooperative.

Some historians believe the castle was constructed in the thirteenth century, while others insist it was in existence in the eleventh century. Until the mid-fourteenth century, the castle belonged to the House of Castro, a family with strong Castilian roots. In 1364 Pedro I gave the property and seigniory of the village to the House of Andrade, whose head at the time was Fernán Pérez de Andrade. He was such a skillful politician that in the confusion following the murder of Pedro he was able to get Enrique to ratify his title in 1376. This same Fernán enriched the community with seven churches, seven hospitals, seven monasteries, and seven bridges.

The castle was rebuilt about 1480. An English ambassador in the early seventeenth century stayed here and called it "a very fine castle." But power diminished in the nineteenth century so that in the twentieth all that remained was the tower.

Navarra

NAVARRA, BOTH A REGION AND A PROVINCE, IS LO-
cated in northeastern Spain between the regions of Vascongadas and Aragón, extending from the Pyrenees south
to the Ribera and Ebro rivers. It is a region of verdant
mountain pastureland and arid yet fertile farmland. Near
the Basque country, Navarrese homes are whitewashed and
roofed with red tile, while in the northeastern area they
are built of stone with sharply slanted tile roofs, necessary
because of the harsh mountain climate.

On the plains, cereal crops, olive trees, and vineyards
are productive. Irrigation in the south has made possible
the cultivation of asparagus, beans, artichokes and peppers. Their abundant yield supports a canning industry.

The Vascons, ancestors of today's Basques, inhabited
Navarra and were successful in encounters with the Visigoths. However, they were pushed northward into the
present Basque provinces and into France by rampaging
Moors. Charlemagne entered Spain in 778 and drove out
the Moors, but made the fatal error of destroying city walls

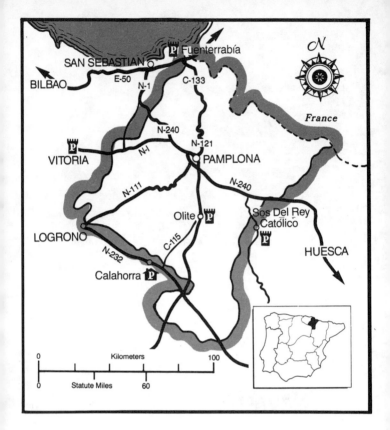

Navarra

surrounding Pamplona. Contingents of Basques, Navarrese, and Asturians attacked and defeated him later the
same year at the famous Battle of Roncesvalles. The twelfth-
century French epic "The Song of Roland" narrates how
Charlemagne's army, led by Roland and twelve Christian
knights, was massacred by mobs of Moors. A slightly later
Spanish epic says that the Navarrese were merely aveng-
ing the French invasion of Spain.

The period from 1234 to 1512 was one of constant struggle and unrest because of the hostility of Navarrese noblemen toward a series of French rulers. In 1512 the duke of
Alba drove the French from the region and claimed Navarra for Castilian King Ferdinand the Catholic.

Through Navarra came French pilgrims en route to Santiago de Compostela, resulting in a great endowment of
Romanesque churches and monasteries, given the Moorish touch of domes and cupolas.

Parador Nacional
Príncipe de Viana

OLITE, NAVARRA

*** govt. rating
Fourteenth-century castle, 39 rooms
Elevator
Opened in 1966
Phone 948/74 00 00

DIRECTIONS: 45 km south of Pamplona.

Turrets and battlements signal arrival in Olite, medieval capital of the kingdom of Navarra. Through an arch and inside the walled city is found the parador, built under three of the original 15 towers of the castle. Guest rooms are tastefully furnished and have balconies whose leaded windows frame a thickly wooded pine grove, portions of the castle, and the low mountains of Navarra. The main salon is delightful, with an enormous fireplace, two circular wrought iron chandeliers, a knightless suit of armor in a niche of honor, and numerous sofas and chairs. The only discordant item in the motif seems to be the TV set.

Culinary specialties of the parador are *pimientos rellenos* (stuffed red peppers), *trucha a la Navarra* (trout), *conejo bardenero a la plancha* (grilled rabbit), *constillas asadas en parrilla* (grilled ribs), *conejo con caracoles* (rabbit with snails), and *magras de cerdo con tomate* (ham cooked in tomato sauce). Two desserts to try are *coronillas de Pamplona* and *alpargatas de Peralta y Estella*. The wine list includes a *blanco* from Ochoa near Olite, a *tinto* from Jaura, and our favorite *rosado*, from *bodegas* of Marqués de Cáceres.

Historians place the date of completion of the castle-fortress in the early fifteenth century. It was built by Carlos III of Navarra and served as his summer residence until his death in 1425. Later, the prince of Viana, grandson of Carlos and son of Blanche of Navarra, spent his childhood here. Until Navarra was annexed to Castilla in 1512, the castle was the scene of conflicts between Aragonese and Castilians. It was leased to the marquises of Cortes in the sixteenth century, suffered severe damage in the eighteenth, and was almost destroyed during the Napoleonic Wars. At the beginning of the present century, restoration was undertaken by the Council of Navarra and in 1964 the remaining structure was incorporated into a parador.

People tell the story that Carlos once hired three matadors to fight several bulls in the courtyard both for his royal entertainment and to foster enthusiasm for the sport.

> *The countryside between Olite and Sos del Rey Católico to the east (where there is a parador) is ever-changing: there are rolling hills, vineyards, small fields of cereals, olive groves, sunflower fields, hillsides terraced and planted in evergreens, and fields of spidery asparagus.*

Valencia

VALENCIA, ALSO KNOWN AS THE LEVANT, IS THE land of the *huerta,* a fertile, irrigated coastal plain where rich alluvial soil and Mediterranean climate allow for several harvests a year. Great quantities of citrus fruits, vegetables, rice, and flowers are produced. Alicante, Castellón de la Plana, and Valencia are the provinces of this region, arrayed along the eastern coast of Spain.

The vast *huerta,* extending from the sea to coastal mountain ranges, has always been watered and enriched by the Turia River. The river separates into eight fingers emptying into the Mediterranean around the city of Valencia. At these eight points, locks have been constructed to keep salt water from polluting the land. These are not large installations, since tides are very slight.

The Moors improved irrigation systems begun by the Romans. The Water Tribunal is a holdover from the Middle Ages. Every Thursday at 10 A.M., representatives from areas irrigated by the eight canals appear before the Apostle Door of Valencia's cathedral. A judge listens to dis-

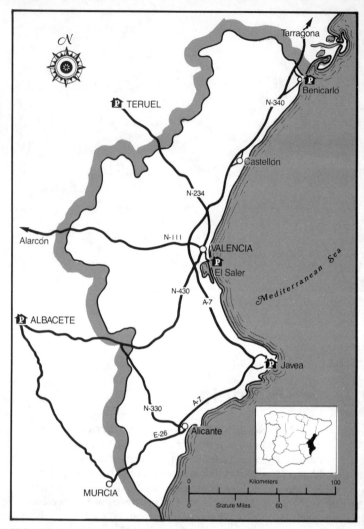

Valencia

putes and makes decisions. If an offender is found guilty
of water misuse, the supply to his *huerta* is cut off. All
proceedings are oral and there is no right of appeal.

Many civilizations have inhabited this region. Prehistoric human beings left evidence of their existence in cave
paintings. Phoenicians roamed from their base in Cádiz
searching for metals. Greeks founded the city of Valencia.
Romans expelled Carthaginians and remained for several
centuries. Next were the Visigoths, followed by the Moors.

After the Reconquest, Valencia came into the kingdom of Aragón in the thirteenth century.

Parador Nacional Costa del Azahar

BENICARLO, CASTELLON
DE LA PLANA

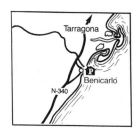

*** govt. rating
Modern, 108 rooms
Gardens, tennis, swimming pool
Opened in 1935
Phone 964/47 01 00

DIRECTIONS: 70 km northeast of Castellón de la Plana.

Facing the Mediterranean and four miles of gently curving beach, the parador is a great place to unwind. Public lounges are numerous, spacious, and comfortable, with floor-to-ceiling windows looking out over gardens stretching to the sea. Each guest room has all the necessary facilities plus a balcony offering vistas of flowering shrubs and palm trees. In 1984–85, the parador underwent refurbishing.

Menu items are heavy on shellfish, since Benicarló has extensive prawn beds off the coast. Here one should certainly have *paella*. Other fish dishes may be seasoned with one of two favorite sauces in the region: *all i pebre*, very peppery, or *ali-oli*, very garlicky.

Miles of luxuriant trees bearing golden fruit have given this part of the Mediterranean coast its name. Azahar means orange blossoms. Benicarló, of remote Greek origin, is but one of many once-tiny fishing villages burgeoning into resort areas. It is a nice town for shopping and tending to banking needs. Try to catch the daily fish auction held around 3 P.M. between the villages of Vinaroz and Peñiscola.

Parador Nacional
Luis Vives

EL SALER, VALENCIA

**** govt. rating
Modern, 58 rooms
Swimming pool, tennis, gardens,
  elevator, golf course
Opened in 1966
Phone 96/161 11 24 and 161 11 86

DIRECTIONS: 12 km south of Valencia.

Set amidst one of the most beautiful and challenging of
Spain's golf courses, Parador Luis Vives is an excellent place
for relaxation, golf, and sightseeing in Valencia. One large
salon, outfitted with upholstered white, natural, and dark
brown wicker furniture, opens onto a terrace, the golf
course, and the Mediterranean beyond. Another, the TV
lounge, has a fireplace and three felt-topped game tables.
Wall decor in public rooms consists of many sketches on
the golf theme as well as a few paintings depicting the
corrida and matadors' agility. Guest rooms have white wicker
furniture with upholstered backs and seats, coordinated
with the colors of bedspreads, drapes, and carpeting. Very
attractive, restful, and harmonious.

As the staple of Valencia is rice, *arroz*, many dishes are
based on rice and accordingly labeled *a la valenciana*. *Paella
a la valenciana* is very popular and comes in several guises.
It may be made with chicken, snails, green vegetables, or
strictly seafood, or what some think is the best, a combination of chicken and shellfish. *Ensalada valenciana* (lettuce,
tomatoes, tuna, anchovy, eggs, and asparagus) makes a

satisfying luncheon. *Merluza a la romana* (white fish fried in batter) and *brochetas de solomillo* (medallions of pork) are other entrees. The house wine is Torres de Serranos *tinto*. With fish and *paella*, however, a dry Utiel or Requena is recommended.

El Saler is located on a narrow, sandy peninsula enclosing La Albufera, a freshwater lagoon teeming with fish, and a favorite resting place for migratory birds. The lake is surrounded by orchards, small villages, and rice paddies. On the southern outskirts of the parador and golf course, notice one of the eight locks protecting La Albufera from the influx of saltwater. There is another one at El Perelló, a kilometer or two farther south.

The 18-hole golf course, 6 km in length, is a series of rolling greens along the Mediterranean, laced with pine trees and pitted with sand traps. A smaller par 3 course that can be played in about two hours sits within the larger course.

TOURING VALENCIA. Valencia is a big city with the big city vices of traffic, noise, and air pollution. Those who are driving should get as close as possible to the city center before parking and hailing a cab to get to the cathedral. The cathedral is the base for a nice walking tour of old Valencia, which was walled until 1868.

After Jaime I drove out the Moors in 1238, the city became one of the most prosperous kingdoms under the crown of Aragón. Built on the site of an Arab mosque, the cathedral was begun in 1262 and completed in the fifteenth century. The octagonal Gothic tower, the Miguelete, is beloved by Valencianos. From its flat roof, Victor Hugo is said to have counted 300 belfries throughout the city. But until Valencia cleans up its air, not much can be seen. The cathedral, built over the course of three centuries, has three different architectural styles inside and out. There are three portals: Romanesque, Gothic, and Baroque. Paintings by Goya, gold work by Cellini, and a purple agate cup said to be the Holy Grail used by Christ at the Last Supper may be seen in the cathedral museum. Next to the cathedral is the Basilica of La Virgen de los Desamparados (Virgin of the Abandoned), with a revered statue of the city's patron saint. Behind the basilica is El Almudín, a medieval granary, now the Paleontological Museum.

The Generalidad or Provincial Council Building is across

from the basilica on Plaza de la Virgen. The fifteenth-century former palace has such intriguing features as ornamented coffered ceilings, friezes of *azulejos*, portraits, and sculpture. The Cortes, or parliament, convened here until the early eighteenth century. The word Generalidad, or in Catalán, Generalitat, is seen on town buildings throughout Aragón, Cataluña, and Valencia. In times past, one of the main duties of the Cortes was to collect the general tax, from which no one could escape. The name has endured.

Behind the Generalidad are two former palaces, one of which now contains the Prehistory Museum. Several narrow streets south and west of the cathedral is the National Museum of Ceramics in an eighteenth-century palace, once belonging to the marquis of Dos Aguas. Don't miss the "typical" Valencian kitchen on the second floor. It may inspire you to buy a supply of tiles and hurry home to remodel your own.

Manises is a small town of potters and pottery workshops open for visiting and buying. It is 8 km from the city center, near the airport. Take a taxi.

Lladro is the most eminent ceramicist on the Iberian peninsula. (Learning how to say Lladro isn't easy: ULYAHdro.) Figurines, large and small, are predominatly porcelain. But in the last few years, he has added a line of bisque ware. If you are interested in fine figurines, look in jewelry, gift, and china stores before you leave home. When you see a piece you favor, make a note, because buying in Spain can save you many dollars. Every town and city in Spain sells Lladros. A Ballard tip: when you see just what you want, buy it on the spot. Don't wait, thinking you will find a better price. You won't.

The Lladro factory and seconds shop (two or three blocks apart) are located in a northeastern section of Valencia called Tabernas Blanques. If you are looking for a particular figurine, as we were, you may not find it in the seconds shop. But tour busloads leave with arms full. Terms are cash and carry there. In other shops, you can use your credit card and pay for shipping home if you can't fit your purchase in your luggage.

Parador Nacional
Costa Blanca

JAVEA, ALICANTE

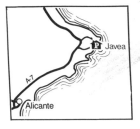

**** govt. rating
Modern, 65 rooms
Swimming pool, gardens, elevator
Opened in 1965
Phone 965/79 02 00

DIRECTIONS: 116 km south of Valencia, 10 km east of the Alicante-Valencia Autopista. Upon entering Javea from the west, turn left at the light signal and follow signs to Playa Arenal and the parador.

The parador faces the sea in extensive gardens graced by stately date palm trees. Bizarre rock formations of the Sierra del Montjo form an unusual southern backdrop. From guest room balconies, vistas take in a small cove almost enclosed by Cape San Martín. Sea air, sight, and sound are enchanting. Furniture is grouped on colorful Alpujarra rugs in lounges and the salon.

The dining room has a view over a terrace, roofed with canvas in summer, to blossoming gardens. It offers *huevos escalfados divorciados* (poached eggs with a tomato cream sauce), *alcachofas salteados con jamón* (artichokes with ham), *merluza con almejas* (white fish with clams), and the specialty *arroz con costra* (rice with various meats and chickpeas, or garbanzos). We hope the same imaginative chef will still be ruling the *cocina,* so that you will be served such delights as a ham-based pâté with melba toast as an appetizer. *Helado crocanti* is a nut-covered ice cream roll.

Javea (Xabia in Valencian) has a nice mixture of new and

old architecture. Thursday is market day but any day is fish auction day at the nearby harbor of Aduanas San Antonio. We wondered if the fantastic haul we saw landed (the largest of any port we visited in Spain or Portugal) was customary. Perhaps so, because the docks and auction building were brand-new. An attached fish market sold many varieties to retail buyers. The inside action dealt solely with wholesalers supplying restaurants, other markets, and institutions.

Vascongadas

VASCONGADAS, THE LAND OF THE BASQUES, IS A fascinating region of geographic contrasts, wedged between Navarra and Castilla La Mancha. Alava, Vizcaya, and Guipúzcoa are the three Basque provinces of Vascongadas. The region extends from the French border south to the Ebro River near Logroño. It also borders the bay whose name is a Basque form of Vizcaya, Biscay; the coastline is marked by rocky abrupt cliffs and small estuaries.

Always seafarers, Basques claim to have hunted whales as far away as Greenland in the eleventh century. Many Basques joined explorers on journeys to the New World. It was Juan Sebastián Elcano, a Basque, who brought Magellan's ship back to Spain after his murder in the Philippines. Other Basques emigrated to North America and became sheep herders. From countless tiny villages huddled along inlets, fishermen have plied their trade for centuries.

Guipúzcoa, Spain's smallest province, lies on the slopes of the Pyrenees at the gateway to France. The mining of

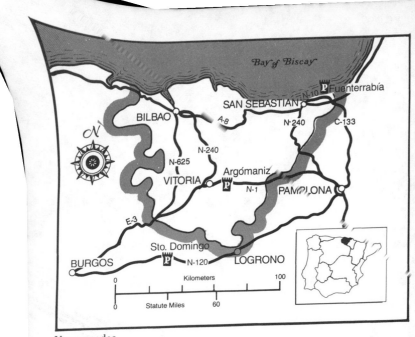

Vascongadas

iron ore in Vizcaya has promoted heavy industry in Vascongadas since the end of the nineteenth century. Alava, largest of the three provinces, has an arid climate similar to that of the Meseta and is an agricultural area of grain fields, olive groves, vineyards, and orchards.

That human beings have inhabited Vascongadas for millennia is proven by ancient cave paintings, by prehistoric dolmens, and by such Iron Age settlements as Hoya. However, the precise origin of the Basques is obscure. Their language, Euskera, is unlike any other, including Spanish and French. To one used to Germanic and Romance languages, it contains a bewildering number of X's and Z's. Dialects of Euskera are spoken in villages. Customs, traditions, and to some extent physical features have remained unchanged. Early in history, Basques instituted a form of democracy, with assemblies made up of heads of families. Farmers maintain old forms of sharecropping handed down from father to son. In oral contracts, families owning land select successors from among their members. Basque women have almost the same powers of inheriting property as do men.

Basques are very individualistic, energetic, hardworking, brave, and freedom loving. They have a passion for contests involving strength and skill. Woodcutters and weightlifters vie for top physical honors while poets are encouraged to display their creative abilities in intellectual competitions. Their favorite sport is *pelota*, or jai-alai, as we know it. While driving through Basque country, notice how many homes have an attached, tall two-sided *pelota* court.

Driving through Vascongadas these days can be confusing because of signage. Some road signs are completely illegible because of spray-painted obliteration or alteration. Village signs are in Castilian/Euskera or more often Euskera/Castilian.

Parador Nacional de Argómaniz

ARGOMANIZ, ALAVA

*** govt. rating
Seventeenth-century palace,
    54 rooms
Elevator
Opened in 1977
Phone 945/28 22 00

DIRECTIONS: 15 km east of Vitoria, 1 km off N-I. Use extreme caution if traveling west on N-I. Go 13 km past Salvatierra and look for a turn-out to the right; stop and wait for a gap in the traffic before turning left, crossing the highway to the parador. Signs to Vitoria will read Gasteiz, as that is the Basque name for the same city. So far, Argómaniz is Argómaniz in Argómaniz.

The majestic stone parador stands on the slopes of Mount Zabalgaña, centered between identical wings with many windows; it is isolated but for a few buildings below it. The original building was the Larrea Palace, built in the middle of the seventeenth century. Don Juan de Larrea was a dean at the University of Salamanca for many years until appointed to high government office by Philip IV. The Don was also a knight of the Order of Santiago.

Argómaniz is a very comfortable parador with a friendly, helpful staff. Over the entry, flanked by small round windows, is the Larrea coat of arms, a tree in five parts under the ducal crown. Long and narrow, with a timber ceiling and arched windows, the reception hall has some handsome sturdy Spanish chests holding potted greenery. A large colorful carpet warms the stone floor. This hall, the bar, and the central portion of the parador were part of the original palace. *Galerías*, square oriel or bay windows, are typical of northeastern Spain. In parador guest rooms, two occasional chairs share a table in the *galería*.

The dining room, with a unique heavily timbered ceiling of beams and rafters, served as the palace granary. The food is exceptional. *Caracoles* (snails) and *perros chicos* (mushrooms) are special delicacies. Scrambled eggs with mushrooms make a good lunch. *Canalones Rossini* and *crema de guisantes* (pea soup) are rewarding choices. The house tart is light and delicious. A rioja *tinto* is the house wine.

ENVIRONS. A stay of two or three days at Argómaniz would afford opportunities for visits to French coastal towns, Vitoria, or Pamplona. In Vitoria's Plaza de la Virgen Blanca is a monument celebrating Wellington's decisive victory at the Battle of Victoria in 1813. The Archeological Museum has interesting Celtiberian and Roman relics.

Pamplona, scene of the yearly "Running of the Bulls," is a heavily industrial city with little to recommend it at other times. Motorists especially should be forewarned of extremely heavy traffic, one-way streets, blatant double parking, and no easily read street signs; park on the outskirts and take a taxi to Ciudad Urbano for a walking tour.

Parador Nacional El Emperador

FUENTERRABIA, GUIPUZCOA

*** govt. rating
Tenth-century castle-fortress,
    16 rooms
Gardens
Opened in 1968
Phone 943/64 21 40

DIRECTIONS: 21 km east of San Sebastián (Donostia in Euskera).
Approaching Fuenterrabía from Spain, signs will read Hondarra-
bia or Ondarrabia, both Euskera names for the town. A clue that
you're getting close will be the Aeropuerto sign. If you see a banner reading Ongi etorri, you are being welcomed to the city. Directional Parador signs may be negligible. Carry on until you reach
a five-point intersection with a statue in the center of the island.
Bear left up the hill.

Parador El Emperador is on a square facing quaint old
leaning houses with balconies. Because of its age, the parador needs almost constant maintenance and restorative
work. At times, only rooms and breakfast are available.
But there is no problem obtaining meals as there are plenty
of Basque restaurants in the town. It would be wise to
check if the parador is open prior to arrival rather than
drop in and take a chance.

Guest and public rooms are decorated in castle style—
heavy, tall, leather-backed chairs, long hall tables with
embroidered runners, old paintings, etchings, tapestries,
heraldic banners, stone wall escutcheons, ancient weapons, flared black iron oil lamp stanchions, and wall receptacles. On the top floor is a banquet hall whose walls are
hung with Rubens-inspired tapestries. Walk over tenth-
century flagstones in the rather monastic courtyard and
notice the well that provided water to troops and citizens
of the town during times of siege.

According to historians the castle-fortress was constructed on this high point overlooking the Bidasoa River
on the border between Spain and France by the king of
Navarra, Sancho Albarca. Additional fortifications and
modifications were made by ensuing rulers, including Ferdinand and Isabella. Their grandson, Carlos V, gave the
structure much the shape it has today (the parador is named
El Emperador after Carlos). The castle, whose walls vary
from six to ten feet in thickness, has played a major role

in the history of Fuenterrabía and has withstood countless assaults, easily believable when studying its pock-marked façade. In 1521, Francis I of France conquered the fortress only to lose it almost immediately to High Constable Iñigo Fernández de Velasco. The castle was under siege by the French for 64 days in 1638; the day the siege ended, September 7, is remembered annually with a great fiesta in Fuenterrabía. During the siege, the mayor offered all of his money to make bullets, a gesture followed by other citizens. In 1794, French bombardment seriously damaged a large portion of the castle. Restoration that began in the late nineteenth century, during the regency of Maria Christina, was finally completed when the Ministry of Tourism included it in the parador network.

A stay of a couple of days in the parador will give you a chance to explore small coastal villages or cross into France. Be sure to stop at the border bank for francs. We didn't, and our credit cards were refused in Biarritz, but accepted in a small waterside restaurant in charming St. Jean-de-Luz.

Hanging on a wall of the parador is a quote from Rubén Darío's "Cantos de Vida y L'Esperanza." In the authors' free translation it reads:

> As long as the world breathes, as long as the clock revolves, as long as friendly waves whisper a dream, as long as there is a passion for living, a noble eagerness, an impossible quest or deed, a hidden America to discover, Spain will live!

RECOMMENDED ITINERARIES

We hope these recommended itineraries will be helpful to you in planning your trip to Spain and Portugal. We have driven the routes following Firestone-Hispania road map number P-41-42. These itineraries are designed so that you won't spend all day adding up kilometers, and we have tried to limit driving time to a maximum of four to six hours a day. When planning your journey, try to avoid a long drive on the first day.

You will notice that we have not designated stops at all the pousadas and paradores. This is not because we find certain ones less desirable—they were simply not as practical for these particular itineraries.

As a general rule, count on averaging 75 to 100 km per hour on major highways (wide red routes on the Firestone map), 120 km per hour on the freeways (*autopistas* in Spain, *autostradas* in Portugal—wide red with a yellow strip down the middle), and 60 to 80 km per hour on most secondary roads (narrow yellow and red). Never hesitate to deviate a bit and travel a secondary road, for it may be on just such a road that you will see unforgettable sights. Remember to maintain at least enough fuel to travel 100 km at all times.

"Early start" in these itineraries means checking out of your lodgings by 9 A.M. "Late arrival" means arriving in the afternoon (by 5 P.M.). Late arrival should be indicated when making reservations. If you can't make it by 5, try to telephone ahead.

Page numbers in parentheses refer to *Paradores of Spain* when in Spain and *Pousadas of Portugal* when in Portugal.

When on the road, we usually snacked midday on cheese, bread and crackers, wine, and fruit. We enjoyed browsing in village markets and shops, keeping our travel larder stocked. Tuck in a corkscrew and kitchen knife when packing. Always keep bottled water in the car.

If a stop en route to a parador or pousada is suggested, do take time for a look around or a snack.

Since we believe that half the fun of any trip comes from anticipation and planning, we have included an enlarged map of Iberia, giving locations of major cities, paradores, and pousadas, so that you may plot your own course.

Buen viaje! Boa viagem!

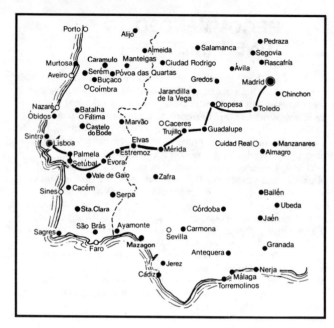

Itinerary 1

7 days, Lisboa to Madrid or vice versa

Day 1, Lisboa to Setúbal (50 km). Leave Lisboa southeast with a stop in Palmela (p. 119) en route to Setúbal (p. 116). *Pousada de São Filipe.*

Day 2, Setúbal to Evora (100 km). Take E-4 northeast to Montemor-o-Novo, southeast on N-114 to Evora (p. 102). *Pousada dos Lóios.*

Day 3, Evora to Estremoz (49 km). Spend most of the day seeing Evora, the Museum of Portugal, before driving northeast to Estremoz (p. 98). *Pousada da Rainha Santa Isabel.*

Day 4, Estremoz to Mérida (125 km). Early start from Estremoz southeast through Borba 5 km to Vila Viçosa (p. 100) for a tour of the palace. Retrace to Borba then east through Elvas (p. 96) and Badajoz to Mérida (p. 142). *Parador Nacional Via de la Plata.*

Day 5, Mérida to Trujillo (90 km). Spend most of the day seeing Mérida's Roman ruins before leaving for Trujillo (p. 145) northeast on N-V. *Parador Nacional de Trujillo.*

NOTE: Page numbers following Spanish locales refer to *Paradores of Spain;* page numbers following Portuguese locales refer to *Pousadas of Portugal.*

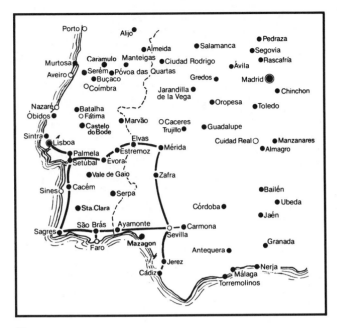

Itinerary 2

Day 6, Trujillo to Guadalupe (82 km). Drive southeast on C- 524 and at Zorita turn left onto C-401 to Guadalupe (p. 139). Twisting secondary roads, but lots of scenery. *Parador Nacional Zurbarán.*

Day 7, Guadalupe to Toledo (205 km via Oropesa). Leave Guadalupe east then head north through Puerto de San Vicente for a stop in Oropesa (p. 85). Leave E-4 at Santa Olalla, head southeast on N-403 to Toledo (p. 89). *Parador Nacional Conde de Orgaz.*

Most of the next day can be spent in Toledo, 70 km southwest of Madrid.

ITINERARY 2
10 days, round trip from Lisboa

Day 1, Lisboa to Evora (158 km). Drive southeast through Setúbal to Evora (p. 102). If interested in purchasing a *tapête*, stop in Arraiolos en route. Try to save several hours for Evora. *Pousada dos Lóios.*

NOTE: Page numbers following Spanish locales refer to *Paradores of Spain;* page numbers following Portuguese locales refer to *Pousadas of Portugal.*

Day 2, Evora to Estremoz (48 km). Budget your day to spend four or five hours visiting the environs of Estremoz (p. 98). Drive 18 km southeast through Borba to Vila Viçosa (p. 100). Take a tour of the palace and a stroll through the old town before checking into the pousada. *Pousada da Rainha Santa Isabel.*

Day 3, Estremoz to Zafra (186 km). Early start from Estremoz. Head east through Elvas (p. 96) and Badajoz to Mérida (p. 142). Spend several hours seeing the Roman ruins and perhaps have lunch at the parador. It's a one-hour drive south to Zafra (p. 147). *Late arrival. Parador Nacional Hernán Cortés.*

Day 4, Zafra to Carmona (170 km). Early start south from Zafra to Sevilla (p. 56). Follow signs to Catedral, park nearby, and take your own walking tour. Specify *late arrival* in Carmona (p. 41), 33 km east of Sevilla. *Parador Nacional Alcázar del Rey Don Pedro.*

Day 5, Carmona to Cádiz (126 km). Early start from Carmona back through Sevilla, where you pick up the *autopista* to Cádiz (p. 39). *Hotel Atlántico.*

Day 6, Cádiz to Arcos de la Frontera (70 km). Go northeast on IV to Jerez (p. 37) for a visit to one or more *bodegas* before proceeding west on C-342 to Arcos (p. 36). *Parador Nacional Casa del Corregidor.*

Day 7, Arcos de la Frontera to Ayamonte (247 km). Leave Arcos east on C-342, then go northwest on C-343, north on the *autopista* A-4 to Sevilla. Leave Sevilla west on N-431 to Ayamonte (p. 37). *Parador Nacional Costa de la Luz.*

Day 8, Ayamonte to São Brás de Alportel (44 km). Ferry from Ayamonte to Vila Real, then 22 km to Tavira, where you will turn northwest onto N-270 to São Brás (p. 107). Time to visit Faro (p. 108) if you wish. *Pousada de São Brás.*

Day 9, São Brás to Sagres (140 km). Lovely drive along the Algarve to Sagres (p. 110). Try to arrive for 3:30 daily movie (in English) about Prince Henry. *Pousada do Infante.*

Day 10, Sagres to Santiago do Cacém (137 km) or Sagres to Setúbal (237 km) or Sagres to Palmela (243 km). Drive north to Santiago do Cacém (p. 114) for lunch and go on to Setúbal or Palmela, or spend the night in Santiago do Cacém. *Pousada de São Tiago, Santiago do Cacém. Pousada de São Filipe, Setúbal. Pousada de Palmela, Palmela.*

50 km to Lisboa from Setúbal or 150 km to Lisboa from Santiago.

ITINERARY 3
8 days, round trip from Lisboa

Day 1, Lisboa to Batalha (148 km). Drive north on E-3 then onto N-1. Cut west 28 km for stop in Obidos (p. 41), go through Caldas

---

NOTE: Page numbers following Spanish locales refer to *Paradores of Spain*; page numbers following Portuguese locales refer to *Pousadas of Portugal*.

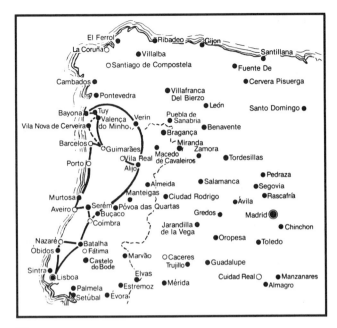

Itinerary 3

da Rainha for stop in Alcobaça (p. 45) and on to Nazaré (p. 43) for visit of two or three hours, perhaps including lunch. Arrive in Batalha (p. 47) for late afternoon visit to monastery. *Pousada do Mestre Afonso Domingues.*

Day 2, Batalha to Murtosa (183 km). Leave Batalha driving north on N-1 through Leiria and Coimbra (p. 53). At Santo António Agueda, cut west to Aveiro (p. 64) for visit of two or three hours. Drive east from Aveiro and cut north at Angeja, through Estarreja to Murtosa (p. 63). *Pousada da Ria.*

Day 3, Murtosa to Guimarães (115 km). If it's Thursday, you will want to head for Barcelos's market (p. 68), skirting Porto. Or you can visit Porto (p. 65) for several hours, then head for Guimarães (p. 67). Might be wise to specify *late arrival* in any case. *Pousada Santa Maria da Oliveira or Pousada Santa Marinha da Costa.*

Day 4, Guimarães to Valença do Minho or Vila Nova de Cerveira (92 km). Drive north from Guimarães for a visit to Braga (p. 70). The area from Ponte de Lima to Ponte da Barca has several *solares*, manor houses, you might want to visit. Get a list from the Por-

NOTE: Page numbers following Spanish locales refer to *Paradores of Spain;* page numbers following Portuguese locales refer to *Pousadas of Portugal.*

tuguese National Tourist Office before leaving home. Stay either in Vila Nova (p. 73) or Valença (p. 75). *Pousada de Dom Dinis or Pousada de São Teotónio.*

Day 5, Valença do Minho or Vila Nova de Cerveira to Bayona (60 km). Enjoy morning hours in Valença before crossing international bridge into Spain at Tuy (p. 162). Get pesetas at border bank. Leave Tuy driving southwest through Laguardia before arriving in Bayona (p. 152). *Parador Nacional Conde de Gondomar.*

Day 6, Bayona to Verin (205 km). Beautiful drive through southern Galicia and Orense, then southeast to Verin (p. 164). *Parador Nacional Monterrey.*

Day 7, Verin to Alijó (136 km). Drive south from Verin into Portugal. In autumn, you will see wonderful grape harvest scenes if you drive southeast from Chaves through Valpacos and Mirandela, then southwest on N-15 before turning south to Alijó (p. 82). *Pousada Barão de Forrester.*

Day 8, Alijó to Buçaco (224 km). Travel west to Vila Real and Highway N-2, south through Viseu (p. 92) to Buçaco (p. 56). *Palace Hotel.*

231 km south from Buçaco to Lisboa.

ITINERARY 4
8 days, Lisboa to Madrid or vice versa

Day 1, Lisboa to Batalha (148 km). Drive north on E-3 then onto N-1. Cut west on Highway 366 for a stop in Obidos (p. 41), through Caldas da Rainha to Highway 8 for a stop in Alcobaça (p. 45) and on to Nazaré (p. 43) for two or three hours' visit and perhaps lunch. Arrive in Batalha (p. 47) for late afternoon visit to monastery. *Pousada do Mestre Afonso Domingues.*

Day 2, Batalha to Buçaco (110 km). Two choices of sights en route to Buçaco. EITHER leave Batalha heading southeast and go 13 km for a visit to Fátima (p. 49). Tomar (p. 51) is 31 km southeast of Fátima. Leave Tomar north on N-110 through Penela and cut over to N-1 at Condeixa for a stop in Conímbriga (p. 53), on through Coimbra to Buçaco (p. 56). OR bypass Fátima and Tomar and head directly for Coimbra (p. 53) for a visit of several hours. Take N-1 north to Highway 234, east to Luso, then follow signs to Buçaco (p. 56). *Palace Hotel.*

Day 3, Buçaco to Valença do Minho or Vila Nova de Cerveira (245 km). If it's Thursday, get an early start north to Barcelos (p. 68) for its market. If not, you may opt to spend several hours in Porto (p. 65) before proceeding north to Valença (p. 75) or Vila Nova de Cerveira (p. 73). *Pousada de São Teotónio or Pousada de Dom Dinis.*

NOTE: Page numbers following Spanish locales refer to *Paradores of Spain;* page numbers following Portuguese locales refer to *Pousadas of Portugal.*

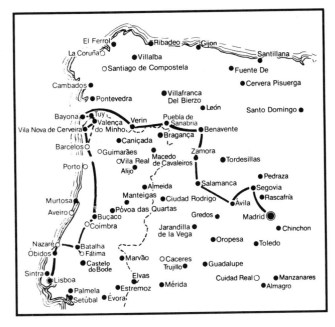

Itinerary 4

Day 4, Valença do Minho or Vila Nova de Cerveira to Bayona (60 km).
Enjoy the morning in Valença before crossing the international
bridge into Spain at Tuy (p. 162). Remember to buy pesetas at the
border bank. You may want to stroll through Tuy before driving
northwest to Bayona (p. 152). *Parador Nacional Conde de Gondomar.*

Day 5, Bayona to Verin (205 km). Beautiful drive through southern
Galicia and Orense, then southeast to Verin (p. 164). *Parador Nacional Monterrey.*

Day 6, Verin to Zamora (240 km). Drive east through Puebla de
Sanabria (p. 106). Stop in Benavente (p. 94) before continuing south
to Zamora (p. 119). *Parador Nacional Condes de Alba y Aliste.*

Day 7, Zamora to Avila (162 km). Plan a visit of two to three hours
in Salamanca (p. 106), 62 km south of Zamora, before continuing
southeast to Avila (p. 93). *Parador Nacional Raimundo de Borgoña.*

Day 8, Avila to Segovia (65 km). Divide your day between Avila
and Segovia (p. 113). *Parador Nacional de Segovia.*

88 km to Madrid.

NOTE: Page numbers following Spanish locales refer to *Paradores
of Spain*; page numbers following Portuguese locales refer to *Pousadas of Portugal.*

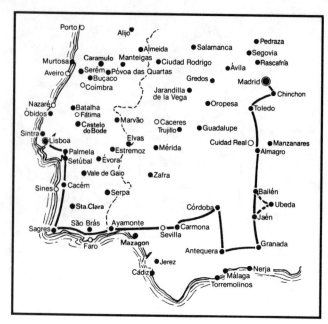

Itinerary 5

ITINERARY 5
10 days, Lisboa to Madrid or vice versa

Day 1, Lisboa to Santiago do Cacém (150 km). Drive southeast to Setúbal (p. 116) or Palmela (p. 119) for a visit, then on to Santiago do Cacém (p. 114). *Pousada de São Tiago.*

Day 2, Santiago do Cacém to Sagres (137 km). Easy drive south and spend most of the afternoon in Sagres (p. 110). *Pousada do Infante.*

Day 3, Sagres to Ayamonte (180 km). Interesting drive east along the Algarve to Vila Real, where you ferry into Spain at Ayamonte (p. 37). *Parador Nacional Costa de la Luz.*

Day 4, Ayamonte to Carmona (186 km). Early start from Ayamonte through Huelva to Sevilla (p. 56). Follow signs to Catedral, park nearby, and take walking tour of Sevilla's monuments. Specify *late arrival* in Carmona (p. 41), 33 km east of Sevilla. *Parador Nacional Alcázar del Rey Don Pedro.*

Day 5, Carmona to Córdoba (105 km). Short drive, allowing several hours of sightseeing in Córdoba (p. 44). *Parador Nacional La Arruzafa.*

NOTE: Page numbers following Spanish locales refer to *Paradores of Spain*; page numbers following Portuguese locales refer to *Pousadas of Portugal*.

Day 6, Córdoba to Granada (229 km). Drive south to Antequera (p. 33), then east to Granada (p. 47). *Parador Nacional San Francisco or, if no vacancy, Alhambra Palace Hotel.*

Day 7. A full day for sightseeing in Granada. *Parador Nacional San Francisco.*

Day 8, Granada to Almagro (267 km). You may want to stop for a morning coffee break at the spectacular parador in Jaén (p. 49), or take time for a visit to Ubeda (p. 57). Either way, specify *late arrival* in Almagro (p. 77). *Parador Nacional de Almagro.*

Day 9, Almagro to Toledo (139 km). Leave Almagro east and drive to C-517, then head north on N-420 to N-IV and Madridejos, northwest on C-400 to Toledo (p. 89). *Parador Nacional Conde de Orgaz.*

Day 10, Toledo to Chinchón (66 km). Most of the day for shopping and sightseeing in Toledo before departing northeast to Chinchón (p. 79). *Parador Nacional de Chinchón.*

33 km northwest to Madrid.

13 days, round trip from Madrid

Day 1, Madrid to Toledo (70 km). Drive southwest on N-401 to Toledo (p. 89). *Parador Nacional Conde de Orgaz.*

Day 2, Toledo to Guadalupe (205 km). Drive northwest 47 km and join N-V at Santa Olalla. Stop in Oropesa (p. 85). Proceed southwest to Guadalupe (p. 139). You might consider having dinner at the monastery across the street from the parador. *Parador Nacional Zurbarán.*

Day 3, Guadalupe to Mérida (130 km). Leave Guadalupe southwest on C-401, then N-V to Mérida (p. 142). *Parador Nacional Via de la Plata.*

Day 4, Mérida to Estremoz (135 km). Drive west through Badajoz and Elvas (p. 96). At Borba, cut southeast 5 km to Vila Viçosa (p. 100) for visit of two or three hours before proceeding to Estremoz (p. 98). *Pousada da Rainha Santa Isabel.*

Day 5, Estremoz to Evora (69 km via Arraiolos). If interested in purchasing a *tapête*, leave Estremoz driving west to Arraiolos, then 21 km southeast to Evora (p. 102). *Pousada dos Lóios.*

Day 6. Another day for sightseeing in Evora. *Pousada dos Lóios.*

Day 7, Evora to Lisboa (158 km). Early start for a visit to Setúbal (p. 116) and Palmela (p. 119) before arrival in Lisboa (p. 28).

Days 8 and 9, Lisboa.

NOTE: Page numbers following Spanish locales refer to *Paradores of Spain;* page numbers following Portuguese locales refer to *Pousadas of Portugal.*

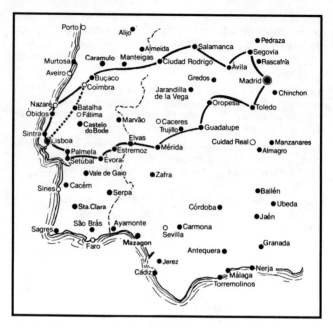

Itinerary 6

Day 10, Lisboa to Buçaco (231 km). Get an early start. Choose between two routes: EITHER Sintra (p. 35), Mafra (p. 39), Nazaré (p. 43), Alcobaça (p. 45), and on to Buçaco (p. 56). OR drive the *autostrada* north for stops in Batalha (p. 47), Conímbriga (p. 53), and Coimbra (p. 53), and on to Buçaco. *Palace Hotel.*

Day 11, Buçaco to Ciudad Rodrigo (214 km). Head east on Highway 234 to N-16, through Guarda (p. 91), cross into Spain at Fuentes de Oñoro and on to Ciudad Rodrigo (p. 98). *Parador Nacional Enrique II.*

Day 12, Ciudad Rodrigo to Avila (189 km). Leave Ciudad Rodrigo northeast on E-3. Stop for visit in Salamanca (p. 106) before continuing to Avila (p. 93). *Parador Nacional Raimundo de Borgoña.*

Day 13, Avila to Segovia (65 km). Allow most of the day for the sights of Avila before driving to Segovia (p. 113). *Parador Nacional de Segovia.*

88 km to Madrid.

NOTE: Page numbers following Spanish locales refer to *Paradores of Spain;* page numbers following Portuguese locales refer to *Pousadas of Portugal.*

ITINERARY 7
15 days, Barcelona to Lisboa or vice versa (central route)

Day 1, Barcelona to Tortosa (193 km). Drive south via the Barcelona-Valencia *autopista*. Take the Tortosa exit 14 km north through the Ebro valley to Tortosa (p. 130). *Parador Nacional Castillo de la Zuda.*

Day 2, Tortosa to Alcañiz (91 km). Take your choice of secondary roads northwest to Alcañiz (p. 64). *Parador Nacional La Concordia.*

Day 3, Alcañiz to Sigüenza (252 km). A day of winding secondary roads but you will have Day 4 to rest. Leave Alcañiz south on N-211 to Caminreal, south then west on N-211, now a principal highway, to Alcolea del Pinar, then northwest on C-114 to Sigüenza (p. 87). *Parador Nacional Castillo de Sigüenza.*

Day 4. A day of relaxation, with possible trips to Santa María de Huerta (p. 108) and Medinaceli (p. 109), besides a stroll through Sigüenza. *Parador Nacional Castillo de Sigüenza.*

Day 5, Sigüenza to Segovia (236 km). Leave Sigüenza south on C-204, then pick up E-4. If you wish to avoid Madrid, take the airport freeway north past the airport, through Alcobendas, across N-1 to C-601, north and west through Navacerrada, and north on N-601 to Segovia (p. 113). *Parador Nacional de Segovia.*

Day 6, Segovia. Visit La Granja and have lunch at Hostería Nacional Pintor Zuloaga in Pedraza (p. 104). *Parador Nacional de Segovia.*

Day 7, Segovia to Madrid. Leave you car and luggage at the parador and take the train into Madrid (p. 81). There are many trains daily arriving and departing both Atocha and Chamartín stations. A convenient hotel is the Chamartín (p. 82).

Days 8 and 9, Madrid.

Day 10, Madrid to Avila. Take the train back to Segovia, pick up luggage and car, and head southwest to Avila (p. 93). *Parador Nacional Raimundo de Borgoña.*

Day 11, Avila to Ciudad Rodrigo (189 km). Drive northwest on N-501 for stop in Salamanca (p. 106) en route to Ciudad Rodrigo (p. 98). *Parador Nacional Enrique II.*

Day 12, Ciudad Rodrigo to Manteigas (135 km). Cross into Portugal at Fuentes de Oñoro, go through Guarda (p. 91), following signs to Covilhã. Take N-18 south for 27 km and turn west on 232 to Manteigas (p. 90). It's another 12 km to the pousada. *Pousada de São Lourenço.*

Day 13, Manteigas to Buçaco (156 km). Leave the pousada heading north through Gouveia, pick up N-17, head southeast to Poiares,

---

NOTE: Page numbers following Spanish locales refer to *Paradores of Spain;* page numbers following Portuguese locales refer to *Pousadas of Portugal.*

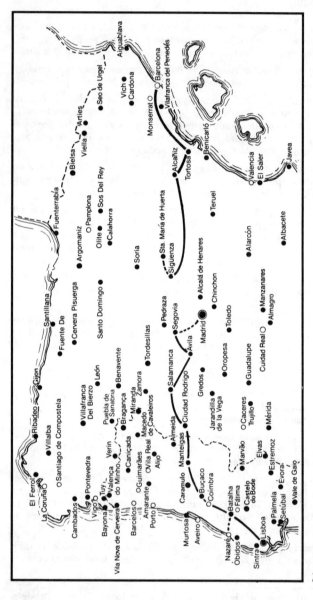

Itinerary 7

northeast on Highway 2 for 13 km, and pick up signs to Buçaco (p. 56). *Palace Hotel.*

Day 14, Buçaco to Batalha (110 km). After morning hours enjoying the environs of the Palace Hotel, drive south to Coimbra (p. 53) for a visit of two or three hours before proceeding south to Batalha (p. 47). *Pousada do Mestre Afonso Domingues.*

Day 15. Another day based in Batalha for trips of your choice: Tomar (p. 51), Fátima (p. 49), Nazaré (p. 43). *Pousada do Mestre Afonso Domingues.*

148 km to Lisboa.

ITINERARY 8
15 days, Galician tour from Lisboa to Madrid or vice versa

Day 1, Lisboa to Batalha (148 km). Drive north on E-3 then onto N-1. Cut west 28 km for stop in Obidos (p. 41), through Caldas da Rainha for a stop in Alcobaça (p. 45) and on to Nazaré (p. 43) for visit of two to three hours, perhaps lunch. Arrive in Batalha (p. 47) for late afternoon visit to monastery. *Pousada do Mestre Afonso Domingues.*

Day 2, Batalha to Murtosa (183 km). Leave Batalha driving north on N-1 through Leiria and stop in Coimbra (p. 53) for two-hour visit. Leave Coimbra north on N-1. At Santo António Agueda, cut west to Aveiro (p. 64) for two-hour stop. Drive east from Aveiro and cut north at Angeja to go through Estarreja to Murtosa (p. 63). *Pousada da Ria.*

Day 3, Murtosa to Valença do Minho or Vila Nova de Cerveira (200 km via Porto or 237 km via Barcelos). If it's Thursday, drive north, skirting Porto, through Guimarães (p. 67) and Braga (p. 70) for the market in Barcelos (p. 68). Or you may choose to visit Porto (p. 65) for a couple of hours before driving north on N-13 to Vila Nova or Valença. They are 12 km apart. *Pousada de São Teotónio or Pousada de Dom Dinis.*

Day 4, Valença do Minho or Vila Nova de Cerveira to Bayona (60 km). Enjoy morning hours in Valença (p. 75) before crossing international bridge into Spain at Tuy (p. 162). Get pesetas at border bank. Leave Tuy driving southwest through Laguardia for spectacular scenery before arriving in Bayona (p. 152). *Parador Nacional Conde de Gondomar.*

Day 5, Bayona to Cambados (88 km). Leisurely day along the scenic *rías* (estuaries) of Galicia; go through Vigo and Pontevedra (p. 157) to Cambados (p. 154). *Parador Nacional del Albariño.*

NOTE: Page numbers following Spanish locales refer to *Paradores of Spain;* page numbers following Portuguese locales refer to *Pousadas of Portugal.*

Itinerary 8

Day 6, Cambados to Santiago de Compostela (82 km). Easy drive north to Santiago (p. 159), allowing most of the day for this exciting, historic city. *Hotel Reyes Católicos.*

Day 7, Santiago de Compostela to Villalba (92 km). Try for one of the six rooms at the parador in Villalba (p. 165). If unsuccessful, spend another night in Santiago. There is plenty to do and see. *Parador Nacional Condes de Villalba.*

Day 8, Villalba to Ribadeo (73 km). Leave Villalba northeast on N-643 for Ribadeo (p. 158). You may want to check into parador before exploring small nearby coastal villages. *Parador Nacional de Ribadeo.*

Day 9, Ribadeo to Villafranca del Bierzo (190 km). Drive south on N-640 through Lugo then onto N-VI to Villafranca (p. 118). *Parador Nacional Villafranca del Bierzo.*

Day 10, Villafranca to Zamora (215 km). Drive southeast on N-VI to Benavente (p. 94) for lunch before continuing to Zamora (p. 119). *Parador Nacional Condes Alba y Aliste.*

NOTE: Page numbers following Spanish locales refer to *Paradores of Spain;* page numbers following Portuguese locales refer to *Pousadas of Portugal.*

Day 11, Zamora to Tordesillas (67 km). Spend the rest of the day and days 12 and 13 in the area around Tordesillas (p. 116). Take a castle tour of your own (p. 117), returning each night to the very comfortable parador. *Parador Nacional de Tordesillas.*

Days 12 and 13, Tordesillas. Parador Nacional de Tordesillas.

Day 14, Tordesillas to Avila (136 km). You will have most of the day for the sights of Avila (p. 93) if you get an early start from Tordesillas. *Parador Nacional Raimundo de Borgoña.*

Day 15, Avila to Segovia (65 km). Early start from Avila for many hours in Segovia (p. 113). *Parador Nacional de Segovia.*

88 km to Madrid.

ITINERARY 9
15 days, coastal trip from Barcelona to Lisboa or vice versa

Day 1, Barcelona to Tortosa (193 km). Leave Barcelona heading south on either the *autopista* or N-340 to Vilafranca del Penedés (p. 133) for a visit to the wine museum. Then continue to Tortosa (p. 130). There is a Tortosa exit from the *autopista*. *Parador Nacional Castillo de la Zuda.*

Day 2, Tortosa to El Saler (194 km). Rejoin the *autopista* for drive south through Castellón and Valencia to El Saler (p. 174). Plenty of time for a game of golf. *Parador Nacional Luis Vives.*

Day 3. Another day for a visit to Valencia. *Parador Nacional Luis Vives.*

Day 4, El Saler to Javea (119 km). Leisurely day to enjoy beautiful surroundings of Javea (p. 177), southeast of El Saler. *Parador Nacional Costa Blanca.*

Day 5, Jávea to Mojácar (207 km). Drive southwest on the *autopista* to Alicante then take N-340 to Puerto Lumbreras (p. 86) for lunch and perhaps a stop at the parador. At Vera, travel south on C-323 to Mojácar (p. 53). *Parador Nacional Reyes Católicos.*

Day 6, Mojácar to Nerja (278 km). Rejoin N-340 south to Almería. If it's lunchtime, stop at the Club de Mar Restaurant in Almería (p. 54). Drive along the Mediterranean to Nerja (p. 54). *Parador Nacional de Nerja.*

Day 7, Nerja to Torremolinos (70 km). Easy drive with plenty of time to stop off in Málaga (p. 50) for lunch at the Gibralfaro parador. On to Torremolinos (p. 59). *Parador Nacional del Golf.*

Day 8. A day in Torremolinos for golf or an excursion to Mijas, Casares (p. 60), or Ronda. *Parador Nacional del Golf.*

NOTE: Page numbers following Spanish locales refer to *Paradores of Spain;* page numbers following Portuguese locales refer to *Pousadas of Portugal.*

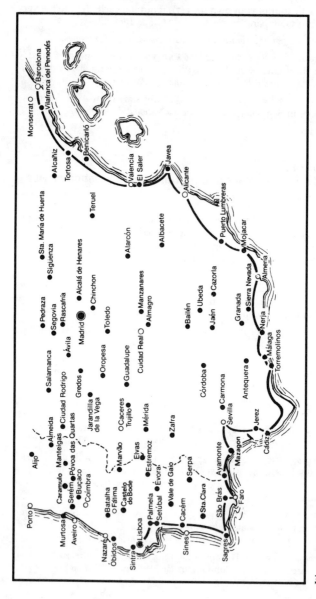

Itinerary 9

Day 9, Torremolinos to Cádiz (244 km). A day of exceptional scenery along coastal Highway N-340 as you round the southern tip of Spain and head northwest to Cádiz (p. 39). *Hotel Atlántico.*

Day 10, Cádiz to Mazagón (211 km). A rather roundabout route to Mazagón. You may want to stop in Jerez (p. 37) to visit a *bodega* or two before traveling the *autopista* to Sevilla, then west on 334, turning south just before reaching San Juan del Puerto to Mazagón (p. 51). *Parador Nacional Cristóbal Colón.*

Day 11. Another day for Mazagón as a base while you see sights of the Coto de Doñana (p. 52). *Parador Nacional Cristóbal Colón.*

Day 12, Mazagón to São Brás de Alportel (147 km via Faro). Drive northwest to Huelva to pick up N-IV at Ayamonte (p. 37), where you will ferry into Portugal at Vila Real de Santo António. Drive south for a look at Faro (p. 108) before turning north and going 18 km to São Brás (p. 107). *Pousada de São Brás de Alportel.*

Day 13, São Brás de Alportel to Sagres (140 km). Leave São Brás west to Loulé, then 13 more km to join N-125, the coastal route. You will have time for many stops. Albufeira is a quaint fishing village with many stores to shop. Lagos (p. 112) is another such town. From there, just 43 km to Sagres (p. 110). *Pousada do Infante.*

Day 14, Sagres to Setúbal or Palmela (216 km). This looks like a long haul on the map but it is an easy drive. Stop in Santiago do Cacém (p. 114) for lunch at the pousada before continuing to Setúbal (p. 116) or Palmela (p. 119). *Pousada de São Filipe or Pousada de Palmela.*

Day 15, Setúbal, Palmela, and environs. Visit the Fonseca winery in Azeitão (p. 121) or explore Sesimbra (p. 121). *Pousada de São Filipe or Pousada de Palmela.*

50 km to Lisboa.

ITINERARY 10
22 days, round trip from Lisboa

Day 1, Lisboa to Obidos (149 km). Stop in Sintra (p. 35) and lunch at Hotel Palácio dos Seteais before driving north to Mafra (p. 39), then on to Obidos (p. 41). *Pousada do Castelo.*

Day 2, Obidos to Batalha (72 km). Leave Obidos driving north through Caldas da Rainha for a stop in Alcobaça (p. 45) before proceeding 13 km northwest to Nazaré (p. 43) for a visit and lunch. It's 26 km to Batalha (p. 47). *Pousada do Mestre Afonso Domingues.*

Day 3. Another day based in Batalha to allow trips to Fátima (p. 49) and Tomar (p. 51). *Pousada do Mestre Afonso Domingues.*

NOTE: Page numbers following Spanish locales refer to *Paradores of Spain;* page numbers following Portuguese locales refer to *Pousadas of Portugal.*

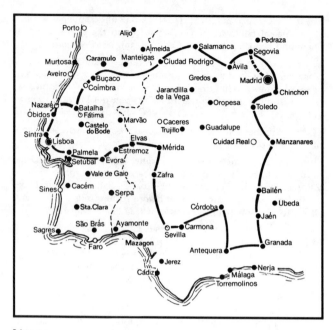

Itinerary 10

Day 4, Batalha to Buçaco (110 km). Leave Batalha driving north on
N-1 with a brief stop in Conímbriga (p. 53) and three to four hours
in Coimbra (p. 53) before proceeding northeast to Buçaco (p. 56).
Palace Hotel.

Day 5, Buçaco to Ciudad Rodrigo (217 km). Leave Buçaco heading
east a few kilometers before turning south at Santa Comba Dão
onto N-234 then northeast on N-17 to pass through Guarda
(p. 91). Cross into Spain at Fuentes de Oñoro and on to Ciudad
Rodrigo (p. 98). *Parador Nacional Enrique II.*

Day 6, Ciudad Rodrigo to Avila (189 km). Early start from Ciudad
Rodrigo to allow for several hours in Salamanca (p. 106) before
proceeding to Avila (p. 93). *Parador Nacional Raimundo de Borgoña.*

Day 7, Avila to Segovia (65 km). Allow several hours for Avila before proceeding to Segovia (p. 113). *Parador Nacional de Segovia.*

Day 8, Segovia. Perhaps visit La Granja and have lunch in Pedraza
(p. 104). If you don't want to drive in Madrid (p. 81), check train
schedules (several a day) and make arrangements with parador to
leave luggage and car. *Parador Nacional de Segovia.*

NOTE: Page numbers following Spanish locales refer to *Paradores
of Spain;* page numbers following Portuguese locales refer to *Pousadas of Portugal.*

Days 9, 10, and 11, Madrid.

Day 12, Segovia to Chinchón (161 km). Early train from Madrid to Segovia. Pick up luggage and car and drive southeast to Chinchón (p. 79), skirting Madrid. Specify *late arrival. Parador Nacional de Chinchón.*

Day 13, Chinchón to Toledo (70 km). Not a long or difficult drive, allowing most of the day for Toledo (p. 89). *Parador Nacional Conde de Orgaz.*

Day 14, Toledo to Jaén (273 km). Stop off at the parador in Manzanares (p. 83) or Bailén (p. 38) for a rest or refreshment before continuing to Jaén (p. 49). *Parador Nacional Castillo Santa Catalina.*

Day 15, Jaén to Granada (97 km). Easy drive so you can have most of the day for Granada (p. 47). *Parador Nacional San Francisco.*

Day 16, Granada to Córdoba (229 km). Drive west from Granada on N-342. Have lunch at the parador in Antequera (p. 33). Then turn north on N-331 to Córdoba (p. 44). *Parador Nacional La Arruzafa.*

Day 17, Córdoba. Day to explore and rest. *Parador Nacional La Arruzafa.*

Day 18, Córdoba to Carmona (105 km). Early start, heading southwest on N-IV to Carmona (p. 41). Check into parador then take a bus into Sevilla (p. 56). *Parador Nacional Alcázar del Rey Don Pedro.*

Day 19, Carmona to Mérida (245 km). Plan to have lunch at the parador in Zafra (p. 147) en route to Mérida (p. 142). *Parador Nacional Via de la Plata.*

Day 20, Mérida. A full day to explore the ancient city. *Parador Nacional Via de la Plata.*

Day 21, Mérida to Estremoz (124 km). You will have time to stop en route for a visit to Vila Viçosa (p. 100) before arriving in Estremoz (p. 98). *Pousada da Rainha Santa Isabel.*

Day 22, Estremoz to Palmela (155 km). Early start to allow two or three hours in Evora (p. 102) before continuing to Palmela (p. 119). *Pousada de Palmela.*

44 km to Lisboa.

ITINERARY 11
21 days, northern route from Barcelona to Lisboa or vice versa

Day 1, Barcelona to Seo de Urgel (187 km). Leave Barcelona heading northwest through Manresa with a stop at the parador in Cardona (p. 127). At Basella, join C-1313 to Seo (p. 129). *Parador Nacional de Seo de Urgel.*

NOTE: Page numbers following Spanish locales refer to *Paradores of Spain;* page numbers following Portuguese locales refer to *Pousadas of Portugal.*

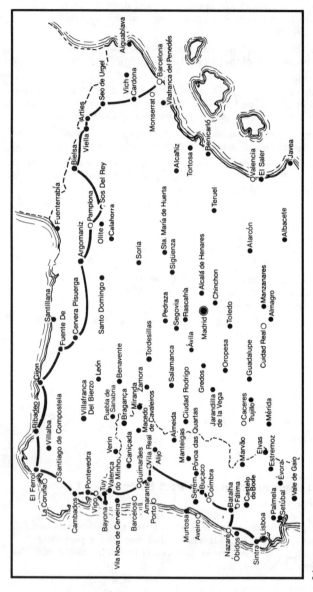

Itinerary 11

Day 2, Seo de Urgel to Viella (164 km). Backtrack south on C-1313 about 6 km and turn west onto a road appearing only on regional maps; go for 78 km in second or third gear to Sort. In any of several small towns, pick up some *queso* (cheese), *pan* (bread), and a bottle of wine so that when you reach the acme of the route (6734 feet) at Puerto de la Bonaigua you can ice the wine in roadside snow. Unforgettable lunch in the midst of the Pyrenees. Stop at the parador in Arties (p. 125) for a look around and a chat with the young administrator, who speaks English. Just a few km to Viella (p. 134). *Parador Nacional Valle de Arán.*

Day 3, Viella to Bielsa (164 km). Leave Viella via the 6-km tunnel. After you have gone 38 km look for a road west to Castejón. At Castejón, turn south then west to Ainsa. Drive north from Ainsa 34 km to Bielsa, then 14 km more west to the parador (p. 65). These roads are narrow with no center stripe—adequate, but might be a little scary in occasionally heavy summer traffic. *Parador Nacional Monte Perdido.*

Day 4, Bielsa to Sos del Rey Católico (245 km). Return to Ainsa, where you turn west on C-138 through Broto to Biescas, then south to Sabinanizo, west to Jaca, and take C-134 for about 10 km beyond Berdún. Turn south on C-137 for 34 km to Sos del Rey Católico (p. 66). A long, rather hard drive, but rewarding scenery. Watch out for herds of sheep! *Parador Nacional Fernando de Aragón.*

Day 5, Sos del Rey Católico to Argómaniz (156 km). Leave Sos del Rey Católico heading northwest through Sangüesa and in 5 km turn west onto N-240 to Pamplona (p. 182). You will have time for two or three hours in Pamplona. It is simplest to park on the outskirts of the old town and take a cab to begin a walking tour. It's 94 km to Argómaniz (p. 181). *Parador Nacional de Argómaniz.*

Day 6, Argómaniz. A day for a junket into France (remember to get francs at a border bank) or a visit to the parador in Fuenterrabía (p. 183). *Parador Nacional de Argómaniz.*

Day 7, Argómaniz to Cervera de Pisuerga (174 km). Leave Argómaniz heading through Vitoria southwest to Burgos if you wish. This route will add about 65 km. Otherwise, at Pancorbo, cut west on N-232 through Poza de la Sal and Portillo, go northwest to Aguilar de Campóo, then go 25 more km to Cervera (p. 97). *Parador Nacional Fuentes Carrionas.*

Day 8, Cervera to Fuente Dé (85 km). Drive north on C-627 then west through Potes to Fuente Dé (p. 101). Breathtaking scenery in the Picos de Europa. *Parador Nacional Río Deva.*

Day 9, Fuente Dé to Gijón (206 km). Retrace route to Potes, turn north to Panes, west on C-6312 to Cangas de Onis, and pick up N-634 west to the turn-off north to Gijón (p. 70). In Cangas de Onis, there's a Romanesque bridge over the Sella River. Used now

---

NOTE: Page numbers following Spanish locales refer to *Paradores of Spain;* page numbers following Portuguese locales refer to *Pousadas of Portugal.*

only for foot traffic, it is strangely humped in the middle. You are in sacred Spanish territory because it was in nearby Covadonga that tribal leader Pelayo defeated the Moors in 722. He was then made king of Asturias and established his court in Cangas. *Parador Nacional Molino Viejo.*

Day 10, Gijón to Ribadeo (156 km). Winding scenic drive west on N-632 then N-634 to Ribadeo (p. 158). *Parador Nacional de Ribadeo.*

Day 11, Ribadeo to El Ferrol (146 km via C-642 or 188 km via Villalba). Take your choice of two routes to El Ferrol (p. 156). You might enjoy seeing the parador in Villalba (p. 165). *Parador Nacional del Ferrol.*

Day 12, El Ferrol. Take a bus trip from here into La Coruña. *Parador Nacional del Ferrol.*

Day 13, El Ferrol to Santiago de Compostela (97 km). Drive north around the bay, then south on N-VI to Betanzos, south on C- 542 for shortcut to N-550 and on into Santiago (p. 159). *Hotel Reyes Católicos.*

Day 14, Santiago de Compostela. Hotel Reyes Católicos.

Day 15, Santiago de Compostela to Bayona (113 km). Leave Santiago heading south on E-50 and at Puentecesures, turn southwest on C-550 for a drive and stop at parador in Cambados (p. 154), then through Sanjenjo, Pontevedra, Vigo, and the coastal road to Bayona (p. 152). *Parador Nacional Conde de Gondomar.*

Day 16, Bayona to Guimarães (128 km). Drive east through Gondomar to join N-550 and proceed to Tuy (p. 162). Cross the international bridge, remembering to stop and change money. Linger a while in Valença do Minho (p. 75), then head south through Braga (p. 70) to Guimarães (p. 67). *Pousada Santa Maria da Oliveira or Pousada Santa Marinha da Costa.*

Day 17, Guimarães to Amarante (53 km). Short drive southeast, to allow time to relax in Amarante (p. 80). *Pousada de São Gonçalo.*

Day 18, Amarante to Buçaco (204 km). Drive east to Vila Real, south on N-2 through Viseu (p. 92), through Santa Comba Dão to Buçaco (p. 56). *Palace Hotel.*

Day 19, Buçaco to Batalha (110 km). Take time for a walk through the forest before driving through Luso to pick up N-1 at Mealhada. Stop for a visit in Coimbra (p. 53). Leave Coimbra south through Condeixa for a look at Conímbriga's Roman ruins (p. 53) before arrival in Batalha (p. 47). *Pousada do Mestre Afonso Domingues.*

Day 20, Batalha and environs. Visits to Fátima (p. 49) and Tomar (p. 51). *Pousada do Mestre Afonso Domingues.*

Day 21, Batalha to Sintra (128 km). Drive from Batalha southwest to Nazaré (p. 43) for a visit, then on to Alcobaça (p. 45) for a tour

NOTE: Page numbers following Spanish locales refer to *Paradores of Spain;* page numbers following Portuguese locales refer to *Pousadas of Portugal.*

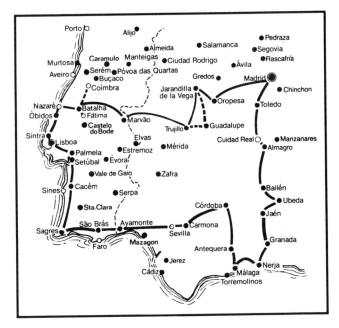

Itinerary 12

of the monastery, southwest for another monastery, at Mafra (p. 39), before arrival in Sintra (p. 35). *Hotel Palácio dos Seteais.*

Day 22, Sintra. Visit the two palaces in Sintra and the one in Queluz (p. 38), with lunch at Restaurante Cozinha Velha. *Hotel Palácio dos Seteais.*

30 km to Lisboa.

ITINERARY 12
24 days, round trip from Malaga

Day 1, Málaga to Córdoba (178 km). Drive north on N-321 with a stop in Antequera (p. 33) en route to Córdoba (p. 44). *Parador Nacional La Arruzafa.*

Day 2, Córdoba to Carmona (105 km). Spend the morning in Córdoba, then head southwest on N-IV to Carmona (p. 41). *Parador Nacional Alcázar del Rey Don Pedro.*

Day 3, Carmona. Explore Carmona, then take a bus into Sevilla (p. 56). *Parador Nacional Alcázar del Rey Don Pedro.*

NOTE: Page numbers following Spanish locales refer to *Paradores of Spain;* page numbers following Portuguese locales refer to *Pousadas of Portugal.*

Day 4, Carmona to São Brás de Alportel (230 km). Early start from Carmona west through Sevilla and Huelva to Ayamonte (p. 37), where you take a ferry to Vila Real, Portugal. At Tavira, cut north on N-270 to São Brás (p. 107). *Pousada de São Brás de Alportel.*

Day 5, São Brás de Alportel to Sagres (141 km via Faro). Enjoy a scenic drive along the Algarve west to Sagres (p. 110). *Pousada do Infante.*

Day 6, Sagres and environs. Trips to Lagos (p. 112) and Albufeira. *Pousada do Infante.*

Day 7, Sagres to Palmela (243 km). Leave Sagres north on N-120 to Santiago do Cacém (p. 114) for a rest and perhaps lunch before continuing to Palmela (p. 119). *Pousada do Castelo de Palmela.*

Day 8, Palmela to Lisboa (56 km). A leisurely day for visits to Setúbal (p. 116) and Fonseca winery in Azeitão (p. 121) before late arrival in Lisboa (p. 28).

Days 9 and 10, Lisboa.

Day 11, Lisboa to Obidos (120 km). En route to Obidos (p. 41), stop in Sintra (p. 35) and Mafra (p. 39). *Pousada do Castelo.*

Day 12, Obidos to Batalha (72 km via Nazaré). Leave Obidos heading north through Caldas da Rainha (p. 44) for visit to Alcobaça (p. 45) before continuing to Nazaré. Drive north from Nazaré 26 km to Batalha (p. 47). *Pousada do Mestre Afonso Domingues.*

Day 13, Batalha and environs. Visits to Fátima (p. 49), Tomar (p. 51), or Coimbra (p. 53). *Pousada do Mestre Afonso Domingues.*

Day 14, Batalha to Marvão (159 km). Leave Batalha heading south through Porto de Mos, Constância, Alpalhão. Stop in Castelo de Vide (p. 93) before arrival in Marvão (p. 92). *Pousada de Santa Maria.*

Day 15, Marvão to Trujillo (179 km). Return to N-118 (N-521 in Spain) and drive east through Cáceres to Trujillo (p. 145). If you had an early start, you might want to turn north at Membrio and go 31 km to Alcántara for a look at the Roman bridge, then south on 523 through Cáceres to Trujillo. This will add more kilometers but not too many if you love Roman ruins. *Parador Nacional de Trujillo.*

Day 16, Trujillo to Jarandilla de la Vera (107 km directly, 190 km via Guadalupe). Either go directly to Jarandilla (N-V to Navalmoral de la Mata, and then north 33 km to Jarandilla) or visit Guadalupe en route. Leave Trujillo heading south on C-524. Drive northeast at Zorita on C-401 to Guadalupe (p. 139). Leave Guadalupe heading north through Navalmoral de la Mata to Jarandilla (p. 140). *Parador Nacional Carlos V.*

Day 17, Jarandilla de la Vera to Madrid (212 km). Return to Navalmoral de la Mata then head east on N-V. You may want to stop in Lagartera (p. 86) and Oropesa (p. 85) or purchase pottery in Talavera before continuing to Madrid (p. 81).

NOTE: Page numbers following Spanish locales refer to *Paradores of Spain;* page numbers following Portuguese locales refer to *Pousadas of Portugal.*

Days 18 and 19, Madrid.

Day 20, Madrid to Toledo (70 km). Early start southwest, to spend most of the day in Toledo (p. 89). *Parador Nacional Conde de Orgaz.*

Day 21, Toledo to Almagro (139 km). Leave Toledo south on N-401 to Ciudad Real, then go 23 km southeast to Almagro (p. 77). *Parador Nacional de Almagro.*

Day 22, Almagro to Ubeda (162 km). Easy drive south to Bailén, then east to Ubeda (p. 57). *Parador Nacional Condestable Dávalos.*

Day 23, Ubeda to Granada (173 km via Jaén). Drive southwest through Baeza for a stop in Jaén (p. 49) before continuing to Granada (p. 47). *Parador Nacional San Francisco.*

Day 24, Granada. Full day of sightseeing. *Parador Nacional San Francisco.*

179 km to Málaga. Take time to stop in Nerja (p. 54) en route.

ITINERARY 13
52 days, Ballards' choice, Barcelona to Madrid or vice versa

Day 1, Barcelona to Aiguablava (155 km). Leave Barcelona heading northeast along the coast through many enchanting villages before arriving in Aiguablava (p. 123). Allow a full day for this drive for you will want to make several stops. *Parador Nacional Costa Brava.*

Day 2, Aiguablava. Visits to Pals and La Bisbal or a drive north to fishing village and artists' enclave of Cadaqués. *Parador Nacional Costa Brava.*

Day 3, Aiguablava to Cardona (220 km). Leave Aiguablava heading north through Bagur then west to Gerona for the *autopista* south. Exit at Martorell (or sign to Montserrat). Visit Montserrat before continuing north through Manresa to Cardona (p. 127). *Parador Nacional Duques de Cardona.*

Day 4, Cardona to Benicarló (300 km). Retrace yesterday's route and enter Barcelona-Valencia *autopista* at Martorell, south to Benicarló (p. 173). A lot of kilometers, but fast going on the *autopista*. Maybe even time for the wine museum at Vilafranca del Penedés (p. 133). *Parador Nacional Costa del Azáhar.*

Day 5, Benicarló to El Saler (136 km). Early start heading south on the *autopista* to El Saler (p. 174), where there is a golf course. *Parador Nacional Luis Vives.*

Day 6, El Saler to Alarcón (214 km). Leave El Saler through Valencia west on N-111 to Alarcón (p. 74). *Parador Nacional Marqués de Villena.*

NOTE: Page numbers following Spanish locales refer to *Paradores of Spain;* page numbers following Portuguese locales refer to *Pousadas of Portugal.*

Itinerary 13

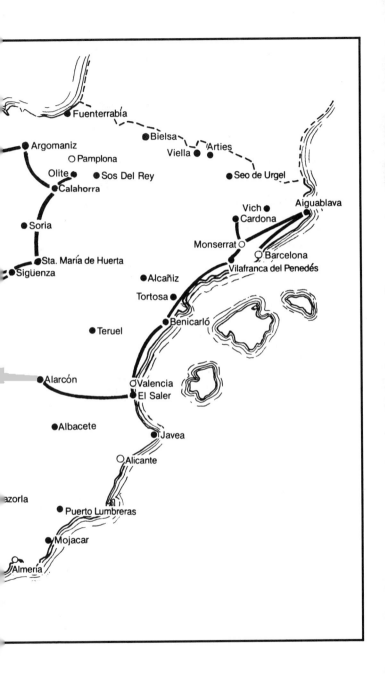

Day 7, Alarcón to Toledo (214 km). Drive northwest on N-111 to Tarancón, west through Aranjuez, south to Toledo (p. 89). *Parador Nacional Conde de Orgaz.*

Day 8, Toledo. Parador Nacional Conde de Orgaz.

Day 9, Toledo to Ubeda (268 km). Leave Toledo heading southeast on C-400 and pick up N-IV at Madridejos, south to Bailén (p. 38), east on N-322 to Ubeda (p. 57). *Parador Nacional Condestable Dávalos.*

Day 10, Ubeda to Granada (173 km via Jaén). Early start from Ubeda southwest through Baeza for stop in Jaén (p. 49) before continuing to Granada (p. 47). *Parador Nacional San Francisco.*

Day 11, Granada. Parador Nacional San Francisco.

Day 12, Granada to Torremolinos (195 km). Stop in Nerja (p. 54) before continuing through Málaga (p. 50) to Torremolinos (p. 59). *Parador Nacional del Golf.*

Days 13 and 14, Málaga. Lunch at the parador, drive to Ronda, Casares (p. 60), Mijas, or along the coast toward Gibraltar. *Parador Nacional del Golf.*

Day 15, Torremolinos to Córdoba (192 km). Back through Málaga, north through Antequera (p. 33) to Córdoba (p. 44). *Parador Nacional La Arruzafa.*

Day 16, Córdoba. Bus tour of the city or independent exploration. *Parador Nacional La Arruzafa.*

Day 17, Córdoba to Carmona (105 km). Early start from Córdoba to Carmona (p. 41). Check into parador then take bus into Sevilla for walking tour. *Parador Nacional Alcázar del Rey Don Pedro.*

Day 18, Carmona to Mérida (231 km). Another early start, heading back through Sevilla north to Zafra (p. 147) for a rest and perhaps lunch before going on to Mérida (p. 142). *Parador Nacional Via de la Plata.*

Day 19, Mérida and Roman ruins. Parador Nacional Via de la Plata.

Day 20, Mérida to Marvão (161 km). Leave Mérida heading east through Badajoz. Stop at pousada in Elvas (p. 96) before driving north on N-246 through Portalegre to Marvão (p. 92). *Pousada de Santa Maria.*

Day 21, Marvão to Estremoz (78 km). Retrace yesterday's route through Portalegre, then take N-18 to Estremoz (p. 98). Time en route for a visit to Vila Viçosa (p. 100). *Pousada da Rainha Santa Isabel.*

Day 22, Estremoz to Evora (61 km via Arraiolos). Drive east from Estremoz on N-4 to Arraiolos. Even if not interested in buying, do take time to visit the shops to see the beautiful locally made

---

NOTE: Page numbers following Spanish locales refer to *Paradores of Spain;* page numbers following Portuguese locales refer to *Pousadas of Portugal.*

carpets before continuing southeast to Evora (p. 102). *Pousada dos Lóios.*

Day 23, Evora. Pousada dos Lóios.

Day 24, Evora to São Brás de Alportel (199 km). Drive south, possibly stopping in Beja (p. 107), then over to N-2 and south to São Brás de Alportel (p. 107). *Pousada de São Brás de Alportel.*

Day 25, São Brás de Alportel to Sagres (141 km). Early start from São Brás to allow stops in Faro, or any of many coastal villages. Good shopping in Albufeira and Lagos. *Pousada do Infante.*

Day 26, Sagres and environs. Pousada do Infante.

Day 27, Sagres to Setúbal or Palmela (216 km). Drive north on N-120 for a stop in Santiago do Cacém for 1 P.M. lunch then on to Setúbal or Palmela. *Pousada de São Filipe or Pousada do Castelo de Palmela.*

Day 28, Setúbal, Troia Peninsula, Azeitão. Pousada de São Filipe or Pousada do Castelo de Palmela.

Day 29, Setúbal to Lisboa (50 km). Majority of day in Lisboa.

Days 30, 31, and 32, Lisboa (p. 28).

Day 33, Lisboa to Sintra (30 km). Take the coastal route to Sintra (p. 35). Hotel Palácio dos Seteais.

Day 34, Sintra to Batalha (167 km). Early start from Sintra north for visits to Mafra (p. 39), Obidos (p. 41), Alcobaça (p. 45), and lunch at seaside cafe in Nazaré (p. 43). *Late arrival* in Batalha (p. 47). *Pousada do Mestre Afonso Domingues.*

Day 35, Batalha and environs. Trips to Fátima (p. 49) and Tomar (p. 51). *Pousada do Mestre Afonso Domingues.*

Day 36, Batalha to Buçaco (110 km). Drive north through Leiria on N-1 for short stop in Conímbriga (p. 53). Try to allow at least three hours in Coimbra (p. 53) before continuing 32 km northeast through Luso to Buçaco (p. 56). *Palace Hotel.*

Day 37, Buçaco to Murtosa (111 km). Enjoy early morning walk in Buçaco forest before driving back through Luso to N-1, north to Santo António Agueda (you might want to stop in Serém at gracious Pousada de Santo António [p. 61] for a cup of coffee), west to Aveiro for a visit of two or three hours. Leave Aveiro (p. 64) to Angeja, north to Estarreja, southwest to Murtosa (p. 63). *Pousada da Ria.*

Day 38, Murtosa to Valença do Minho or Vila Nova de Cerveira (237 km/225 km via Barcelos, 200 km/188 km via Porto). If it's Thursday, enjoy market day in Barcelos (p. 68). If not, you may choose to spend several hours in Porto (p. 65). In any case, leave Murtosa and head back through Estarreja, north to Ovar, and east to

NOTE: Page numbers following Spanish locales refer to *Paradores of Spain;* page numbers following Portuguese locales refer to *Pousadas of Portugal.*

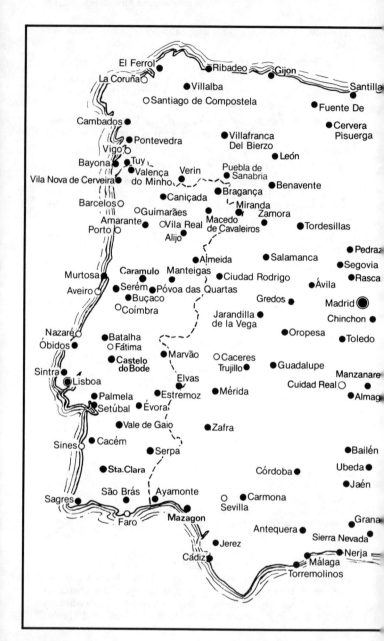

Your choice

Highway N-1. From either Porto or Barcelos, travel scenic N-13 along the coast to Valença do Minho (p. 75) or Vila Nova de Cerveira (p. 73). *Pousada de São Teotónio or Pousada de Dom Dinis.*

Day 39, Valença do Minho to Bayona (60 km). Enjoy shopping in the morning in Valença. Cross the international bridge into Spain and Tuy (p. 162). From Tuy, drive southwest to Laguardia and north to Bayona (p. 152). *Parador Nacional Conde de Gondomar.*

Day 40, Bayona to Santiago de Compostela (113 km). Leave Bayona and go northeast through Vigo, Pontevedra (p. 157), west through Sanjenjo, north to Cambados (p. 154) for a visit and rest. Retrace a few kilometers and then cut east and north on C-550 to Santiago de Compostela (p. 159). *Hotel Reyes Católicos.*

Day 41, Santiago to Ribadeo (147 km). Drive northeast from Santiago de Compostela on C-544 and then pick up N-VI and at Bahamond turn northeast on N-634 for lunch at the parador in Villalba (p. 165). Take N-634 again north to Ribadeo (p. 158). *Parador Nacional de Ribadeo.*

Day 42, Ribadeo to Gijón (211 km). Take the coastal route and at Avilés turn north to Cabo Peñas and down to Luanco and into Gijón (p. 70). *Parador Nacional Molino Viejo.*

Day 43, Gijón to Santillana del Mar (193 km). Leave Gijón heading south on C-630 to Noreña, east on N-634 past San Vicente de la Banquera, then C-6316 to Santillana (p. 110). Go at once to the reception center at the caves of Altamira and put your name on the list for possible entry to the caves. *Parador Nacional Gil Blas.*

Day 44, Santillana del Mar to Cervera de Pisuerga (112 km). Drive east a few kilometers to pick up N-611 south to Aguilar de Campóo, then west 25 km to Cervera de Pisuerga (p. 97). *Parador Nacional Fuentes Carrionas.*

Day 45, Cervera to Argómaniz (267 km via Burgos). Retrace the 25 km to Aguilar de Campóo, then south to Burgos if you wish. Otherwise go from Aguilar to La Nuez de Arriba and east on N-232 all the way to Vitoria and Argómaniz (p. 181). *Parador Nacional de Argómaniz.*

Day 46, Argómaniz to Olite (144 km or 155 km if via Calahorra). Drive south through the rich Rioja wine country. Wine tasting at bodegas in Laguardia. Follow the secondary road north of the Ebro River. You might have lunch at the parador in Calahorra (p. 96) before turning north to Olite (p. 169). *Parador Nacional Príncipe de Viana.*

Day 47, Olite to Sigüenza (259 km). Get on the Zaragoza *autopista* at Tafalla. Exit at signs to Soria (p. 115), take N-111 south to Medinaceli (p. 109), and go west to Sigüenza (p. 87). *Parador Nacional Castillo de Sigüenza.*

NOTE: Page numbers following Spanish locales refer to *Paradores of Spain;* page numbers following Portuguese locales refer to *Pousadas of Portugal.*

Day 48, Sigüenza to Segovia (236 km). Leave Sigüenza south on C-204, then pick up E-4. If you wish to avoid Madrid, take the airport freeway north past the airport, through Alcobendas, across N-1 to C-601, north and west through Navacerrada, and north on N-601 to Segovia (p. 113). *Parador Nacional de Segovia.*

Day 49, Segovia to Avila (65 km). Morning in Segovia, rest of day in Avila (p. 93). *Parador Nacional Raimundo de Borgoña.*

Day 50, Avila to Jarandilla de la Vera (144 km). Mountain roads as you cross the Sierra de Gredos. Leave Avila heading south on C-502. At Arenas de San Pedro turn west to Jarandilla de la Vera (p. 140). *Parador Nacional Carlos V.*

Day 51, Jarandilla de la Vera to Guadalupe (77 km). South through Navalmoral de la Mata to Guadalupe (p. 139). *Parador Nacional Zurbarán.*

Day 52, Guadalupe to Oropesa (91 km). Drive south then east through Puerto de San Vicente and north to Oropesa (p. 85). Plenty of time to shop in Lagartera. *Parador Nacional Virrey Toledo.*

148 km to Madrid.

Train Itineraries

We have prepared three train itineraries. The times given may change from season to season and year to year, but they will give a general idea of how to take a parador vacation by train. An important fact to remember is that you must always have a seat reservation on a Spanish train other than a local, so it's best to make reservations at least one day in advance. In Madrid, trains depart from and arrive at Atocha or Chamartín stations; in Barcelona trains use Sants or Termino stations. Times are given according to the 24-hour system, as they are on train timetables.

ITINERARY 1
6 days, round trip from Madrid

Day 1, Madrid to Avila. Depart 8:40, arrive Avila 10:20 (p. 93). *Parador Nacional Raimundo de Borgoña.*

Day 2, Avila to Salamanca. Depart 11:07, arrive Salamanca 12:49 (p. 106). *Parador Nacional de Salamanca.*

Day 3, Salamanca to Zamora. Depart 12:56, arrive Zamora 13:47 (p. 119). *Parador Nacional Condes Alba y Aliste.*

Day 4, Zamora to Puebla de Sanabria. Depart 14:50, arrive Puebla de Sanabria 16:23 (p. 106). *Parador Nacional de Puebla de Sanabria.*

NOTE: Page numbers following Spanish locales refer to *Paradores of Spain;* page numbers following Portuguese locales refer to *Pousadas of Portugal.*

Day 5, Puebla de Sanabria to Santiago de Compostela. Depart 11:00, arrive Santiago de Compostela 15:54 (p. 159). *Hotel Reyes Católicos.*

Day 6, Santiago de Compostela to Madrid. Depart 11:17, arrive Madrid 19:39.

ITINERARY 2
11 days, round trip from Madrid

Day 1, Madrid to León. Depart 14:40, arrive León 18:54 (p. 102). *Hotel San Marcos.*

Day 2, León to Gijón. Depart 8:43, arrive Gijón 12:40 (p. 70). *Parador Nacional Molino Viejo.*

Day 3, Gijón to Zamora. Depart 6:15, arrive Zamora 11:52 (p. 119). *Parador Nacional Condes de Alba y Aliste.*

Day 4, Zamora to Salamanca. Depart 12:00, arrive Salamanca 12:54 (p. 106). *Parador Nacional de Salamanca.*

Day 5, Salamanca to Mérida. Depart 13:16, arrive Mérida 18:08 (p. 142). *Parador Nacional Vía de la Plata.*

Day 6, Mérida to Sevilla. Depart 18:11, arrive Sevilla 22:00 (p. 56). We suggest staying at a formerly government-owned hotel, *Hotel Alfonso XIII.*

Day 7, Sevilla. Day of sightseeing. You might want to take a bus to Carmona and stay a night in the parador (p. 41). But you would have to return for overnight stay in Sevilla as train leaves so early for the next lap. *Hotel Alfonso XIII.*

Day 8, Sevilla to Córdoba. Depart 8:20, arrive Córdoba 9:27 (p. 44). *Parador Nacional La Arruzafa.*

Day 9, Córdoba to Málaga. Depart 8:35, arrive Málaga 11:50 (p. 50). *Parador Nacional Gibralfaro.*

Day 10, Málaga to Bobadilla to Granada. Depart 9:15, arrive Bobadilla 10:13. Change train to Granada: depart Bobadilla 10:35, arrive Granada 12:36 (p. 47). *Parador Nacional San Francisco.*

Day 11, Granada to Madrid. Depart 14:35, arrive Madrid 20:50 (p. 81).

ITINERARY 3
4 days, round trip from Barcelona

Day 1, Barcelona to Tortosa. Depart 900, arrive Tortosa 11:48 (p. 130). *Parador Nacional Castillo de la Zuda.*

Day 2, Tortosa to Benicarló. Depart 11:48, arrive Benicarló 12:18 (p. 173). *Parador Nacional Costa del Azáhar.*

Day 3, Benicarló to Valencia. Depart 12:18, arrive Valencia 14:12 (p. 175). *Parador Nacional Luis Vives.*

Day 4, Valencia to Barcelona. Depart 10:58, arrive Barcelona 16:55 (p. 126).

There are several local trains daily from Madrid to Segovia (p. 113), Avila (p. 93), and Toledo (p. 89). The marvelous parador in Sigüenza (p. 87) can be visited by train. Departures at 8:25 from Chamartín in Madrid, arrive Sigüenza 10:03. Depart Sigüenza 16:03, arrive Madrid 17:45.

GLOSSARY

ALCAZABA. Palace-fortress of Moorish rulers.

ALCÁZAR. Palace-fortress of Spanish kings.

ALMOHADS. Moors living in Christian Spain from the twelfth to the fourteenth centuries.

ALMORAVIDS. Moors living in Christian Spain from 1057 to 1147.

APSE. Vaulted semicircular recess in church at end of choir.

ARCHIVOLT. Decorative band around an arch.

BAROQUE. Extravagant decoration used from 1600 to 1750.

BYZANTINE. In architecture, buildings of masonry, round arches, low domes; use of frescoes and mosaics; period after 476.

CAPUCHÍN. Monk of a Franciscan order observing vows of poverty and austerity.

CELTS. Indo-European tribes living in southwestern Germany and eastern France from 2000 B.C.

CHALICE. Cup for wine of eucharist or mass.

CHANCEL. Space around altar, usually enclosed, used by clergy.

CHASUBLE. Sleeveless, outer vestment worn by priest during mass.

CHOIR. Part of cruciform church east of the crossing.

CHURRIGUERESQUE. Baroque form of architecture appearing in Spain in the late 1600s and early 1700s.

CISTERCIAN. Member of an order of monks and nuns founded in 1098 in France, under rule of Saint Benedict.

CLOISTER. Covered walkway of arcades opening onto a courtyard.

CORBEL. A bracket projecting from a wall to support an arch.

CORINTHIAN. Type of Greek architecture in which column has tall, slender, fluted shaft, molded base, and bell-shaped capital decorated with acanthus leaves.

DISCALCED. Shoeless, wearing sandals.

DOLMEN. Tomb with two or more upright stone slabs supporting a capstone; typical of the Neolithic age.

DORIC. Oldest and simplest type of classical Greek architecture.

FLEMISH. Pertaining to Flanders, medieval country in western Europe that encompassed the modern regions of western Belgium and adjacent parts of southwestern Netherlands and northern France.

GOTHIC. Architecture originating in France in the mid-1100s; pointed arches, ribbed vaults, fine wood and stone work; use of flying buttresses and ornamental gables.

HERRERIAN. Type of architecture named after Juan Herrera; austere, monastic.

IBERIANS. Ancient inhabitants of Spain and Portugal.

INFANTA. Daughter of Spanish king, not heir to throne; wife of Infante.

INFANTE. Son of Spanish king, not heir to throne.

IONIC. Type of Greek architecture having scrolls on capitals of columns.

JACOBEAN. Style of architecture and literature developed during reign of James I of England (first half of seventeenth century).

LEVANT. Lands in southeastern Spain bordering western shores of the Mediterranean Sea.

MEDIEVAL. Pertaining to the Middle Ages.

MIDDLE AGES. From the late fifth century to around 1350.

MONSTRANCE. Receptacle in which consecrated host (bread or wafer regarded as body of Christ in the mass) is exposed for adoration.

MORISCO. Christianized Moor.

MOZARAB. Christian living under Moorish rule.

MUDEJAR. Christianized Moor; in architecture, Spanish works with Moorish influence, from eleventh to sixteenth centuries; key-shaped arches, decorative ceiling panels.

NAVE. Long part of church from entrance to chancel.

NECROPOLIS. Prehistoric burial ground.

NEOCLASSICAL. Art and architecture based on revival of classical Greco-Roman style in the late eighteenth and early nineteenth centuries.

NEOLITHIC AGE. Circa 8000–6000 B.C.

OGIVAL. Architectural style using diagonal vaulting rib, pointed arches.

PLATERESQUE. Delicate, ornate, architectural decoration of sixteenth century.

PLINTH. Slab beneath base of a column.

POLYCHROME. Use of many and varied colors.

PORTAL. Imposing door or entrance.

PREDELLA. Base of altarpiece.

RECONQUEST. Period in Spain having to do with reconquering territory held by Moors.

REFECTORY. Dining hall of religious building.

RENAISSANCE. Period beginning in fourteenth century, continuing until the seventeenth, signaling rebirth in the arts.

REREDOS. Decorated part of retable or wall.

RETABLE. Ornamental structure above and in back of an altar.

ROMANESQUE. In architecture, period from the ninth through twelfth centuries; heavy masonry construction with narrow openings; round arches; groin and barrel vaults.

ROMERIA. Pilgrimage to shrine, followed by picnic.

SACRISTY. Room of church in which sacred vessels and vestments are kept.

SEE. Center of authority or jurisdiction of a bishop.

TALAYOT. Prehistoric corbeled stone monument in shape of round or quadrangular tower.

TEMPLAR. Member of religious-military order founded by crusaders in Jerusalem about 1118.

TRANSEPT. Part of cruciform church that usually crosses nave at entrance to choir.

TRIFORIUM. Wall at sides of nave, choir, and transept, opening onto gallery.

TRIPTYCH. Set of three connected panels bearing pictures or carvings.

TYMPANUM. Triangular, recessed space enclosed between horizontal and sloping cornices of pediment.

VISIGOTH. Western division of Goths (Germanic tribes), who formed monarchy about 418 and maintained it until 711. Visigothic architecture characterized by rough-hewn stones without mortar; carved friezes of geometric or scroll motifs and Christian symbols; horseshoe arches.

PRONUNCIATION GUIDE

One r is trilled; two r's are an extended trill. J at the beginning of a word is pronounced like the *ch* in German *ach!*

Aiguablava: *aye-(g)wuh-BLAH-vuh* (the g is 'swallowed')
Alarcón: *ahl-ahr-COHN*
Albacete: *ahl-bah-THAY-tay**
Albariño: *ahl-bah-REEN-yoh*
Alcalá de Henares: *ahl-cah-LAH day ay-NAHR-ays*
Alcañiz: *ahl-CAHN-yeeth**
Almagro: *ahl-MAH-groh*
Antequera: *ahn-tay-CARE-uh*
Arcos de la Frontera: *ARE-cose day lah frohn-TAIR-uh*
Argómaniz: *ahr-GOH-mahn-yeeth**
Arties: *ahr-tee-AYS*
Avila: *AH-vee-lah*
Ayamonte: *aye-yuh-MOAN-tay*
Badajoz: *bah-dah-HOTH* (long o)*
Bailén: *bye-LEN*
Barcelona: *bahr-thay-LOH-nuh**
Bayona: *bye-OHN-uh*
Benavente: *behn-uh-VEHN-tay*
Benicarló: *bay-nee-cahr-LOH*
Bielsa: *bee-EHL-sah*
Cádiz: *CAH-deeth**
Calahorra: *kah-lah-OR-rah*
Cambados: *cahm-BAH-dohs*
Cardona: *cahr-DOHN-uh*
Carmona: *cahr-MOHN-uh*
Cataluña: *cah-tah-LOON-yah*
Cazorla: *cah-THORE-luh**
Cervera de Pisuerga: *THAIR-vair-ah day pee-sue-AIR-guh**
Chinchón: *cheen-CHOHN*
Ciudad Real: *thee-oo-DAHD ray-AHL* (hard th)*
Ciudad Rodrigo: *thee-oo-DAHD roh-DREE-goh**
Córdoba: *CORE-doe-bah* (soft d, almost like th in other)
Costa del Azáhar: *COHS-tuh dell ah-THAH-ahr*
Cuenca: *coo-AYN-cuh*
El Ferrol: *ell FEHR-rohl*
El Saler: *ell sah-LEHR*
Fuente Dé: *foo-AYN-tay DAY*
Fuenterrabía: *foo-ayn-tair-rah-BEE-uh*
Fuentes Carrionas: *foo-AYN-tayss car-ree-OHN-ahss*
Galicia: *gah-LEE-thee-ah**
Gerona: *heh-ROH-nuh*
Gijón: *gee-HONE* (hard g)

*Hard th sound.

Granada: *grah-NAH-duh*
Gredos-Navarredonda: *GRAY-dohs nah-vahr-ray-DOHN-duh*
Guadalupe: *(g)wah-dah-LOO-pay* (the g is 'swallowed')
Huelva: *HWHALE-vuh*
Jaén: *hah-EN*
Jarandilla de la Vera: *hah-rahn-DEE-yah day lah VAY-rah*
Javea: *HAH-vay-uh*
Jerez de la Frontera: *HAIR-eth day lah frohn-TAIR-uh*
León: *lay-OHN*
Lérida: *LAY-ree-dah*
Madrid: *mah-DREED*
Málaga: *MAH-lah-guh*
Manzanares: *mahn-thahn-AHR-ayss**
Mazagón: *mah-thuh-GON (long o)**
Mérida: *MAY-ree-dah*
Mojácar: *moe-HAH-car*
Monachil: *MON-ah-keel*
Murcia: *MER-thee-uh**
Nerja: *NAIR-hah*
Olite: *oh-LEE-tay*
Oropesa: *or-oh-PAY-suh*
Pedraza: *peh-DRAH-thuh**
Pontevedra: *pohn-tay-VAY-druh*
Puebla de Sanabria: *poo-AY-blah day sah-NAH-bree-ah*
Puerto Lumbreras: *poo-AYR-toh loom-BRAIR-ahs*
Ribadeo: *ree-bah-DAY-oh*
Rioja: *ree-OH-hah*
Salamanca: *sah-lah-MAHN-cah*
Santa María de Huerta: *sahn-tuh mah-REE-ah day HWHERE-tuh*
Santiago de Compostela: *sahn-tee-YAH-goh day cohm-pos-TAY-luh*
Santillana del Mar: *sahn-tee-YAHN-uh dell MAHR*
Santo Domingo de la Calzada: *SAHN-to do-MEEN-goh day lah cahl-THAH-dah**
Segovia: *say-GOH-vee-yah*
Seo de Urgel: *SAY-oh day ur-HELL*
Sevilla: *say-VEE-yah*
Sigüenza: *sih-GWEN-thuh**
Soria: *SOH-ree-uh*
Sos del Rey Católico: *SOHS del RAY cah-TOE-lee-coh*
Teruel: *teh-rue-ELL*
Toledo: *toh-LAY-doh*
Tordesillas: *tore-day-SEE-yahs*
Torremolinos: *tore-ray-moe-LEE-nos*
Tortosa: *tore-TOH-sah*
Trujillo: *true-HEE-yoh*
Tuy: *TOO-ee*
Ubeda: *OO-buh-duh*
Valle de Arán: *VAH-yay day ah-RAHN*
Verin: *veh-REEN*

*Hard th sound.

Vich: *BEEK*
Viella: *vee-AY-yah*
Villafranca del Bierzo: *bee-yuh-FRAHN-cah dell bee-YAIR-thoh**
Villalba: *bee-YAHL-buh*
Zafra: *THAH-frah**
Zamora: *thah-MOH-ruh**
Zaragoza: *thah-rah-GOH-thah**
Zurbarán: *thur-bah-RAHN**

*Hard th sound.

INDEX BY LOCALE

INDEX BY ESTABLISHMENT

SUBJECT INDEX

HARVARD COMMON PRESS books are available at bookstores or from the Harvard Common Press, 535 Albany Street, Boston, Massachusetts 02118. When ordering from the publisher, include $2 postage and handling; if you live in Massachusetts, also include 5 percent sales tax.

Other travel books published by the Harvard Common Press are listed below. A complete catalog of books is available on request.

POUSADAS OF PORTUGAL: UNIQUE LODGINGS IN STATE-OWNED CASTLES, PALACES, MANSIONS, AND HOTELS
By Sam and Jane Ballard
$8.95 paper, ISBN 0-916782-77-8
192 pages

A companion volume to *Paradores of Spain*, this is the only published guide to the luxurious lodgings owned and operated by the Portuguese government. The Ballards, who have visited every pousada, provide detailed maps, photographs, and suggested itineraries as well as lively descriptions of the accommodations and their historic settings.

BEST PLACES TO STAY IN AMERICA'S CITIES: UNIQUE HOTELS, CITY INNS, AND BED AND BREAKFASTS
Edited by Kenneth Hale
$9.95 paper, ISBN 0-916782-84-0
346 pages

For travelers seeking the charm and personal service of small lodging places, this book describes the best hotels, inns, and B&Bs in the fifty most visited cities in the United States. *Available October 1986.*

BEST PLACES TO STAY IN NEW ENGLAND
By Christina Tree and Bruce Shaw
$9.95 paper, ISBN 0-916782-74-3
364 pages

A guide to the best accommodations in New England—including inns, small hotels, motels, resorts, B&Bs, and farms—grouped according to the kind of vacation experience offered.

HOW TO TAKE GREAT TRIPS WITH YOUR KIDS
By Sanford and Joan Portnoy
$14.95 cloth, ISBN 0-916782-52-5
$8.95 paper, ISBN 0-916782-51-4
192 pages

Traveling with the kids can be fun and easy, once you know some special techniques. Whether you're driving to Aunt Helen's or flying to Zanzibar, this book offers the ABCs of planning, packing, and en-route problem solving.

THE PORTABLE PET: HOW TO TRAVEL ANYWHERE WITH YOUR DOG OR CAT
By Barbara Nicholas
$12.95 cloth, ISBN 0-916782-50-6
$5.95 paper, ISBN 0-916782-49-2
96 pages

If vacation wouldn't be the same without your faithful friend, or you're planning to move your pet along with the rest of your household, you're headed into a maze of requirements and regulations. Find the answers to all your questions in this lively and pragmatic guide.

Exploring Our National Parks and Monuments
Revised Eighth Edition
By Devereux Butcher
$10.95 paper, ISBN 0-87645-122-9
400 pages

"This is very possibly the best available collection of photographs of our national parks. Schools and libraries will find it an admirable guide and sourcebook as will the traveler."—*Library Journal*

A Traveler's Guide to the Smoky Mountains Region
By Jeff Bradley
$19.95 cloth, ISBN 0-916782-63-8
$10.95 paper, ISBN 0-916782-64-6
288 pages

The first comprehensive and critical guide to southern Appalachia, a land of outstanding natural beauty and old-time graciousness.
    "A thoroughgoing, level-headed guide through some fascinating hills!"—*Roy Blount, Jr.*

Inside Outlets: The Best Bargain Shopping in New England
By Naomi R. Rosenberg and Marianne W. Sekulow
$8.95 paper, ISBN 0-916782-66-2
224 pages

A critical, quality-conscious guide to the best of New England's bargain shops. Special features include price-quality ratings, shopping "itineraries" in scenic areas, and over $100 worth of money-saving coupons from New England merchants.

The Best Things in New York Are Free
By Marian Hamilton
$10.95 paper, ISBN 0-916782-75-1
560 pages

A comprehensive guide to every free attraction in New York City, including museums and historic houses, art galleries, films and concerts, tours, libraries, parks, and cultural societies. Over a thousand listings.

The Carefree Getaway Guide for New Yorkers
By Theodore Scull
$8.95 paper, ISBN 0-916782-68-9
208 pages

For restless New Yorkers, Scull describes forty day and weekend trips in New York and its environs, including Connecticut, Pennsylvania, Rhode Island, and New Jersey. All trips are by safe, convenient public transportation, and detailed maps are provided.